The
Oceans
Our Last
Resource

The
Oceans
Our Last Resource

Wesley Marx

Sierra Club Books · San Francisco

THE SIERRA CLUB, founded in 1892 by John Muir, has devoted itself to the study and protection of the earth's scenic and ecological resources—mountains, wetlands, woodlands, wild shores and rivers, deserts and plains. The publishing program of the Sierra Club offers books to the public as a nonprofit educational service in the hope that they may enlarge the public's understanding of the Club's basic concerns. The point of view expressed in each book, however, does not necessarily represent that of the Club. The Sierra Club has some fifty chapters coast to coast, in Canada, Hawaii, and Alaska. For information about how you may participate in its programs to preserve wilderness and the quality of life, please address inquiries to Sierra Club, 530 Bush Street, San Francisco, California 94108.

PORTIONS OF THIS BOOK were previously published in *Reader's Digest, Smithsonian,* and *Cry California.*

LIBRARY OF CONGRESS CATALOGING IN PUBLICATION DATA
Marx, Wesley.
The Oceans: Our Last Resource.
Bibliography: p. 313
Includes index.
1. Marine resources conservation. I. Title.
GC1018.M315   333.91'6417   81–5332
ISBN 0–87156–291–X   AACR2

JACKET AND BOOK DESIGN BY HOWARD JACOBSEN
PRINTED IN THE UNITED STATES OF AMERICA
10 9 8 7 6 5 4 3 2 1

FOR
Judy, Chris, Heather and Ty

CONTENTS

FOREWORD

THE IDEA OF THE INEXHAUSTIBLE sea has long been with us. In fact the possibility that fish stocks were being depleted by over fishing did not occur to anyone until about the middle of the last century, and even then many were not convinced. Much of the concern of the first commission to investigate fisheries problems, called together by Queen Victoria in the 1860's under the chairmanship of Thomas Henry Huxley, was over the matter of limiting the market and keeping up the prices. We have not changed much in that respect in the last 120 years or so.

The use of steam trawlers had barely begun when Huxley concluded that man could not affect the fisheries stocks of northern Europe. Another staunch advocate of the inexhaustible sea, William Carmichael M'Intosh, defended until his last day his conclusion arrived at in the 1880s that "with some exceptions, the fauna of the open sea, from its nature and environment, would appear, to a large extent, to be independent of man's influence." Time has proved these optimistic Victorians wrong, most dramatically so during two great wars in which fishing was suspended long enough for the stocks to improve. Man can obviously have an adverse effect on fisheries, and his effect increases with the sophistication of his gear.

It would seem that this lesson must be learned all over again with each fishery that is developed. If you fish the sea long and hard enough for anything, decline, and possibly ecological change, will set in. Recently we have been talking about harvesting the vast swarms of krill that support blue whales in the Antarctic seas. It has been estimated that the annual mass of Antarctic krill may equal all the rest of the world's fisheries combined. But krill are small animals about two or three inches long, and have indigestible casings or shells. The most likely way to use them would be to husk them and reduce them to paste in large factory ships. But if we harvest the krill, the diminishing population of blue whales cannot return to their feeding grounds and that may be the end of them as a species. And what of the penguins that also depend on krill? Among our own costs will be enormous quantities of oil to send the factory ships halfway around the world for those millions of cans of shrimp paste. And what kind of ocean will there be when we have eaten all the krill?

No, the sea is not inexhaustible and its material resources are not infinite. We still have much to learn about how to harvest the sea wisely, and how to develop means of culturing its living creatures without excessive cost, and we are not always approaching the questions in the right way. But that is the greatest art in science, the art of asking a question so that we can be sure the answer we get applies to that question. The problems raised in this book of harvesting the sea, obtaining minerals and oil, or resolving the socio-political problems related to mariculture should stimulate readers to think harder about our watery planet, and what mankind can really expect from the oceans of the world.

Unfortunately the promise for the next few years is that these matters are to be left ashore as our Administration in Washington sets forth into strange new fiscal seas. It seems to be thought that the ranching, mining and industrial interests whose greater profits are to be returned to developing the country for the common good will take care of all the things the federal government no longer cares to support. A troubling situation.

The Sea Grant College program, authorized by Congress in 1966, was intended to support education and research in fisheries, mariculture, law and other matters related to the sea, and to stimulate active participation in university extension programs with the fishing industry. The basic idea was to support a selected group of maritime colleges and universities to develop skills in the exploitation and management of marine resources after the pattern of the Land Grant colleges. Since the initial Sea Grant colleges, Rhode Island, Oregon State and Washington, were funded in 1968, a sizable empire of activity in universities throughout the country, including Michigan and Wisconsin, has become established. Initial budget cut proposals of the Reagan Administration would abolish the Sea Grant program entirely, and also abolish the Coastal Zone Management program, which has financed state programs to establish estuarine sanctuaries and coastal commissions.

A reconsideration of the Law of the Sea Treaty, the result of years of complicated negotiations and compromises, has been requested by the new Administration too, in part because of intense pressure from private mining interests. This action may make it impossible to arrive at a consensus about the management of earth's last great Commons. This is doubly unfortunate because it is unlikely that deep sea mining is practical at our present state of technology. It would be wiser to study the conditions under which manganese nodules are formed and possibly develop a synthetic process. This, however, calls for support of marine research.

The Administration's policy appears to be one of exploitation of the sea to the utmost, to abandon international agreement for the use of the sea, to drill for oil along every possible part of the coast, even where the prospects are admittedly marginal as along the coast of northern California, and to scuttle all environmental controls for the estuaries and coastal areas. Certainly these are compatible with the views and inclinations of the Secretary of the Interior, the Director of the Bureau of Land Management, the Manager of the Budget, and the Administrator of the Environmental Protection Agency—all persons from inland parts of the country without experience or interest in the sea or coastal problems. This is an astonishing reversal of policy; there has not been less interest by an administration in the United States as a maritime nation since the presidency of Ulysses S. Grant.

But four or eight years is insignificant in the time scale of the oceans. And the problems, perhaps more acute, will still be with us. May this book serve as a guide to the rehabilitation of needed programs and a reminder of questions that demand to be asked.

JOEL W. HEDGPETH

ACKNOWLEDGMENTS

I HAVE BENEFITTED FROM THE assistance and the insights of many people in gathering material for this book. Persons whom I interviewed on the subject of fishery management and who often provided helpful reports include Dr. John McHugh, State University of New York at Stony Brook; Dr. Richard Hennemuth, National Marine Fisheries Service—Woods Hole, Mass.; Richard Stroud and Gilbert Radonski of the Sport Fishing Institute; Langdon Warner of the Environmental Defense Fund, Herb Kameon of the National Coalition for Marine Conservation and John Royal, a Pacific coast fishery union official and member of the Pacific Regional Fishery Council. Dr. Reuban Lasker of the National Marine Fisheries Service Southwest Center—La Jolla and Dr. George Hemingway, the California Cooperative Oceanic Fisheries Investigation Coordinator, permitted me to attend the 1978 and 1979 California Cooperative Oceanic Fisheries Investigations Conferences at Idyllwild, California. Bill Verna, an anchovy bait dealer, permitted me to accompany him twice on board his vessel to seine for anchovy at night.

Dr. George Hunt, Jr. of the Department of Ecology and Evolutionary Biology at the University of California at Irvine directed me to several key references on seabird-fish interactions.

James Keith of the Denver office of the U.S. Fish and Wildlife Service provided his thesis on pelican survival in the Gulf of California. Dr. Gary Brewer, Institute for Marine and Coastal Studies at the University of Southern California, answered a number of questions on forage fish and reviewed Chapters 2 and 3. Dr. James Joseph and Witold Klawe of the Inter-American Tropical Tuna Commission at La Jolla shared with me their knowledge of the uncertain management status of highly migratory fish. Leo Pinkas of the California Department of Fish and Game provided helpful fishery statistic reports. Robert Chapoton of the National Marine Fisheries Service—Southeast Center supplied reports on the menhaden fishery.

Mr. Dan O'Keefe, senior editor with *Reader's Digest*, gave me considerable encouragement and editorial support in completing an editorial project on forage fish.

Dr. Richard Yeo, an aquatic plant expert with the Department of Agriculture at Davis, California, arranged for me to observe seining of carp used to control plants in a farm pond in California's wine grape district. Mr. Tom Jackson of the Denver office of U.S. Fish and Wildlife Service provided information and reports on the testing of grass carp. Vern Hacker of the Wisconsin Department of Natural Resources provided a copy of *A Fine Kettle of Fish*. Leo Ray of Niland, California took me on a tour of his catfish growing operation in the Imperial Valley and shared his thoughts on the future of aquaculture.

In Hawaii, C. Richard Fassler of the State Aquaculture Development Program supplied a number of publications and arranged visits to commercial projects. Bob Hanohano permitted me to participate in seining his prawn ponds and then patiently shared with me his experiences in prawn culture. He also introduced me to Dr. K. Gopalakrishnan of Honolulu Community College. "Gopol" showed me his campus prawn project and explained to me various aspects of aquaculture operations. Jeffry Wallace permitted me to observe prawn ponds at Lowe Aquafarm while Tomohiro Imamura, technical director of Ikko Hawaii Aqua Culture Company, enthusiastically explained the care and culturing of the sweet-tasting tiger shrimp that is flown to Japan.

Tap Pryor of Systemculture and his technical director, Dr. Berry Goldstein, took me on a tour of their oyster culturing operation in Oahu. Tap Pryor also discussed with me his views on the future of aquaculture.

Dr. John Ryther of Woods Hole Oceanographic Institution shared his experiences in visiting Chinese carp growing operations.

Don Moser, editor of *Smithsonian Magazine*, quickly grasped the unique role of carp in human affairs, and, by assigning me to do an editorial project, furthered my research.

Amid last minute preparations for a trip to the Philippines to visit seaweed culture operations, Dr. Maxwell Doty of the University of Hawaii explained his involvement with spreading the culture of *Euchema.* Dr. Isabella Abbott of the University of Hawaii made me aware of Ewa Beach near Honolulu, where I was able to talk with people gathering edible seaweeds. Jeffrey Hunt of Windward Community College provided a copy of his report on a pilot project to raise *Gracilaria.* Jimmy Muraoka of Jimmy's Fish Market in Honolulu described the various recipes for use of edible seaweeds and introduced me to crisp-tasting ogo. Cyrus Tamashiro and Patsy Choy of Tamashiro Market in Honolulu explained how edible seaweeds are procured and prepared for sale. Jerry Kaluhiwa, leader of a pilot seaweed culture project, and Bob Nakata of the Kualoa-Heeia Ecumenical Project explained the practical problems of marine gardening.

Dr. Paul Dayton of Scripps Institution of Oceanography reviewed an early draft of the chapter on the kelp forests and made many helpful corrections and suggestions. Dr. Alan Mearns, presently with the National Oceanic and Atmospheric Administration, explained his work in assessing kelp changes while with the Coastal Water Research Project. Dr. Irwin Haydock of the County Sanitation Districts of Los Angeles explained efforts by the Districts to reduce possible outfall impacts on kelp growth. Dr. Howard Wilcox of the Naval Oceans Systems Center in San Diego and Ab Flowers of the Gas Research Institute explained efforts to develop kelp plantations. Dr. John Ryther of Woods Hole Oceanographic Institution provided reports on his work with aquatic plants.

Lester Feldman and Harold Singer, staff engineers with the California Regional Water Quality Control Board—San Francisco Region, provided reports and information on wastewater treatment issues. James Smith, Office of Water and Water Management in the Environmental Protection Agency, provided a number of helpful EPA research publications on alternative wastewater treatment processes. Charles Phelps of Rand Corporation provided a copy of Rand's excellent report on California water policy. In working with Carlyle Hall and Jan Levine of the Center for Law in the Public Interest, who developed the successful "one man, one vote" legal challenge to the privately-controlled Irvine Ranch Water District, I learned much about the political and legal history of water development in the west. William Woodworth, a member of the Monterey Peninsula Water Management District, supplied material and information on the cistern comeback precise enough to inspire the writer to build his own backyard cistern system.

Dr. Joel Hedgpeth and William Davoren of the U.S. Fish and Wildlife Service Bay Institute in Tiburon, California provided important reference material on the impact of water diversion projects on estuaries, gulfs and inland seas. Dr. Hedgpeth also provided papers and his own writings on the different classifications of bays, estuaries and wetlands.

Robin Saunders, Santa Clara's solar utility engineer, supplied material on that city's solar program. Dr. Paul Yuen, director of the Hawaii Natural Energy Institute, forwarded reports on that state's energy initiatives. Kathleen Courier of Solar Lobby supplied helpful material on federal energy policy. Dr. Delmar Bunn of the Newport Foundation for the Study of Major Economic Issues arranged for me to attend that Foundation's conference on "Solutions to the Energy Problem" at the University of Southern California July 11, 1980. Harvey Meyerson of Senator Spark Matsunaga's office provided helpful material on sail-assisted technology. Bernie Arthur of Skookum Marine Construction in Port Townsend, Washington, sent material on his work in sailing fishboats. Dr. Richard Podgorny, marine sanctuary projects manager for the National Oceanic and Atmospheric Administration, provided documents on new marine sanctuaries. Dr. Hedgpeth and Dr. John Mohr helped educate me on the problems posed by drilling fluids and shortcomings in assessing impacts from these fluids. Odom Fanning of Washington, D.C. forwarded informative Energy Department reports on local energy programs.

Rudy Cassani, legislative assistant to Congressman Mario Biaggi, answered questions on the status of the Superfund bill covering oil spills and provided legislative reports. Gordon Enk of the Institute of Man and Science at Rensselaerville, New York arranged for me to participate in the Institute's Symposium, "Assessing the Social Impacts of Oil Spills," co-sponsored by the Environmental Protection Agency.

I appreciate receiving permission from the conference sponsors to attend the Marine Technology Society's Oceans '77 conference in Los Angeles and the ninth Underwater Mining Institute sponsored by the University of Wisconsin Extension in San Diego in 1978.

Dr. Warren Wooster, Institute for Marine Sciences at the University of Washington, and Dr. Hedgpeth reviewed a draft of chapter 20 and made a number of helpful suggestions and corrections. Dr. Wooster provided copies of his articles on the subject of access for marine scientific research. Harold Stanley of Interstate Electronics Corporation in Anaheim, California provided a copy of that firm's underwater survey of the radioactive disposal site off California's Farallon Islands.

Martine Coursil, information assistant for the New York liaison office of the United Nations Environmental Programme, supplied reports on the Programme's marine activities.

Gilven Slonim, president of the Oceanic Educational Foundation in Falls Church, Virginia, provided materials on his work in expanding the horizons of marine education. Teaching a course on Man and the Oceans in the Program in Social Ecology at the University of California at Irvine provided an opportunity to explore the human marine experience with students capable of asking incisive questions.

The collections at the general library of the University of California at Irvine and at the library of the Long Beach office of the California Department of Fish and Game proved invaluable.

Toba Wheeler and Arlene Terris of Irvine typed the bulk of the manuscript. As always, my wife Judy displayed admirable patience when I was confronted by new research leads and deadlines. Jon Beckmann and Jim Cohee of Sierra Club Books and my agent, Frances Collin, helped bring this book project to fruition.

WESLEY MARX
Irvine, California
March 5, 1981

The
Oceans
Our Last
Resource

I

In Search of Bearings

THE AQUARIUM IN MY DENTIST'S waiting room has all the universal features that unite it with sister aquariums throughout the world. Small, brightly colored fish cruise serenely in an ocean world without tides, sharks, or sea storms. A sunken clipper rests peacefully on a seabed of multi-colored gravel. A Chinese coolie fishes from a submerged porcelain bridge without need of a scuba tank, a diving helmet, or a fishing permit.

I know the larger purpose of this aquarium is to calm me, to divert my thoughts from the upcoming encounter. It does its job well. My thoughts do drift away from the muffled whir of dental polishers to a singular quality that the glass-enclosed ocean exudes: its ability to resist change. No supertankers or super oil spills intrude here. No resort condos or gambling casinos rise in the background. No urban outfall discharges into its clear water. No multinational oil companies or political blocs compete to control its destiny. The flashy fish, the sunken clipper, and the coolie persist, waiting patiently to calm those who follow me.

The future of the ocean outside the glass box is much harder to decipher. Natural, economic, and political changes are converging at an unprecedented rate as we turn increasingly toward marine resources to fulfill human needs and desires. What does this mean for the ocean and for ourselves? We can choose from any number of visions, dreams, and nightmares that purport to answer this question. The ocean does not want for prophets.

To some of the most persistent prophets, the ocean is destined to be a veritable treasure chest of seabed minerals, sea farms, submarine resorts, and as yet undiscovered drugs. The ocean as resource cornucopia would prolong the affluence of industrial nations and bootstrap developing nations into prosperity. Technological wizardry of some sort is viewed as the key that will unlock the treasure chest. Seawater itself would be refined to quench the thirst of sun-drenched, star-crossed southern California and other coastal regions.

The vision of the ocean as resource cornucopia appears to be true for the oil industry, but not for many other seekers. Remember those much-publicized underwater submersibles with names like Beaver, Deep Star, and Sea Quest? They were ready a decade ago to begin unlocking the underwater treasure chest with automated metal arms. Today, most sit idle and empty hundreds of miles away from the sea wind, gathering dust in warehouses. College students who trained eagerly to operate such submersibles now seek employment landward of the tides.

But nagging questions persist. Why do we depend on less, not more, marine-based sources of food? How can China, without a modern fishing fleet, still produce more fish than the United States or Norway? Why is the federal government withdrawing support of saline conversion and selling off existing research units to scrap iron dealers or oil-rich Arab kingdoms? Just what do those fabled mineral nodules that ocean-going mining ships re-

trieve with great fanfare actually contain? Scarce ore . . . or a
tax-free hedge on deep-sea mineral exploration? Is the ocean's
resource potential being carefully assessed by the inhabitants of
a planet that is running out of clean air and clear water in some
urban areas?

Is the ocean as resource cornucopia a hype? With the reso-
lute faith of ancient mariners in search of the Hesperides and the
Antipodes, persistent supporters claim this slightly frayed vision
can still be realized if certain nonmarine barriers are lifted. They
say that national governments should regulate less and subsidize
more. The need to subsidize a national turn to the sea is justified
by invoking the success of similar subsidies in the past, from
imperial Great Britain all the way back to the sea kings of tiny
Minos. The implication is clear. No nation can be a pretender
to global influence without a strong maritime presence, subsidized or not. Stint on public support for a rejuvenated merchant
marine, a modern fishing fleet, and a marine mineral rush and you
subvert national power and prestige. Who wants to lose out on
possibly the greatest—if not the last—big resource bonanza on
this planet?

This is a tantalizing appeal, backed by historical truth. Nobody, including political leaders, wants to be accused of missing
the boat to untold riches while haggling over a modest down
payment. Indeed, the spectacular rise of maritime nations has
been accompanied by some of the most ingenious and desperate
forms of public subsidy yet devised, including mandated fish on
Friday, impressment of seamen, and free ship timber from royal
forests. A coastal village on a soggy marsh once catapulted itself
into prominence by getting other nations to fund much of its
naval infrastructure, from gondolas to galleys. Wrote William
Wordsworth in praise of Venice:

> Once did she hold the gorgeous east in fee;
> and was the safeguard of the west . . .
> she took unto herself a Mate,
> she must espouse the everlasting Sea.

Such impressive allusions can overlook one factor. The maritime expansions of the past, whether undertaken in Phoenician purple, Roman breastplate, Viking horned helmets, or English cockades, were often motivated by domestic failures: grain shortfalls and urban food riots, depleted forests and exhausted farm soils, inflated economies and debased currencies. Desperate nations often expand seaward to ward off domestic unrest, poverty, and decline. Why can they master the world ocean and other continents but not their own overheated economies? Why must they forever engage in feverish political juggling acts to balance imports with exports, revenues with maritime tax subsidies, ship timber demand with forest growth? When does the national turn to the sea become a glorious diversion rather than a fundamental solution?

The ocean as resource cornucopia can inspire a contradictory vision: the ocean as resource grab. This vision can come to coastal resort owners when oil spills smear their sandy front yard, to coastal fishermen when oil platforms punctuate their fishing grounds, and to coastal dwellers who find their bays and estuaries recruited as refinery sites. These people suddenly sense a surprising kinship with native Americans who watched the Spanish horse and the iron horse thunder over the buffalo's prairies. They view marine development not so much as an economic boon as an agent of great cultural change in which there will be big losers as well as big winners.

The ocean as resource grab is not without its own historic precedents. Fishermen and residents who protest reclamation of estuaries echo the same fears of fishermen and residents who once depended on Holland's Zuider Zee and Italy's Pontine Marshes. Today, coastal residents who protest intensive marine oil development are told by their national leaders that they must accept the risk of oil spills and loss of marine values to resolve the global energy crunch.

Concern over the ocean as resource grab, however justifiable, can generate its own paradoxes. Coastal regions may seek to halt offshore oil development while complaining about gas shortages and ignoring energy alternatives to our hydrocarbon high. Can affluent coastal areas like auto-crazed southern California learn to reform the consumptive practices that energize relentless exploitation and regain control over their own political destiny?

The ocean as resource cornucopia and as resource grab can inspire a hybrid vision: the ocean as human garden. If we can disrupt ocean processes, can't we learn to shape, alter, and modify the ocean to more benign human goals? Marine development could serve to enhance, restore, and enrich the marine environment. Guided by this vision, oil platforms might undergo metamorphosis into high-rise marine suburbs. Below deck, fish farms might flourish, nourished by ocean sewage outfalls whose output would be as carefully blended as a purée from a food processor.

We are learning how to revive urban estuaries once considered as biologically dead as Lazarus. The restoration of sea forests off the coast of southern California has generated an ambitious attempt to cultivate seaweed plantations. Mainland China has been doing this for some time. However, the limits of the ocean can be as hard to decipher as its actual resource potential. After blaming overfishing and pollution for depleting some fisheries, government agencies now recognize another possible suspect that can defy human attempts at manipulation: climatic change. Does the often confusing quest to identify forces responsible for marine change doom our ambitions to manage the ocean as human garden?

Sometimes our pretensions at understanding the marine environment can border on the ludicrous. In one recent news story, scuba-diving scientists were quoted as saying that marine animals affected by a harbor oil spill had not only recovered but were "happy." What sort of emotive index do these discerning scientists use? Do they show the starfish, the urchins, and the mussels reports of past oil spills and record their reactions? Can these scientists detect sadness and melancholy in oil spills that might not induce euphoria? Or were the newspaper's readers simply being put on? A photo of one marine diver accompanied the news story. He was smiling, presumably like the starfish below.

The conflicting marine visions can generate a bustling reality: the politicized ocean. Today, national marine agencies, state coastal commissions, regional fishing councils, and international law of the sea conferences produce an unprecedented flow of regulations, standards, treaties, and plans to prescribe proper human behavior in the marine realm. A political melee can result, particularly when the experts compete for each other's jurisdictional turf. The scientific exploration of the ocean has been one prominent victim of this situation. Does global marine exploitation portend the development of political institutions even more remote, distant, and coolly bureaucratic than those that flourish today? Can our use of the ocean serve instead to *expand* freedom and choice?

Amid the heady talk of international marine law, 200-mile economic zones, floating sea cities, and ecological niches, the most common human encounter with marine values may be overlooked. This is not as scientist, planner, engineer, sailor, or tanker broker. It is as a person who visits the seashore to be exhilarated, calmed, or refreshed. Out of this age-old sentiment, older probably than the sail and the rock anchor, springs the major new marine bonanza—not oil, minerals, or new regulatory guidelines, but coastal tourism. The jet-age migration to warm shores dwarfs human movements of the past in volume, speed, and turnover. This urge to enjoy the coastal marine environment can be far more traumatic than oil spills. Each tourist flight can release a broadside of overloaded sewage outfalls, overflowing dump sites, and over-pumped water basins. The inflationary impact of tourism can be just as traumatic. Local residents can't afford to compete with tourists as food prices and apartment rents spiral. Young people may find that fishing and farming no longer pay the rent. They must learn to ape maritime glories of the past as costumed waiters, door captains, or blackjack dealers

. . . or to grow pot in deserted sugar cane fields and to smuggle drugs or political refugees.

Many coastal regions willingly accept such social and environmental disruptions as the necessary price of progress. These regions, as in the past, contend with limited resources and trade deficits. New World gold fleets and long distance fishing fleets no longer offset such crippling deficits. Today, from the Mediterranean to Hawaii, a feverish flow of people armed with sunglasses and credit cards accomplish this. Devising new ways to lure the tourist trade can be more critical than advanced ship design, better fishing gear, or improved fish culture. These regions want saltwater Barnums and Baileys, not marine ecologists or deep-sea miners.

The attraction of the seashore can transcend nationality, religion, and economic systems. It wells up in youths who pole small boats through Bengali marshes, in Los Angeles families who seek relief from urban smog on the Malibu shore, and in elderly British couples watching the sunset in Blackpool. People who never visit the ocean still share in its fascinations as expressed in the work of artists, writers, and musicians. This human affection for the sea can have more genuine depth of feeling than all the overblown slogans about the freedom of the seas and the common heritage of mankind. Can this sense of shared wonder help kindle the sense of global marine community that so far eludes us and that the current competition for marine resources may mock into oblivion? Must the "wild" ocean be retired to a few refuges or to glass boxes in dentists' waiting rooms?

Clearly, the ocean will play a critical role as we act out our ultimate fate on this planet. Yet our current attitudes towards the sea are shot through with contradictions and conflicts, mistaken expectations, and overlooked opportunities. We are just beginning to learn the real meaning of living on a watery planet.

2

Boil

FISHERMEN CALL IT A "BOIL." THE blue sea starts to froth as if it were boiling. As the boil moves slowly along the horizon, a pelican materializes out of a deserted sky. It hovers for a moment, then plunges seaward to penetrate the source of the boil: a huge school of small, silvery fish. Their wriggling bodies make the ocean surface froth. The pelican pops back to the surface, its pouchlike bill filled with some of the wriggling bodies. The one pelican is followed by a hundred, the hundred by a thousand hovering, diving, splashing, gorging pelicans. Screeching sea gulls join this aerial circus to compete for scraps that fall from the pelicans' bills.

Other predators converge on the boil from below: the sleek, torpedolike forms of tuna and barracuda. The tuna attempt to encircle the school so the tight formation will turn into panic-stricken chaos. Sharks displace the gorging tuna and barracuda and then blindly bite each other as the feeding frenzy spirals. Blood streaks the boil.

Caught between seabirds above and marine predators below, the small fish continue to move as one unit, twisting and veering, moving up and down, trying to shake their tormentors. The school will succeed and survive out of sheer abundance. The seabirds, tuna, and sharks eventually recede. The sea is blue again.

Today, a new predator stalks these telltale boils with huge walls of webbing. The global fishing industry, which once used boils as clues to bigger fish, now prefers to catch the smaller fish. It does so with a relentless efficiency that could jeopardize the living oceans.

The boil is a critical link in the marine food chain. Large land animals such as buffalo, elephants, deer, and horses can graze casually on mountain meadows and prairies, but the ocean contains few equivalent large forage plant systems. Yet the ocean teems with life. Marine pastures are formed by tiny plants and animals—plankton—that drift with the currents. Baleen or filter-feeding whales graze on these mobile pastures, but most large marine animals can't. They must pursue the small, filter-feeding fish found in the boils—sardine, anchovy, menhaden, herring, and related species. (Scientists group them into the suborder *clupeoids*.)

If such a food chain prevailed on land, elephants and buffalo might pursue rodent packs, which in turn would pursue tiny plants drifting across the landscape like dust clouds. Without forage fish, our most esteemed sport and commercial fish would be on short rations. They are valuable to us without even being caught.

Forage fish appear to reproduce as haphazardly as a dandelion giving up its tiny seeds to summer breezes. On moonlit nights, a female may emit up to 10,000 eggs. In a year's time, a female menhaden may emit up to 700,000 eggs. The hatched young, smaller than your thumbnail, enter a hostile world with few natural defenses. They cannot sting, bite, poison, or outswim predators. Squirrels and other small land animals can scamper up trees or down burrows, but the open ocean offers few sanctuaries. Adults do not protect their struggling young. Indeed, adults may consume their progeny amid the plankton pastures. The young destined to survive will form a crucial elite. From 50 to 99 percent of the eggs that are spawned will not make it.

After consuming their yolk sac, the newborn fish literally collide with their first meal of tiny marine plants and animals. With this newfound energy, the minute fish sense their power to guide themselves. The body deepens. Scales form. A remarkable evolutionary imprint asserts itself. Without milling about or bumping into each other, the tiny fish begin to move together as one. They may form a school less than three months after being cast randomly into the waters.

By schooling, the small fish can band together as one large object to scare off smaller predators. Once under attack, the school's outer members may satiate predator appetites and spare most of the school. One school can be as wide as three football fields, over 90 feet deep, and can contain a population of millions. These millions of fish swim with a close precision that only a drill instructor for the Marines could appreciate.

Forage fish can swim with their mouths agape, filtering two gallons of water a minute to extract their microscopic diet. At every aquatic turn, these marathon feeders can face stabbing beaks or ripping teeth. Forage fish grow a foot long and weigh six pounds, but most are as long and as light as your pen. They can live six years and longer, but few will die of old age. Their final resting place is often the stomach of a tuna, seal, or seabird. They are universal fodder, as critical to marine life systems as prairies and meadows are to life systems on land.

People close to the sea have sensed this relationship for some time. In 1556, long before the advent of marine ecologists and environmental impact reports, the Dutch painter Pieter Brueghel depicted a huge, beached fish in one of his paintings. Men on ladders were cutting open the fish's belly. Out of the belly and the mouth spilled a glut of small fish. The painting was entitled "Big Fish Eat Little Fish." Brueghel had it right over 400 years ago.

Human beings have also exploited select forage stocks as food. The Pacific sardine off California, once a cheap source of canned protein, helped millions of Americans get through the hard times of the Depression. The anchovy has livened up countless pizzas. For over three centuries, the North Sea herring has served as a protein staple for millions of Europeans. British herring fishermen would chant:

We who plow the North Sea deep
Though never sowing, always reap
The harvest which to all is free.

Other forage stocks were considered too oily and not as tasty as tuna, salmon, and other preferred species. Scorned by the civilized palate, clupeoids often wound up as fertilizer or bait. As a boy fishing on California sport charter boats, I remember that the burning question concerning the use of the northern anchovy was whether it should be hooked in the mouth or the tail in order to catch "real" fish.

A shift in world food production has transformed forage fish into gold mines of the sea. Since World War II, poultry and pig ranchers have used artificial feeds instead of household garbage to expand production. Feed supplements must be cheap, nutritious, and in ample supply. Forage fish ground up into fishmeal can serve this purpose.

In order to serve as feed for pigs and chickens, forage fish must be caught in quantities far in excess of fish caught for human consumption. One ton of fishmeal requires 5 tons of forage fish. In one year, Peru surpassed such fishing giants as Russia and Japan in tons of fish landed by catching 12 million metric tons of just one fish, the 6-inch-long anchoveta. The 12 million tons became less than 3 million tons of meal.

The schooling behavior that helps forage fish ward off natural predation assists such massive human predation. By schooling, forage fish do everything but swim into the fishing vessel and operate the machinery. Sardine and herring schools become mobile veins of biological ore, to be detected by electronic probes and extracted by walls of webbing. The telltale boils help alert eager fishermen to their presence. And schools show up clearly on sonar screens even when they're well below the sea surface.

A huge net is deployed around the sonar "signature." Whirring winches retrieve it and tighten it into a sodden bag of tiny, writhing bodies whose scales flash silver under night work lights. A suction hose transfers this squirming cargo to the hold. One school can contain up to 10,000 tons of "raw" product, and one cast of a mechanized net can retrieve over 200 tons. Man himself could not train these fish to fit so perfectly the needs of industrial fishing operations.

The tons of wet biomass sloshing around in the holds of a hunter-vessel would overwhelm a conventional cannery. A special reduction plant is required. The plant, with its metal stacks, looping pipes, and storage tanks, resembles a refinery or mine smelter. You smell a reduction plant before you see it. The most accurate set of directions I ever received came while in search of a reduction plant in coastal New Jersey: "Just follow the stink."

Forage fish that enter this plant in huge suction hoses depart in limp brown bags of meal. Inside, machinery steam cooks, presses, dries, and grinds tons of fish—heads, bones, guts, and all —into tan-colored, powdery meal. One steam cooker can cook 35 tons every hour. Oil squeezed out of the lifeless bodies helps to make margarine, lipstick, and explosives. There is not much left for scavenging cats and gulls.

Through such industrial ingenuity, one critical element in the marine food system can be diverted to barnyards thousands of miles away from the sound of foghorns and bell buoys. Six-pound chickens and 200-pound hogs can gorge themselves on marine protein literally snatched from the jaws of tuna and the bills of pelicans. Our own dietary preferences fuel this massive protein diversion. Each American consumes about 53 pounds of fish yearly, but less than one-quarter of this is consumed in the form of fish. We consume the rest mainly as eggs, chicken, ham, and sausage from poultry and pigs nourished in part on fishmeal.

Everybody would appear to benefit by fishing further down the food chain: the poultry producers and consumers, the fishermen, the coastal hamlets turned fishing boom towns. National governments will even subsidize construction of fishing fleets to cash in on the commercial clamor for clupeoids. Fishmeal exports can secure sorely needed foreign exchange for nations battling trade deficits. Peru has obtained up to one-third of its foreign exchange by pursuing the anchoveta.

The case for exploiting the gold mines of the sea seems persuasive until you consider the economic and ecological backlash. Just how abundant are these fish? How great is the danger of disrupting the food chain?

Our exploitation of forage stocks was producing disturbing results even before the global demand for fishmeal skyrocketed. During the 1930s, the largest fishery in the United States flourished off California. Its target was the Pacific sardine. Catches began to fluctuate dramatically by the 1940s, and by the 1950s the Monterey canneries immortalized by John Steinbeck began closing. Scavenging gulls moved on to cultivate rotting garbage dumps and other new food sources.

Some scientists were confident that the sardine would return. Because of this prospect, other nations hurried to build up their own forage fisheries to cash in on California's misfortune and profit from the fishmeal boom. Fishing vessels were built to travel faster. Nets were made larger. Airplane spotters were recruited to expand a vessel's range of detection. Fish schools show up like inkspots from the air, and the spotter can direct the set of the net with the precision of an artillery spotter bracketing gunfire.

Some idle California canners were surprised to find that Spanish-speaking businessmen were anxious to buy their rusting equipment. The buyers were gearing up to exploit the Peruvian anchoveta.

Because of the frenetic global hunt for forage fish, the world marine fish catch soared, growing in annual jumps of 8 percent. But in the 1970s the catch leveled off, growing at 2 percent or less a year.

What happened?

During the late 1960s and early 1970s, the forage fisheries declined abruptly: herring and menhaden catches off our Atlantic coast, the herring fishery off Norway, the sardine fishery off South Africa. "The harvest which to all is free"—the North Sea herring fishery—plummeted, unable to feed both humans and livestock. The traditional chant of herring fishermen became a bitter parody.

Scientists refer to these spectacular declines as population collapses or crashes—and no wonder. Peru's anchoveta fishery went from a record 12 million metric tons in 1970 to less than 2 million metric tons by 1973. For Peru, the massive buildup of the fishing industry became an economic curse. Reduction plants became as useless as smelters next to a played-out mine. The air is fresh again in many coastal towns. For the unemployed, this is a mixed blessing.

Since 1955, the number of menhaden reduction plants along the U.S. Atlantic coast has dropped from 28 to 9. In California, some sardine canneries have reopened—as restored theme restaurants that import marine entrées from as far away as South Africa.

Such collapses can stun marine scientists as well as coastal communities and national political leaders. Describing the anchoveta collapse as "another clupeoid misadventure," U.S. fishery expert Garth Murphy concluded, "Clearly, something is wrong with our approach to these kinds of resources."

What accounts for such collapses? Because of natural causes, forage fish populations fluctuate much more dramatically from year to year than tuna and other stocks higher on the food chain. Just a few degrees difference in water temperature or a change in ocean currents can result in a poor year for the survival of newborn fish. However, the population usually bounces back once favorable climatic conditions return.

That's why some scientists expected the Pacific sardine to bounce back. But it didn't. Had overfishing, on top of unfavorable climatic conditions, triggered the collapse? In 1967, almost two decades after the sardine collapse, California decided to ban sardine fishing at the behest of scientists. Few sardine fishermen were left to protest.

The fishery advisers who had originally urged Peru to fish the anchoveta intensively now urged more caution. But to Peru, as to other nations before and since, the clupeoid collapses were an economic goad rather than an ecological omen. World fishmeal prices were soaring.

In 1972, two years after the record anchoveta catch, Peru's coastal waters became warmer. Heavy rains triggered floods that rampaged through the coastal boom towns. Fishing vessels returned to port with empty holds. The fishery and Peru's economy were in the hot, humid grip of El Niño. Cooler waters have long since returned, but not the anchoveta in its former abundance. Peru's experience confirmed what many scientists first began to suspect in California: that overfishing on top of poor climatic conditions can trigger forage fishery collapses.

Today, fishermen who set a net on the North Sea herring or the Pacific sardine may be jailed or fined. Such public penalties seek to insure recovery of the marine gold mines. With such protection, depleted predator stocks such as salmon, halibut, and certain marine mammal species can recover in some cases. What about depleted forage stocks? The Japanese sardine shows signs of recovery . . . some forty years after it was intensively exploited.

Fishery officials don't expect the Pacific sardine to recover before the turn of the century, if ever. No one is predicting when the North Sea herring, the Norwegian herring, the Peruvian anchoveta, and the South African sardine will recover. When we risk fishing further down the marine food chain, we may get only one roll of the dice.

And we can lose more than forage fish with a bad roll. When Peru's anchoveta declined, so did a major anchoveta predator—the bonito, which is similar to the tuna. For a nation reeling from the loss of its major export, this related decline was another economic blow, since the bonito was Peru's major domestic food fish. Peru's seabird population also declined, from 28 million to a low of a half million. Ergo, another economic setback. Guano (bird droppings) deposited on desert islets by these anchoveta predators supplies a fertilizer industry. Today, in some coastal towns, children and pelicans compete for scraps in garbage dumps.

Why are seabirds so vulnerable to such collapses? Pelican expert James Keith of the U.S. Fish and Wildlife Service observes that, when feeding by itself, a pelican will recover a fish on fewer than half its dives. With a boil or "pile-up," this success rate jumps to 90 percent, according to Keith. "It is not the biomass of fish in the ocean, but the pile-up which is important for the pelican," says Keith. Alternative prey that could sustain fish predators may swim at depths beyond a seabird's diving capability.

The fate of a small fish off New England adds another foreboding dimension to such collapses. The sand lance is so named because it will plunge into the sandy seabed to evade bluefish, porpoises, and other predators. While Atlantic menhaden and herring stocks recede under exploitation, sand lance stocks proliferate. (At low tide, clam diggers will see these fish clustered like huge piles of silver ore.) Is this just a coincidence? All three species compete for similar food sources, including their own young. Some scientists now feel that the sand lance population has expanded because its food competitors are being systematically removed. Furthermore, its expanded population can serve as a lid to block recovery of the stressed stock. To Richard Frank, former administrator of the National Oceanic and Atmospheric Administration (NOAA), the sand lance "may significantly impair the ability of herring stocks to return to their former levels."

Our fishing strategies thus not only can exhaust a forage stock but can militate against its recovery by altering the very composition of a coastal ecosystem. Do stocks favored by such selective fishing pressures provide the basis for new gold mines of the sea? Replacement species are often smaller, shorter-lived species with little economic value. According to Richard Frank, the sand lance is a "smaller, less economically desirable species." If we gardened like we fished, we would be uprooting vegetables so crabgrass could expand.

Clearly, we must recognize the critical role of forage fish or risk disrupting the marine ecosystem and our own expectations of the ocean as a protein source. The pelican skimming along the waves, the seal sunning itself on a rock, the tuna cruising in the blue depths, and the anchovy school swimming just below the surface may appear to have separate fates; but in reality, their fates are inextricably intertwined. Yet we tend to manage each fish species separately. We assign catch quotas or limits on a species-by-species basis with little or no regard for the complex ways that fish interact with each other, or for climatic changes. Imagine what would happen if we managed a cattle herd without regard for the condition of the range.

Scientists now urge that fishery resources be managed on a multispecies or ecosystem basis. Congress recognized this need in passing the landmark Fisheries Conservation and Management Act (FCMA) in 1976. This act extends our fishery jurisdiction 200 miles seaward to control foreign fishing efforts. Realizing that domestic fishing must also be controlled, Congress has mandated the secretary of commerce, through the National Marine Fisheries Service (NMFS) and regional fishery councils, to prepare management plans. These plans must "prevent overfishing" and "rebuild overfished stocks." The act declares that "interrelated stocks of fish shall be managed as a unit or in close coordination." The secretary of commerce shall maintain a "comprehensive program" of "biological research concerning the interdependence of fisheries or stocks of fish."

Congress obviously wants to give our coastal ecosystems a new lease on life. But this lease may be foreclosed by the very officials responsible for complying with Congress's mandate. In a recent (1979) report to Congress, the highly respected General

Accounting Office (GAO) criticized NMFS and the fishery councils for "limited long-range planning." Stock assessment lacks "knowledge concerning the interrelatedness among species." In other words, we still manage fish stocks separately, as if they existed in zoo cages.

Ominously enough, the race to exploit can ensnare more key forage stocks. The secretary of commerce has adopted a plan to exploit the northern anchovy off the Pacific coast for fishmeal. One justification for this is that we can now predict and control our fishing pressures on these sensitive stocks. But can we? The anchovy management plan candidly concedes, "The impact of an anchovy fishery on other fish species, birds and mammals cannot be predicted with accuracy." What can be stated with accuracy is that in the coastal waters off California, where the Pacific sardine has already been depleted, the anchovy is now the major food source for bluefin tuna, albacore (the white-meat tuna), the Pacific bonito, and other important commercial fish. It is also the primary food source for the endangered brown pelican.

Can the fishery be closed in time if overfishing occurs? The plan states frankly: "Whether such an action would come in time to forestall a long period of highly depleted anchovy stocks is problematical." Can tuna, pelicans, dolphins, and pilot whales find other prey? According to the plan, "There is no clear indication that equivalent alternatives exist in the ocean; most likely alternatives will be less efficient sources of nutrition." Nesting success of the California pelican colony dropped sharply in 1978. A team of scientists surmised that the parents abandoned nests because of a lack of anchovies to raise their young. Peru's seabirds behave in a similar manner. California shares another disquieting link with Peru's experience: a sharp decline in bonito stocks.

During hearings on the anchovy management plan, scientists with NMFS (this acronym is often pronounced as if it were "nymphs") contended that annual surveys of newly hatched fish (larva) would serve to monitor the anchovy's shifting abundance. Conservation and recreational fishing representatives, including Herb Kameon of the National Coalition for Marine Conservation, criticized these surveys as being unreliable. Dr. Gary Brewer, a fishery scientist with the University of Southern California who samples extensively in coastal waters, described the surveys as "painfully crude." One federal survey resulted in stock estimates two to three times higher than estimates by California fishery officials.

As it turns out, NMFS scientists are concerned with their survey method too. In 1980, Dr. Gary Stauffer of NMFS's Southwest Fisheries Center disclosed that the larva survey requires "unverifiable assumptions." He urged a new survey method based on egg production. This method resulted in a 1980 anchovy biomass estimate so low that, under the anchovy management plan, no reduction fishery would be permitted. The Pacific Fishery Management Council chooses to maintain catch quotas based on the old method while the new one is "calibrated." Unimpressed, the California Fish and Game Commission will only allow onshore reduction plants to process half the federally approved quotas. Dr. Brewer regards the egg production survey as a definite improvement.

What about closing the gap on scientific understanding of how fish interact? In a 1980 NMFS report, scientists Daniel Huppert and Alec MacCall stated, "The long-term studies needed to develop an inter-species model for management purposes are not now being done, nor is it obvious that they will be funded in the future." Simply put, scientists are not receiving the funding to carry out Congress's mandate.

Meanwhile, 300 miles to the south, Mexico is developing its own forage fishery in a joint venture with a U.S. fishmeal producer, Zapata Corporation of Houston, Texas. The target is the very same northern anchovy stock that triggers controversy north of the border. Mexico imposes no regulations of any kind on its anchovy fishermen, much to the consternation of U.S. fishermen. In a recent fishery conference in California, Mexican fishery scientist Alejandro Villamar disclosed that, based on Mexican catch statistics, the anchovy fishery is "at or near maximum exploitation limits." Younger fish dominate the catch and fishermen must expend more effort to maintain past catch levels. Can the United States and Mexico agree to manage the anchovy jointly before their respective fishing efforts make such an issue academic? So far the only major accord has been to exchange more foreboding catch data.

Finally, pressures to fish further down the food chain jeopardize the existence of the ocean's largest living creatures. In the Southern Ocean, which encircles Antarctica, swarms of small, shrimplike krill sustain what large whales remain as well as countless seals, penguins, and seabirds. Industrial nations with idle fishing fleets now pursue krill for food and fishmeal. Japan's krill fleet intends to double its present annual catch of 21,000 tons. But Dr. Sidney Holt, a fisheries adviser to the United Nations' Food and Agriculture Organization, warns that it might be more prudent "to leave the Southern Ocean in its relatively pristine state for the time being, while the great whales recover, while mankind learns much more about the dynamics of that rich biological system, and while strong international institutions are developed, which would one day be capable of organizing a rational use of the area for the benefit of mankind." It would be ironic indeed if we saved the great whales from harpoons only to starve them by harvesting krill for chicken feed.

3

The Last
Hunting Grounds

THE MODERN FISHING CAPTAIN, with all his mechanized gear, cannot escape one constraint that binds all hunters: the need to find new hunting grounds. I began to appreciate this better while looking at the fate of the world fish catch since the collapse of the forage fish stocks. The spectacular rate of growth in the catch during the 1950s and 1960s slowed to less than 2 percent annually during the 1970s. Nutrition experts once banked on the fishing industry as one answer to world food shortages, but the world fish catch is no longer able to keep abreast of the annual growth in world population.

Given the collapse of the forage fisheries, how has the catch managed to remain relatively stable? Catch pressures have shifted to fish higher on the food chain to the point that cod and tuna catches now approach, if not exceed, their sustainable yield. Commercial fish landings in California remain at about the same level as forty years ago. Most of the fish landed then came from coastal waters and included the now-depleted Pacific sardine. Today, about half the landings consist of tropical tuna caught far beyond California's coastal waters.

Won't expanded fishery jurisdiction by coastal nations help augment catches? This jurisdictional shift often only serves to reallocate the catch of fleets from distant nations to those of coastal nations that are able to build up their own fishing fleets. At the same time that Russia and Japan cut back their catches in U.S. coastal waters, U.S. tuna and shrimp fishermen find they must do the same off prime Latin American fishing grounds.

Many fish stocks mock a nationalistic approach to fishery management. "All the Sea is their native country," wrote Spanish cleric Martin Sarmiento of tuna in 1757. The tuna haven't changed their highly migratory habits since then and neither have swordfish and marlin. Nations which can agree to manage these wanderers jointly will, in the long run, be better off than those nations which compete to deplete these stocks with the most efficient technology available. Regional fish commissions, such as the Inter-American Tropical Tuna Commission (IATTC) in La Jolla, California, offer the independent, technical expertise to do this. Agreement is not always easy to come by, particularly when the parties include an industrial nation with an established fishery and a developing nation trying to build up its fleet so it can share in the economic benefits of joint conservation. The United States and Mexico, already competing for the anchovy, can't agree on how to manage transboundary tuna. Catch quotas that IATTC Director James Joseph considers prudent are being exceeded. Failing agreement, consumers can expect to see the price of tuna spiral as overfishing exacts its toll. The big game angler partial to trophy tuna and billfish in the tradition of Ernest Hemingway and Zane Grey can expect lean times too.

What about those much-publicized projections that the world fish catch can be doubled? Some projections may assume that catches in the open ocean will approximate those in coastal waters. However, coastal waters are generally far more productive and nutrient-rich. About 90 percent of the world's fish catch comes from three percent of the ocean's area, the coastal waters already under intense fishing pressures.

Some projections are based on catching plankton. These tiny, drifting plants and animals can be costly and energy-intensive to catch in quantities sufficient for human consumption. Moreover, while forage fish like plankton, their taste is not so appealing to us.

Other projections count on bigger catches from tropical waters. However, the dense, single-stock concentrations common in temperate or sub-arctic waters are not as common in tropical waters, where marine life communities are much more diverse. When you snorkel coral reefs in the Carribean or Hawaii, you are observing a much greater variety of life, but in populations less dense than the salmon and anchovy schools you might see in colder waters. There may also be a higher incidence of potentially toxic marine life in tropical communities, as reflected in Polynesian taboos against eating many species. The diverse tropical communities appear to rely on such chemical warfare to balance predator pressures. These unique tropical life communities could be just as easily disrupted by single-species removal as marine ecosystems in colder waters.

Such constraints suggest how fishermen can run out of new hunting grounds, even on the watery planet. The hunter as well as the hunted can become doomed, as indicated by the rusting reduction plants in Peru and the dusty whale harpoons that serve as decor in thematic cocktail lounges.

As hunting grounds become more limited, the hunters can clash more frequently. While invariably couched in the language of conservation, national claims to extended fishery jurisdiction more often reflect an intent to exclude other hunters, namely foreign fishermen. The British invoked conservation in banishing the Dutch herring fishery from its coastal waters in the seventeenth century. So did Iceland in banishing British fishermen

---

from its coastal waters in the twentieth century. Domestic fishermen can even engage in tribal squabbles over hunting rights. Recreational fishermen feel that commercial marlin and swordfish catches should be cut back; commercial fishermen contend that such fish should go for food rather than sport. With recreational marine fishing already a multi-million-dollar business in the United States, such clashes may intensify. Recreational fishermen have been most vocal in urging more conservative catch quotas on forage fish used as fishmeal.

While catches decline and policy conflicts escalate, national fishing strategies can continue to vacillate between costly subsidies, technical fixes and wishful projections. Shrimp fishermen, caught between the fuel crunch and cutoffs from foreign shrimping grounds, lobby Congress to suspend default provisions on federal vessel loans. At the same time, canners lobby to extend federal subsidies to *onshore processing facilities.* Congressman Paul McCloskey (R.-CA) considers this "unabashed barrel of pork . . . about as reasonable as expanding ship mortgages to cover loading docks or ferry terminals."

As living marine resources shrink, the quest for more efficient gear can border on the ludicrous. Some sport fishing journals trumpet the availability of electric-powered reels. Other gear improvements only intensify the basic predicament. Some Florida commercial fishermen deploy wire traps in productive reef areas. Such gear is inexpensive, easy to repair and, compared to active fishing, requires a minimum of effort. Bloody bait in the trap can add to the catch efficiency.

To Lyman Rogers of the Florida League of Anglers, these traps "are as deadly to reef populations as the use of dynamite." The traps are the latest and most perverse example of gear improvements that trigger incidental kills of "non-target organisms." (Such language is reminiscent of the euphemisms practiced in the Vietnam War.) The traps can ensnare many non-commercial species, including the colored tropical reef fish that attract tourists and delight skin divers. Can't these innocent victims be released when the trap is retrieved? Yes, at least those that survive starvation, cannibalism and fatal gas embolism caused by rapid ascent to the surface. Lost or "ghost" traps can continue their killing ways indefinitely. The widespread use of such traps has been linked to decimated reef fish populations off Jamaica and the Virgin Islands.

Current attempts to restore marine turtle populations can be set back by incidental kills of turtles in nets. Some 63 percent of fish discards from shrimp nets is composed of table-quality bottom fish.

Must we fish indiscriminately up and down the marine food chain, regardless of our ability to control such exploitation, just to maintain our supply of marine protein? The answer is an emphatic no. We have a whole range of alternatives. We can increase the supply of marine protein without casting a single net. If we invest in better sewage treatment and urban runoff control, we can lift the quarantine that exists on 27.5 percent of this nation's commercial shellfish beds. We can't blame foreign fishermen for this statistic. We can protect critical marine habitat from being buried by real estate projects. Two-thirds of the fish most important to sport and commercial fishermen along the Atlantic and Gulf coasts depend on estuaries to feed and spawn.

We can invest in better handling and storage facilities to cut fish loss through spoilage. On a global level, improved fish storage could supply consumers with an additional five million tons of fish a year, according to the United Nations' Food and Agriculture Organization.

While the commercial fish catch is regulated, the number of commercial fishermen often is not. Imagine what would happen if we limited the number of trees to be cut in our national forest but not the number of corporate cutters. This "unlimited entry" invariably fosters the excessive fishing capacity that can make the marine hunt as frenzied as a boil. At one time, Peru had enough reduction capacity to process the whole world catch into fishmeal. During the Cuban refugee influx, I was surprised to read that U.S. commercial fishermen were so heavily involved in illegal transport of refugees. Yet, when there are too many fishermen and not enough fish, this is what excess fishing capacity can lead to. So many commercial fishing vessels were detained by U.S. officials that commercial fishing ports were pleading for early release of impounded vessels so the fishing season would not go down the drain.

Economists such as Francis Christy of Resources for the Future urge governments to institute limited entry systems to avert such costly and inefficient overcapacity. Both Washington and Alaska are attempting to institute such systems for salmon. Ironically, government policies can actually contribute to over-capacity. The General Accounting Office found that, under a federal loan program administered by NMFS, forty-five vessels have been constructed to fish depleted groundfish stocks off New England. This subsidized jump in fishing overkill was cited as a rationale by the New England Regional Fishery Council to *increase* catch quotas on the stressed stocks.

A law that bans U.S. fishermen from using foreign vessels prompted Congress to provide such subsidies. Ship builders pushed through this law. It may be time to give U.S. fishermen the same market access as U.S. car buyers and get taxpayers out of this subsidy bind.

The frantic competition to hunt down stressed stocks emphasizes the need to enforce critical catch quotas. But quota enforcement can serve to protect fishermen rather than fish. GAO found that, "Fishermen frequently land their catch at night when enforcement personnel are not on duty or at remote ports that are not patrolled. The extent of unreported catches is unknown but has been estimated to be as high as 40 percent of reported catches." Better quota enforcement could protect fish as well as fishermen who comply with quotas. Funds to subsidize more fishing overkill might be diverted to this purpose.

Commercial fishermen are often in a unique position to undercut Congress's mandate to "prevent overfishing." GAO found that composition of the New England Council "is heavily weighted toward persons employed in the fishing industry. Environmentalists, scientists and consumer groups are noticeably absent." As the value of living marine resources expands to such "non-consumptive" uses as whale watching or reef snorkeling, the public opportunity to determine wise use should be expanded as well. At the same time, both recreational fishermen and marine animal watchers should be prepared to help foot the bill to protect living marine resources. Only a minority of coastal states require sport fishermen to buy annual fishing licenses. NMFS is only now beginning to undertake a comprehensive study of the recreational marine catch; the most recent data available is a *decade old*, according to NMFS.

Incidental kills of fish accidentally caught in nets can be reduced through better gear design, including wider mesh. Panels in wire traps can be designed to degrade and render ghost traps harmless. The size, number and mesh of these traps can be controlled too. Florida has banned wire traps because of the slowness of federal fishery officials in enacting such controls.

Some tasty fish have distasteful names—ratfish, dogfish and gag. We can change regulations that *require* use of common fish names, however unappealing or misleading. If we learn which of the so-called "trash" fish are quality table fish we can gain marine protein at a less intense level of fishing.

In a world of more than four billion people we must also think long and hard on the waste of marine protein that occurs when we convert fish to livestock feed. Nutrition expert Dr. Jean Mayer observed in *Science,* "More food would be provided for man if a smaller percentage of the fish were used as animal feed." Today, British officials would forgo a fishmeal industry if it would insure the return of the North Sea herring as a food fish. If the U.S. menhaden fishery were diverted from animal feed to human food, U.S. supplies of edible fish would double, according to NMFS. (Both menhaden and anchovy can be tasty if properly prepared.)

Would such a shift put the livestock industry on short rations? Pig and poultry ranchers have already learned to rely on other feeds—soybeans, cottonseed meal, bone meal, and meat scraps—that are cheaper and in more dependable supply than forage fish. As a result, poultry production can continue to expand while the forage fish catch declines or stagnates.

By more efficient use of existing fisheries, we could gain time to develop more reliable fishery management plans and give our coastal species a better chance to recover from past mistakes. When we overfish the small forage fish of the sea, we tinker with perhaps the most critical link in the marine life system. We had better know what we are doing. We can restore rundown auto engines; a rundown ocean is another matter.

In terms of territory gained by the global trend towards 200-mile-wide coastal fishing zones, the United States is the biggest winner, with some two million square miles of coastal waters. But without a broader perspective on fishery management, this resource windfall could go the way of denuded forests and exhausted farm soils. These management reforms are not going to come easily. The commercial fishing industry has often opposed limited entry systems, even with grandfather clauses. The protection of critical estuarine habitat can collide head on with the traditional use of bays as urban sewage sinks, real estate reservoirs, and industrial quays.

The fate of tuna and billfish becomes entrained in the overriding question of whether nation-states can evolve a sense of global community on a fluid planet. Such heated policy conflicts can divert attention from the opportunities provided by aquatic resources.

4

Aquaculture: Hitches in the Dream

IN WASHINGTON'S PUGET SOUND, a man casts pellets on the shallow, inshore waters. A hundred juvenile salmon rise to feed. Such a scene represents one of humanity's most cherished ambitions: to raise rather than just hunt fish on the watery planet.

Human demand for fish is rising as never before, while the supply of natural or wild fish stocks is limited by overfishing and pollution. The opportunity for aquaculture would seem to be better than ever. The aquatic farmer would guarantee a regular supply of fish to restaurants and markets that must contend with natural and artificially induced fluctuations in wild stocks. Consumers would have an alternative supply of fish protein that might help keep fish prices down. Nations could cut fish imports and restore their balance of trade.

In some respects, aquatic animals seem designed to meet the dream specifications of a cattle rancher or hog raiser. It takes eight or nine pounds of grain to put one pound on a beef steer, but only one and a half to two pounds of grain to put one pound on some species of fish. Fish, being cold-blooded, retain the temperature of their environment and do not need to expend calories to maintain a constant body temperature, as warm-blooded animals do.

Cattle take about 960 days to raise before they can be marketed. Hogs take 240 days. Some marine animals, such as shrimp, require about 200 days. This fast growth can become another potential benefit for the aquatic farmer.

No farmer would attempt to stack cattle four deep in a feedlot, but this can be easily accomplished with fish or shellfish in the water column of a pond. Moreover, prime soils or grazing lands are not necessary for aquatic herds. Coastal swamps, wet-lands, or other low-cost lands will do just fine.

Given such tantalizing opportunities, it is not surprising to see daily media reports on projects to raise salmon, abalone, lobster, or shrimp. Indeed, one critical question for a prospective aquatic farmer is what to raise: fish, shellfish, a seaweed like giant kelp? One species or a mixture of species? Freshwater or marine species? A high-value species with proven market potential or a low-cost species that must be sold in large volume?

Let's say you choose a marine species, as many operators in the United States have done. (The cultivation of marine species is known as mariculture.) Now you need a site, preferably as close to the shore as possible so you can culture the organisms in the actual marine environment or pump seawater to artificial rearing ponds. Low-cost coastal sites are not easy to come by. You may have to compete with resort developers, the U.S. Navy, condo-minium developers, and oil companies looking for coastal refinery and port sites. Unlike the U.S. Navy or Exxon, you need high-quality seawater. Urban pollution can further constrain the range of sites available, not to speak of the growing threat of oil spills.

Somehow you manage to obtain a site. Now you must invest in a physical plant, which can range from simple rearing ponds to complex processing facilities. Feeds can range from low-cost grains to high-protein fortified foods. You may have to procure "trash" or "rough" fish to raise a high-value fish. You must hire and train workers and hope that a competitor doesn't pirate them. You must cope with natural hazards. One shrimp farmer was doing pretty well in Florida until his cultured shrimp escaped into nearby coastal waters during a hurricane. Commercial shrimpers had a field day harvesting the liberated shrimp.

Your fish may be fine one day, only to be floating belly up the next morning. Water temperatures can change overnight. You may be better off choosing a species that is relatively tolerant to temperature changes (such as mullet) than investing in temperature-sensitive animals that can be killed off after one cold night. Water temperatures can affect your work force as well, since workers have easier access to a warm-water site than to a cold-water site that necessitates the use of wet suits.

Perhaps you have made the right choice and have anticipated such difficulties. Now you may face a factor that optimistic government reports on aquaculture don't mention: government regulations. Want to take advantage of the sheltered waters of a bay or estuary for pens? Public easements for navigation and fisheries may override your need for exclusive use. Need to dispose of water that accumulates waste matter in the rearing ponds? The Environmental Protection Agency (EPA) may impose discharge standards on you.

Say you manage to overcome regulatory hitches as well as the natural and economic risks. Your fish are doing fine until they are exposed to a disease. You must then pay for drugs, if indeed drugs for the disease are available. The more intensive the aquaculture operation, the greater the risk of disease.

Such problems suggest why aquaculture can be a high-risk enterprise. Considerable front-end capital costs may not be recovered for some years, if ever. This is why many aquaculture operators in the United States choose to rear high-value species such as shrimp, lobster, or salmon. With the existing strong market for such species, capital costs can be more readily recovered. However, such species may require expensive coastal sites and high-protein feeds. These capital costs can exclude one prospective class of investors—commercial fishermen—while favoring large corporations that are attracted to aquaculture by rising fish prices. This situation can inspire a new set of political problems reminiscent of the range wars that once engulfed the wild west.

A pair of salmon swim slowly through the cool depths of the north Pacific Ocean. Their undersides are bloated after gorging on a school of slender anchovy. While they look alike, one salmon is a unique blend of bioengineering and corporate drive. Salmon eggs have been hatched in artificial enclosures before being released into the wild for some time now. Hatcheries have mainly been operated by state and federal agencies, since there is little profit to be made by raising fish that will be caught by somebody else. However, salmon return to their home stream to spawn. Based on this spawning urge, wouldn't it be possible for a salmon hatchery to retrieve adult salmon it had originally hatched?

This premise has inspired the creation of private salmon ranches along the Oregon coast. The rancher rears juveniles in inland hatcheries, releases them to graze on the ocean commons, and waits for their return. The rancher may immunize his salmon against marine diseases. He figures he only needs to recapture 2 or 3 percent of the salmon he releases, thanks to the premium price salmon fetch in the world market. By fattening his aquatic herd on the ocean commons, the rancher avoids the highest cost in aquaculture: artificial feed. With the herd defecating as well as grazing in the open ocean, EPA remains aloof. In 1972, private salmon ranchers released 51,150 salmon. By 1979, they were releasing 18 million annually.

Salmon ranching would appear to benefit both sport and commercial fishermen. The 97 percent of salmon not recaptured remain to augment wild stocks depleted by overfishing, pollution, and loss of stream spawning habitat. To some fishery officials, private salmon ranching could eliminate the need for public hatcheries while increasing state fishery revenues. Salmon, so prone to man's environmental alterations, may benefit from more thoughtful intervention.

A controversial decision by a federal judge in the state of Washington has added impetus to salmon ranching. In the early 1970s the federal government and certain Pacific Northwest Indian tribes brought suit to clarify treaty rights involving fishery resources granted to these tribes in 1856. At that time, guaranteeing native Americans fishing rights to apparently abundant fish in exchange for tribal lands seemed like a good deal to the white man. After seeing fish stocks diminished by urban pollution, destruction of spawning habitats, and commercial salmon fleets, the tribes had to comply with catch restrictions imposed by state officials. The tribes felt that the 1856 treaty was being used to guarantee injustice rather than fish. After a lengthy trial, Judge George Boldt found that the treaty Indians did have special rights. This did not surprise either the Indians or the apprehensive state officials and their principal constituency, the commercial salmon fishermen and canners. The overriding question was how much of a special right. Judge Boldt declared the Indians were entitled to up to 50 percent of harvestable salmon in Puget Sound and the northern two-thirds of the Washington coast.

The initial response of shocked Washington officials was to fight the decision in the courts and in the press while blaming the Indians for careless fishing practices. A Supreme Court majority compared Washington's reluctance to enforce Boldt's order to the resistance of southern states to desegregation. The Court ordered the federal government to manage the state salmon fishery.

The Supreme Court later returned control to the state, but with the warning that federal officials will intervene again if the state remains defiant. Cooler heads are beginning to prevail. "It's not the Indian fishermen who have caused supplies of once plentiful fish to vanish," observed the *Seattle Post-Intelligencer.* "It's pollution, poor logging practices, thoughtless placement of dams, and a sprawling population. What's needed are ecologically sound conservation and management practices." If salmon stocks can be restored, there will be more for everybody. Amid this social stress, one would think that private salmon operators, with their surplus stocks, would be welcomed with open arms.

Instead, they encounter stiff opposition. The major corporation involved in Oregon salmon ranching is Weyerhauser Lumber. Historically, fishermen and Weyerhauser have been involved in bitter disputes over the degree to which lumbering practices destroy salmon stream habitat and deplete salmon stocks. This is not the sort of relationship that breeds mutual confidence. Can't Weyerhauser make up for its environmental sins by releasing more young salmon? Commercial fishermen observe that the salmon favored by most ranchers, including the Weyerhauser subsidiary (Oregon Aqua Foods), is the chum. The chum is the salmon least likely to bite on fishermen's hooks and lures. Some commercial fishermen fear that salmon ranchers will breed salmon hybrids trained to evade or jump fishing nets. Weyerhauser has supported legislative bans against such genetic manipulation in an attempt to defuse such fears, but the fishermen remain skeptical.

The ranchers seek temporary river fishing closures to expedite recapture operations when the salmon return. The fishermen feel that these closures are unjust because they occur at key fishing periods. The fishermen also don't like the gear employed by the ranchers, which makes use of electric shocks to stun the salmon. The fishermen are concerned that this gear can harm other fish in the river, including the wild salmon. The fishermen are also mindful that river recapture provides the salmon rancher with a significant cost advantage over people who must pursue salmon on the open ocean in gas-guzzling vessels.

Salmon ranchers, unlike fishermen, own their own processing plants. They can store temporary surpluses, including those of the fishermen. Because of this capability, some fishermen fear that corporate ranchers will eventually control the pricing and marketing of both cultured and wild stocks. With corporations riding the marine range, the fishermen envision a day when too many salmon will be the main problem. As one commercial salmon troller told a congressional subcommittee, "When the day comes that the starving masses are fed on aquacultured salmon, that will be the end of the troll industry, because the troll industry cannot afford to fish a product that becomes so ordinary that it does, in fact, feed the starving masses, or whatever."

While authorized to release up to 180 million salmon annually, private ranches release but a fraction of this number. They are short of eggs. Local stocks are not fecund enough. Sport and commercial fishermen want eggs from public hatcheries to benefit public programs to restock wild runs. Oregon Aqua imports chum eggs from a nation that does not grapple with such private-public conflicts, the Soviet Union.

What if an egg boom materializes and the cultured releases turn out at full authorized strength? Commercial fishermen are concerned that the cultured fish may interbreed with the wild fish, creating a genetically degraded hybrid that is less hardy or fit. The fishermen and the Oregon Environmental Council convinced a judge to enjoin a Crown Zellerbach ranch project because of such genetic specters.

Many commercial fishermen want Weyerhauser and Crown Zellerbach to confine their role in fishery development to cleaning up their lumbering act. Because of such mutual suspicion, commercial fishermen and private salmon ranchers agree on only one point: the need to control the population of harbor seals and other salmon predators. Harbor seals don't discriminate between wild and cultured salmon. Apart from this issue, the commercial fishermen have been seeking to ban private salmon ranching. Since there are many more fishermen than ranchers in the voting public, the winner on this legislative front should come as no surprise. While Oregon permits private salmon ranching, Washington, which happens to house the headquarters of Weyerhauser, does not. Undaunted, Weyerhauser is looking south to California. The commercial fishing industry is not as strong politically in California, thanks in part to past overfishing. Weyerhauser proposed to establish a $4 million ranch in Humboldt Bay in northern California.

Weyerhauser heard a familiar refrain. "Weyerhauser is the 69th largest company in the United States. Are we going to turn over the public resources to these types of people?" observed Zeke Grader, of the Pacific Coast Federation of Fishermen's Associations. "The small family farmer is almost extinct, and the same thing is going to happen to the salmon fishermen." The California Resources Agency has been spending millions to improve salmon habitat and upgrade water quality in coastal waters and rivers. "When a public agency has invested so much time and effort in restoring salmon, why should we turn it over to a corporation for a profit-making operation?" wondered Resources Agency Secretary Huey Johnson.

The appetite of the salmon is of concern too. "Salmon feed on anchovies, herring, shrimp, and small crab," says Johnson. "We don't know what the impact on Humboldt Bay would be if that many fish were released into it." Johnson prefers to reserve the lower end of the marine food chain for salmon hatched in state-run hatcheries. This smacks of a double standard to Weyerhauser. "You find all the arguments are made against our fish and not the state's fish," observed a Weyerhauser official. So far, Weyerhauser's ranching ambitions in California remain unfulfilled.

Some private salmon operators have found a more sympathetic audience in Chile. Salmon are not natural to the rivers and coastal waters of Chile, and Chile would like to host a population of such prime commercial fish. Chile is permitting an American firm, the Campbell Soup subsidiary Domsea, to stock its rivers to see whether the salmon will become naturalized. Rich potential grazing grounds for salmon lie to the south of Chile—the krill pastures that the industrial fleets covet for fishmeal. If the salmon do take to their new home and obtain their fair share of krill, Chile and Domsea may be confronted by another problem. Chile and Argentina can't agree on a common marine border. Argentine fishermen may take salmon that stray into what Argentina considers its own coastal waters.

The state of Washington will permit private salmon operations that confine salmon to cages and pens so they won't roam the marine range. This can increase the risk of disease through crowding, requires expensive feeds, and eliminates the opportunity to help replenish wild stocks. Operators who transfer hatched salmon to aquatic feedlots in Puget Sound can lose 60 percent of the fish due to shock of transfer. The stock may shrink another 10 to 30 percent. Water conditions can be unfavorable. Young salmon can cannibalize each other. (Lobster also revert to this behavior in pens and raceways; their concerned caretakers are considering the use of blind lobster.) Only subadults in pan-size dimensions of a pound or less can be raised in pens. Despite such constraints, the market demand can make it all worthwhile. Domsea, with 250 pens in Puget Sound, raised 660,000 pounds of pan-size salmon in 1978–1979.

Ironically, some commercial fishermen who oppose private salmon ranching now ranch salmon themselves. Washington does permit salmon ranching by cooperative nonprofit groups. Recapture is limited to "ripe" salmon needed to supply next year's brood and to salmon that can be sold to meet capital and operating expenses. Commercial fishermen's associations willing to help restore salmon runs rather than berating the Boldt decision now ranch under this provision. Alaska has a similar provision. In 1976, Alaskan cooperative groups released 3.7 million salmon. The next year there were 160,147 returns. By 1979, releases amounted to 30 million; returns, 558,000.

This concept attracts Indian tribes as well. Unlike many other tribes, the Lummi Indians of Puget Sound retained rather than traded away their sheltered tidelands. Today, these tidelands serve as the site of a 750-acre diked seawater pond used to raise pan-size salmon for sale. The Lummi operate a school financed by a federal loan that teaches aquaculture skills to urban Lummi who wish to return to the tribal lands. The Lummi also culture oysters.

Such cooperative projects lack the capital to expand as rapidly as a large corporation. But they do enable commercial fishermen and native Americans to benefit from mariculture rather than perceive it as a threat to their future existence. In Japan, the government encourages fishermen to form ranching cooperatives for profit. Too often, new farming technology progresses by putting small farmers out of business. This social tragedy should be avoided in mariculture.

Even if such economic and political problems are resolved, mariculture must recognize the same ultimate constraints that limit the commercial fishing industry. The marine food chain can no more handle unlimited numbers of salmon or tuna ranches than it can support unlimited demands for canned sardines and fishmeal. Move cultured animals to bay cages and you become dependent on how well the bay water quality is maintained. The need to feed the penned animals can add to the pressures to rely on fish geared to the luxury trade. The late Dr. Pieter Korringa of the Netherlands Institute for Fisheries Investigation suggested that developing nations could raise oysters for export and, with the proceeds, could buy ten times as much salted fish to meet the protein needs of their own people.

5

Fish of Honor,
Fish of Scorn

IN THE MAGICAL SHADOW OF DIS-
neyland in California, fireworks bloom in the night sky like giant,
force-fed flowers. I am here to observe a new habitat for the most
despised and revered fish on this planet. I walk across the grounds
of a hotel that features as much running water as a sewage
treatment plant. Fountains gush, a mini-waterfall thunders.
Within earshot of a Tahitian war dance, I look down upon an
illuminated pond. There, unperturbed by the throbbing drums,
the fireworks, and the gawking tourists, are the carp. They stream
by like a rainbow on the move.

The ornamental carp (koi) reside in a nation where attitudes
toward carp range from awe to outrage. The august *Transactions
of the American Fisheries Society* recently devoted a special issue

to one carp species. Few native species have been so honored and this particular carp is not native to the Western Hemisphere. Based in part on information in this issue, some thirty-five states have accorded this carp another honor of sorts by banning it. It ranks as one of this nation's premier unwanted animals, right up there with the giant toad and the walking catfish.

Scott Soule, the koi keeper at the Disneyland Hotel, personifies the contradictory attitudes carp can inspire. One morning, he banged on the metal railing along the foot bridge over the koi pond. Carp from throughout the pond converged in a splashing, milling, squirming swarm of color at his feet. "We have 374 carp," Soule observed. "They represent about $20,000 worth of fish." (Koi collectors have paid $20,000 for just one carp with prized color patterns.) Some of the carp extended their heads above water and opened their toothless mouths wide. Soule dipped his hand into a white plastic bucket and cast small pellets on the pond waters. The splashing increased, turning the water white. The vivid colors of the koi—red, black, white, gold— became blurred, like color film shot too slowly. They were being fed by a man who once supervised the kill of carp by the thousands.

Scott Soule spent over two decades with the California Department of Fish and Game, during which time he supervised the killing of thousands of carp. As he cast more pellets to the koi, Soule recalled some of the tactics he used: "We would spread toxic chemicals, but some carp would always find refuge in a submerged spring or a bank cave." Sometimes, Soule and other wardens would drag large nets through shallow lakes to trap carp. Soule grimaced as he recalled the physical exertion. "You'd get the net into shore and then you often had to hand carry the big carp to a disposal truck. Boy, were they strong and squirmy. They would almost beat you to death."

Why did fishery managers like Soule participate in nationwide carp purges? The story goes back to the 1870s, when European immigrants to North America were homesick for a prize food fish reared in Old World ponds. To their despair, the common carp *(Cyprinus carpio)* was not native to the New World. This potential market for carp impressed the U.S. Fish Commission, a new federal agency that was established by Congress in 1871, in part because of concern over diminishing stocks of salmon, trout, and other popular native fish. Why not import a fish that farmers could raise in ponds to augment U.S. fish production?

At the time, this question seemed rhetorical. The carp's reputation was as secure as that of the salmon, tuna, or trout. Nations as diverse as China and Germany shared a common appreciation and appetite for this husky, large-scaled member of the minnow family. Fish culture owed its very existence to carp. While carp species differ in spawning, feeding, and habitat preferences, they are all relatively hardy. They can flourish in turbid, sluggish waters with low oxygen levels that would repel other fish, and they grow to edible size rapidly. Unlike trout or salmon, they do not require expensive supplemental feeds.

As early as 1000 B.C., the Chinese had discovered that they could double or triple pond production by stocking different types of carp. The grass carp would graze on rooted aquatic plants, the silver and the bighead on plankton. Mud carp and common carp would feed on bottom organisms. To stock just one carp species was to waste space and food. To enrich the food base, Chinese farmers would add vegetable discards and swine manure. This ancient stocking technique is now known as polyculture.

By the 19th century, carp culture was common in Germany, Poland, Czechoslovakia, Austria, Hungary, and Yugoslavia. To immigrant Americans from these regions, carp was a treat, a sort of aquatic turkey associated with birthdays, weddings, and holidays. To Izaak Walton, the carp was "the queen of the rivers, a stately, good and very subtle fish."

Despite their apparent affinity for still or slow-moving waters, carp are strong swimmers and can leap two or three feet into the air. They can negotiate river rapids and clear small waterfalls. They can even jump clear of ornamental carp ponds, much to the distress of their owners. They can leap over nets and, on occasion, even collide with their would-be harvesters. The high-flying carp became a symbol of strength and success, as ubiquitous in some nations as the American eagle or the British lion. According to one Chinese legend, carp that would jump Dragon's Gate waterfall in the Yellow River would be transformed into dragons able to fly to heaven. In Japan, parents fly the carp flag *(koinobori)* in the traditional hope that their offspring will be as strong as the carp.

The U.S. Fish Commission was not about to say no to a potential fish bonanza cum cultural legend. By 1877, passenger vessels carrying European immigrants to Ellis Island were also carrying carp culled from Europe's finest ponds. The carp's hardy nature was equal to the transatlantic crossing. The carp keeper would agitate the water with his hands to restore oxygen in the carp tanks, and would add a block of ice to thwart rising temperatures.

The European imports converged upon the U.S. Carp Ponds in Baltimore and the Potomac flats of Washington, D.C. Another virtue of the common carp, its ability to reproduce in artificial enclosures, promptly manifested itself. An initial shipment of 347 German carp populated the federal ponds with thousands of young carp within a year's time. The carp were distributed by railroad, wagon, and mule to eager farmers in Georgia, ranchers in Texas, gold miners in California, and German immigrants in Wisconsin. Prospective carp raisers did not have to file environmental impact reports. They only needed a letter of endorsement from their local congressmen.

Some congressmen or their secretaries must have suffered writer's cramp. By 1881, the Commission had distributed 143,-696 fish to 5,758 applicants. Maryland received 22,424 carp. Some 16,580 carp were shipped to Texas. Maine received 116; Colorado, 20. "Do not neglect us," implored I.D. Pasco of Nye County, Nevada, in a letter to the Commission. "We are all Uncle Sam's boys and will appreciate the fish beyond any other section . . . Our greatest obstacle would lie in the Indians; a mean, stupid pack, that only think of stealing as a virtue; but once fairly started we can manage them." Nevada was not neglected. By

1883, the Commission was accepting applications from Canada. It had to expand its distribution system to keep ahead of the prolific carp.

Commission officials distributed advice too. Charles Smiley supplied the answers to 118 common questions. Question 49: "Will it harm carp to cut ice in a pond where they are?" Answer: "No. They will be so fast asleep in the mud they will not care." Question 89: "How can one guard carp from frogs, tadpoles, water rats and turtles?" Answer: "Kill the frogs, tadpoles, rats and turtles."

The superintendent of the U.S. Carp Ponds had his own predator problems. Dr. Rudolph Hessel found twenty-five young carp in the stomach of one snake. "Snakes are more injurious than cranes, herons and other birds," observed Hessel to U.S. Fish Commissioner Spencer Baird. "I kill them by shooting, oftentimes seeing only a small part of the head in the water."

The carp farmers of America seemed fully capable of protecting and nurturing their aquatic stock. Abel Wright of Griffin, Georgia wanted Commissioner Baird to know, "I have exterminated the bull-frog and snake tribe and all is quiet on the lake at night now, and not a ripple is made by his snakeship." Griffin also disclosed his special carp feed: damaged crackers from Atlanta. Such encouraging field reports led Smiley, the Commission's answer man, to opine, "Every rural community is destined to have its fish ponds in the same abundance that it has its pig pens or its poultry yards." Hessel, the snake sniper, observed, "The carp is almost as familiar to our people as any other kind of domesticated animal." California, a hot spot for carp culture, was shipping carp by the trainload to the east. You could lunch on carp at the Waldorf-Astoria Hotel.

Unfortunately, the carp farmers became victims of their own success and the carp's fecundity. According to one observer, carp became "a worthless drug on the market." The price dropped to $1\frac{1}{2}$ cents per pound. A penny and a half went a lot further in the 1880s than it does today, but it still wasn't much. Moreover, the disillusioned farmers had to compete with fishermen who were catching pond carp that had escaped into public waters.

The federal government had stopped distributing carp by 1897. As ponds were deserted, drained, or planted with grain, more carp escaped to public waters. The federal program to stock farm ponds was serving instead to stock the nation's lakes, streams, and rivers. The common carp felt at home in the New World. In 1894, Dr. David Starr Jordan, a fishery scientist and president of Stanford University, reported that it was "very common" in California's largest natural lake, Clear Lake. Jordan's attitude toward this hardy immigrant differed from that of the U.S. Fish Commission. "In California, this species is a nuisance, without redeeming qualities."

Many sport fishermen and waterfowl hunters concurred. They felt that the carp's spread and the decline of some popular game species was no coincidence. Carp were accused of eating native wildlife out of house and home. The common carp's habit of uprooting aquatic plants and muddying the water in the process was presented as evidence for this. *Forest and Stream* observed sardonically in 1891, "We shall next hear that the carp has utterly destroyed the salmon industry of Alaska and driven the seals out of the Bering Sea." An 1894 editorial in the *San Francisco Evening Bulletin* expressed a more popular view. "If everyone of these fish could be removed from the water to the land and there employed as fertilizer, a substantial gain would be made." The "disgusting fish" was ranked with the thistle, the English sparrow, and other infamous imports. Concern over the carp's environmental trespasses escalated to concern over its personal habits. In 1897, a Canadian fishery official claimed the carp "suffers from fish leprosy" and was fond of "coarse and loathsome food." Needless to say, no koinobori were swimming in the New World sky.

Fishery officials once besieged with requests to distribute carp were being implored to purge carp from North America. Public supervisors of "rough fish control" began spending millions to sieve rivers, drain lakes, draw down reservoirs, fence wetlands, and poison ponds ("chemical rehabilitation"). The now infamous carp was a boon for devotees of chemical pest control. In New York State, two researchers force-fed over 1,600 chemicals to carp in an attempt to come up with a selective poison. One day they received a letter from Israel. A fish farmer wanted to know if their research might help him to protect his ponds from unwanted fish—but the fish he was raising were carp!

The object of this environmental warfare continued to flourish and to colonize quarry pits, gravel pits, and other new habitats spawned by the urbanization of North America. Some public officials opted for a new strategy: catching carp for sport and profit. No regulations would encumber success. The nets, spears, and bows and arrows that would land you in jail if used on many game species could be used on carp. Carp could be caught with virtually anything short of dynamite. And there were no bag or size limits to curtail fishing success.

By the time this policy switch occurred, European immigrants and their children preferred to catch or eat tuna, lobster, salmon, shrimp, striped bass, and other aquatic life that was unencumbered by the specter of "leprosy" and other inspired invective. As Canadian zoologist Hugh McCrimmon noted in 1968, fishery agencies attempting to promote carp fishing had "over a 75-year period caused a public distaste for the carp which would seem difficult to overcome even by creative promotion and public education."

Why do fishermen and hunters still bag waterfowl and bass with the "aquatic pig" still loose in the waterscapes of North America? A 1964 publication of the Department of the Interior, *Carp: A Sometime Villain,* observed that "carp have gained such a bad reputation that there is a tendency to blame them, sometimes unjustly, for any and all damage to aquatic habitat." The carp can become a scapegoat for changes caused by human beings that are far more adverse to native fish and waterfowl. Dammed rivers, changing water levels, lower oxygen levels, increased silt runoff, pollution, depletion of popular game—all tend to favor the carp's survival over more sensitive species. The common carp's habit of uprooting aquatic plants in its search for insects and other small organisms is still considered detrimental to plant-eating waterfowl and to fish that require clear waters. But most state fishery agencies now prefer to protect and restore our rivers rather than purge carp. If nations chose their symbolic animals on the basis of environmental hardiness, koinobori flags rather than bronze eagles would prevail in the United States.

With the carp here to stay, public attitudes have shifted again, inspired less by public edict than by grass-roots appreciation. A bait shop in California's Sacramento–San Joaquin Delta area displays color snapshots of proud fishermen with their prize salmon, striped bass, and sturgeon. One fisherman holds a husky, bronze-tinted carp. His broad smile indicates he has no need to apologize for landing a "trash" fish.

Sport fishermen do not have to jet into the wilderness to catch carp; the hardy fish can flourish in urban America. One day, caught in a traffic jam on a freeway in southern California, I noticed a group of people clustered at the base of a flood control dam. Water was being released along the dam tailrace, but this alone did not seem to constitute a spectator sport. After exiting the crowded freeway, I hiked down to the bank of the river below the dam release. One smiling gentleman in levis, an undershirt, and a baseball cap on backwards lifted up a fish chain from the water. Six fine carp dangled on the chain. The carp were running! The proud fisherman, Richard Rodriguez of Ontario, California, then filled me in on the components of his customized carp bait: strawberry soda, Cheerios, and cornmeal. The balled-up product remained sticky but firm, even when cast into the dam tailrace. Mr. Rodriguez seemed as fulfilled as a deep-sea fisherman on a chartered swordfish vessel. That evening, he would fry the carp in a skillet and season the fillets with chili pepper. (Other carp dough baits rely on peanut butter, oatmeal, or boiled dumplings seasoned with cheese. The Izaak Walton League recommends a combination of cornmeal and strawberry jello, seasoned with cinnamon. "If you get hungry while fishing, pour a beer and eat the bait," observes one Wisconsin fishery publication.)

The Arizona Game and Fish Department has even stocked urban recreational lakes with common carp to accommodate the needs of young anglers. With a new generation of anglers being weaned on carp, outdoor magazines may have to start running photo spreads on trophy carp.

Defying traditional carp taboos, Rockford, Illinois hosts an annual Rock River International Carp Catching Championship. The event, sponsored by the Winnebago County Council of Sportsmen's Clubs, has attracted up to 500 competitors. Not everybody competes with fishing poles. "Hoggers" prefer to catch carp by hand. They crawl along river shallows feeling for carp amid sunken logs and junked refrigerators. Once "in touch," the hogger attempts to insert his thumb and fingers in the carp's mouth or gills to secure a winning grip. It makes for a wet, chilly, and muddy hunt, but hogging may rank as the fairest encounter in sport fishing. One champion hogger, pipefitter Lloyd Gaines of Winnebago, Illinois, has caught up to twenty-five carp in an hour. Gaines prefers to hog in late May and June, when carp enter the shallows to spawn.

Gaines says the Rockford event began "tongue in cheek. We wanted to call attention to the debris and pollution degrading the Rock River. The waters are a lot cleaner now. We catch bass as well as carp." Children who play on swings and slides in Winnebago County owe a debt to the carp as well. Donations by carp contestants go into a County fund for public recreation and playground projects.

With the New World resigned to the existence of the carp, the time would seem ripe to consider its use as a major food fish once again.

6

The Pond Versus the Ocean

THE GRASS CARP MIGHT BE CON-
sidered the king of the carps. It is the powerful swimmer whose
aquatic leaps inspire Chinese poets and Japanese artists. "If they
do jump, they are in a class with tarpon," observed Ronald Pelzman in a report for the California Department of Fish and Game.
Its body, more elongated than the hump-backed common carp,
lacks the barbels or sensory organs that hang from the jaw of
other carps. Unlike the bronze tints of the common carp, the
grass's coloration is dark green with silvery sides and undersur-
face. Its habitat extends into colder waters, including an icy river
in Siberia, the Amur. A common carp, to the delight of Chinese
farmers and U.S. hoggers, can reach 50 pounds in size. A grass
carp can reach 100 pounds. But the common carp has enjoyed

more popularity because until recently the grass carp could not be spawned in ponds.

When thunder sounded, Chinese "frymasters" would rush upriver with fine-mesh nets. Thunder signalled the advent of the rainy season, and grass carp like to spawn when the rivers run high and turbulent. The young grass carp fry netted by the frymasters would be used to stock ponds. The spread of the grass carp was thus limited by the distance fry could be transported. By the 1950s, the Chinese had learned to induce spawning in the grass carp by means of hormone injections. Grass carp can now be airlifted around the world and spawned in tanks thousands of miles away from their original habitat.

In Europe, the grass has been crossbred with other carp species in attempts to develop a hardier, hybrid food carp. In 1963, 70 grass carp were airlifted from Malaysia to a hatchery operated in Stuttgart, Arkansas by the Bureau of Sport Fisheries (now the U.S. Fish and Wildlife Service). These aliens spawned 1,700 fry. American interest in the grass carp centers on its food preferences rather than its edibleness. Rather than rooting on the bottom like the common carp, the grass carp grazes on submerged aquatic plants like duckweed and on filamentous algae such as "pond moss." Like other carps, the grass carp has comb-like pharyngeal teeth in its throat that grind up the plant leaves before they reach its stomachless gut. Cattails and other emergent plants are too stalky for the grass carp to handle.

The Corps of Engineers, which must keep our waterways navigable, has spent millions on herbicides and mechanical harvesters to remove aquatic plants, which can foul propellers as well as fishing lines. The plants, like the common carp, tend to survive such control efforts. The fact that the grass carp will devour these plants for free and without toxic aftereffects excites officials who do battle with duckweed and other submerged plants. To botanist Richard Yeo, an aquatic weed expert with the U.S. Department of Agriculture in Davis, California, the grass carp is an "aquatic cow that will eat and eat." The grass carp can eat up to its own weight in a day's time, which is why some individuals can grow up to 100 pounds. It can withstand cold winter waters that can kill another imported plant eater, a tropical fish called tilapia. And it can thrive in canals that would not support the tropical manatee, another biological control agent. Furthermore, the grass carp does not roil the waters, unlike the common carp.

Arkansas uses grass carp to control aquatic plants in over 100 lakes. Within a year's time, 100 grass carp "practically eliminated" submerged plants that had covered 40 percent of Marysville Lake, according to the Arkansas Game and Fish Commission. Catfish farmers in Arkansas commonly stock grass carp to control plants that interfere with harvesting operations.

This track record intrigues people around the world with aquatic plant problems. Some 1,000 grass carp have been recruited to graze down plant explosions in the Panama Canal system. An extensive network of irrigation canals that serves the Imperial and Coachella Valleys in California has been plagued by a single submerged plant species that can cut canal flow rates in half. The plant, hydrilla, becomes dense enough to raise water levels by a foot, increasing seepage losses through the canal banks. The plant's prodigious growth rate qualifies it as a research candidate in projects to produce fuel from biomass. "Nothing eradicates it," observes Keith Atkinson, assistant manager of the Coachella Valley Water District. "It can reproduce four different ways."

To irrigation district officials, the grass carp could be a savior. "But the California Department of Fish and Game does not like the grass carp," says Atkinson. "They will consider its use only if it is sterile."

Christopher Lal is with the inland fisheries branch of the California Department of Fish and Game in Sacramento. He began his career in fishery management by encouraging farmers to grow carp in India, where he was born. People who settled in the coastal lowlands would excavate earth pits to set their homes on mounds above flood levels. The pit would become a carp pond.

"The ponds became as common as swimming pools in Beverly Hills," he recalls. The boom in ponds created a lucrative occupation: "You could tell the carp frymasters. Their fingers were loaded with gold."

Mr. Lal showed me a department booklet that lists prohibited species. The rogue's gallery includes the piranha, the giant toad, the mongoose, snapping turtles, cobras, the African clawed frog, the freshwater stingray, and the flying fox (a large bat that sucks fruit). Why is the grass carp, which cannot bite, sting, poison, snap, or consume crops or chickens, on this wildlife hit list?

The department's position paper on grass carp asserts that it "might become an even greater 'pest' than the common carp." Lal explains that "the grass carp eats the same plants that serve as shelter for juvenile fish and provide food for many of our waterfowl. In its juvenile stage, the grass carp subsists on plankton and could become a food competitor to existing juvenile species."

The grass carp, like other carps, cannot be considered a strict or "obligate" herbivore. Scientists at Louisiana State University have observed the grass carp preying on the young of that state's esteemed crawfish.

California's concerns are shared by thirty-four other states that ban grass carp. While working to rehabilitate the common carp's reputation, Wisconsin fishery official Vern Hacker is not ready for the grass. Hacker feels that, as the grass carp removes rooted aquatic plants, "pea-soup algae will use the nutrients" once taken up by the plants. Rooted plants can survive under winter ice, but the algae will die, decay, and suppress oxygen. Winter fish kills could result, according to Hacker.

Hacker is also concerned that the grass carp may eventually wander into the Great Lakes and create more problems for one of humankind's most stressed ecosystems. Pollution, canal links and overfishing of native species have paved the way for invasion by alien species, including the blood-sucking, parasitic sea lamprey and the prolific alewife. Canada and the United States must engage in multi-million dollar eradication efforts to prop up an aquatic ecosystem chronically out of balance.

Such caution is a major policy legacy from the common carp's New World debut. Today's random global exchange of biota, expedited by air freight, underlines the need for such caution. Hydrilla itself is not native to the United States. A tropical plant, it was first introduced to this country to provide greenery in aquarium tanks.

Even the ocean is not immune from such biological boomerangs. The marine worm that chomps on wooden pilings in the San Francisco Bay area immigrated from Europe on ship hulls. The oyster drill, which damages oyster beds in Washington's Puget Sound and mussel beds in France and the Low Countries, came from Japan via imported oyster spat. The possibility of a sea-level Panama Canal linking the Carribean and the Pacific could result in the world's largest random exchange of biota. The fate of our urban rivers, lakes, and ponds can tell us much about what lies in store for the ocean.

Can't grass carp be contained in ponds and lakes? Fishermen in the Mississippi River system can already catch grass carp. After escaping in overflows from Arkansas ponds, it has found its way as far north as Illinois.

Won't this wild population be limited by the grass carp's special spawning needs? Grass carp that escaped from irrigation canals in Russia have reproduced in their new river habitats. The Mississippi and its tributary rivers are considered to have suitable spawning sites, including turbulent water in dam tailraces. Scientists who have done research on the grass carp would not be surprised if it eventually reproduces in the Mississippi River system.

The Mississippi travels of the grass carp have led many states to increase their vigilance. According to Lal, California game wardens learned that one rancher had imported grass carp to stock an irrigation pond. The wardens received a court order to go in and remove the illegal aliens. The ranch owner is now suing the state for alleged damages to his property during the removal operation, and the state is seeking recovery of removal costs, including the cost of aerial overflights to see if pond weeds returned, unhindered by any remaining grass carp.

Florida, which spends up to $6 million a year to combat hydrilla, has permitted grass carp to be stocked in water bodies considered escape-proof. In one research project, the Corps of Engineers installed backup escape barriers to stop grass carp from wandering beyond one lake's outlet. Scuba divers inspected the barriers monthly. Precautions even included plans for corrective actions if "security is breached." "Renovation" was defined as "killing every fish of every species of every size in the lakes to positively eliminate every single white amur." ("White amur" is an alias used by agencies that prefer not to have the grass carp associated with the reputation of the common carp.)

A recent breeding discovery in Europe may pave the way for expanded use of the grass carp in the United States. In Hungary, female grass carp have been crossbred with male bighead carp to produce sterile offspring. (Gonads in these sterile hybrids can be so undeveloped that scientists can't tell the sex of the offspring.) A commercial carp breeder in the United States, J.M. Malone of Lonoke, Arkansas, can now produce this sterile hybrid. A sterile hybrid would remove the risk of reproduction if it escaped into natural waters. California, among other states, is willing to consider use of sterile hybrids, pending results from a research project being conducted by Tom Jackson of the Denver, Colorado office of the U.S. Fish and Wildlife Service.

Jackson has 500 sterile hybrids imported from Arkansas swimming in holding tanks in a greenhouse. "We want to see if wardens in the field can learn to distinguish between regular grass carp and the sterile hybrids." Results are promising. "The hybrid appears to have a smaller eye pupil and a shorter pectoral fin." With such identification aids, public officials can certify sterile hybrids prior to interstate shipment.

Some 2,500 hybrids have been stocked in screened-off irrigation canals in the hydrilla-cursed Imperial Valley. Says Jackson, "We will be observing their environmental impact, how effectively they graze hydrilla and the type of security and handling they require." Jackson does not want to defoliate the canals. "This is not a search and destroy mission," says Jackson. "We are not looking for a biological desert." The project seeks to establish a balance between water delivery needs and enough plant growth to sustain canal fish populations that already attract anglers. The sterile hybrids could even become part of the fishery, according to Jackson. Some carp can live for a century or more.

If the hybrids prove their mettle in the desert canals while retaining their sterility, Jackson forsees some interesting ramifications for the western states. Fish production might be greatly expanded in irrigation canal systems, and water delivery could be improved. As in the farm ponds of China, the grass carp could play a key role in bringing biological harmony to artificial waterways. The physical character of canals resembles an intensive form of aquaculture known as raceway culture. To make carp grow faster, Indonesian farmers will place their fish in bamboo cages in a natural raceway, a swift-moving stream fertilized by nutrient-rich sewage from upstream communities. In Idaho, fish farmers raise trout in concrete raceways fed by well water and high-protein energy feeds.

The opportunity to reconsider inland fish culture and the role of "trash fish" in human affairs comes at a timely moment. In the nineteenth century, people could afford to bypass carp. Meat and fish protein were cheap and abundant. Protein may still be abundant at the supermarket, but it's no longer cheap. The annual world fish catch leveled off in the 1970s, and fish, once the cheap protein alternative, can be as expensive as meat. The United States, like other industrial nations, has relied on capture of "wild" marine stocks for most of its fish production. Aquaculture only contributes 3 to 4 percent of the nation's total fish production. Much of our aquaculture efforts emphasize monoculture of high-cost, high-risk marine species: shrimp, salmon, lobster, and pompano.

China, virtually alone among the large nations, relies more on inland fish production and the versatile, hardy, and accommodating carp. What does this do for its total production of fish? Fishery experts once wrote off Chinese fish production figures as inflated and a form of propaganda. With diplomatic relations reopened, Western scientists can now travel in China. In 1978, Dr. T.V.R. Pillay headed an eighteen-member study team on fish farming in China. Pillay estimated the nation's annual inland fish production at 2.5 million tons. This figure makes China by far the world's largest producer of inland fish. Based on this figure alone, China would rank seventh among other nations in total fish production. Another visitor to China, biologist John Ryther of Woods Hole Oceanographic Institute, made a different estimate at about the same time. While cautioning that his estimate requires more verification, Dr. Ryther estimates annual inland production at 17.5 million tons—nearly one-fourth of the world's total annual marine catch.

These estimates exceed China's own estimate of 1.6 million tons (mainly carp) annually. Why such a wide range of estimates? The science of statistics is not a high Chinese priority. "They can't even agree on their *human* population," observes Shao-Wen Ling, an aquaculture expert who has taught at the University of Washington and the University of Miami. Both Ryther and Shao-Wen Ling identify one possible motive for underestimates: fish farmers may want to be humble about their ponds' production to avoid any taxes or demands for higher community shares. China's increasing use of pesticides and loss of ponds to reclamation programs may inhibit production in some areas.

If we combine the low estimate with China's marine catch, China becomes the world's third largest producer of fish, behind Japan and Russia and ahead of the United States, according to the Food and Agriculture Organization. Inland fish production accounts for one-quarter of China's total production; it's about 10 percent in Japan, and 3 to 4 percent in the United States.

China's inland fish production is almost equal to the United States' total catch of food fish. China would rank behind the United States if this inland fish production were not included.

The fish farmer in China does not need huge, fuel-guzzling fleets subsidized by government loans to harvest his ponds. China can thus produce more fish than the United States with much less capital investment and without stressing the marine ecosystem to the point of no return. The wisdom of China's historical choice in fish production becomes more apparent.

China is now expanding into mariculture. Its choices here are instructive too. In addition to marine animals, China cultures marine algae and other so-called seaweeds for human consumption.

Other areas in southeast Asia, such as Indonesia, practice similar strategies. Warm-water temperatures in these areas permit longer growing periods. In temperate and subarctic regions, organisms may hibernate and reduce their growth rates during winter. Warm water also permits operators to work year-round in the water and to hand-tend their operations. They raise both freshwater and saltwater species. For saltwater species, they choose mullet, which, like the carp, is a herbivore and is relatively tolerant to temperature and salinity changes. Fish farmers in Israel rear both carp and mullet.

Why aren't American farmers into aquaculture? This brings us to an interesting point. The few successful U.S. projects, such as catfish and crawfish farming, have been developed by inland fish farmers, particularly in southern states. Their efforts haven't been as publicized as the more glamorous salmon ranching and abalone farming projects. Fish ponds yield half the nation's supply of catfish. The inland fish farmer doesn't have to compete with coastal resort developers or oil port authorities for a site. He has his own land. For water, he may rely in part or entirely on rain. He minimizes his risk by relying, as does the Chinese farmer, on a diversified crop system. To secure two crops from an acre of land in one growing period, a Louisiana farmer may rotate rice and crawfish culture. He does not require the level of public financial assistance that construction of a modern ocean-going vessel or a coastal shrimp pond system represents. The American farming community wants more emphasis on inland fish production in U.S. fishery policy. Their own track record and the Chinese experience suggest the wisdom of doing this.

To their dismay, Congress passed a bill in 1978 to make the National Marine Fisheries Service the agency responsible for federal aquaculture efforts. Inland fish farmers prefer the Department of Agriculture. President Carter vetoed the bill because of liberal federal funding provisions designed to underwrite high-risk mariculture projects.

Farmers are not interested in the magnitude of public support beleaguered mariculture investors seek. As Porter Briggs of the Catfish Farmers of America testified before a congressional subcommittee, "We do not want to see people come into this industry who are grantsmen or promoters who understand how to get money from these projects. When they fail they dump their product on the market and it hurts the price and also it is a poor quality product on the market and that hurts us in the eyes of the consumer." Farmers are more interested in field assistance.

In one pilot project in Arkansas, the U.S. Department of Agriculture is attempting to identify fish that are suitable for polyculture. Auburn University, which has been involved in aquaculture since 1934, is using two Chinese carp, the grass and the silver, in a polyculture project. Auburn aquaculture director E.W. Shell forsees carp being canned and used, like tuna, in salads. Are carp too bony? Dr. Shell feels that, with modern processing methods, this will be no more of a problem than it is for such popular "bony" fish as salmon.

Dr. Shell is high on another plant-eating "rough" fish that is almost as hardy as the carp, an African native called tilapia. Hickory Ridge Fisheries raises tilapia in power station cooling ponds and sells 1,000 pounds of the firm, sweet-tasting fish a week in the Oklahoma City area. Fish Breeders of Idaho raises tilapia in geothermal raceways and markets 2,000 pounds a week in Los Angeles, Seattle and San Diego. By hatching fertilized eggs in its mouth, a female tilapia protects its young from heavy predation. Catfish and other predators must be stocked so ponds do not become over-populated with young tilapia.

But, argue mariculture promoters, many Americans won't eat freshwater fish like carp. That's the fat-lipped, hump-backed fish that thrives in polluted, muddy waters. Are we really that unwilling to change our consuming preferences over time? Remember when Americans were not supposed to buy Japanese cars . . . or eat tacos . . . or enjoy avocado dip? Carp is already consumed with zest by some Americans, particularly those of Polish, Austrian, Hungarian, Czech, and—of course—Chinese descent.

Should the public sector intervene to help change our food preferences to enhance fishery development? This approach might be cheaper than funding capital-intensive fishing fleets or hurricane-prone shrimp farms. To help create a "nursery of seamen" based on expanded fishing fleets, some English kings decreed that citizens must eat fish on Wednesday, Friday, and Saturday. I doubt that such a policy would get very far in a modern-day democracy.

The federal government can and does use its purchasing power to develop markets for new products. Large public agencies with "semicaptive" food clientele—the military, federal prisons, school systems—could be encouraged to buy carp. This approach runs critical risks. If not carefully prepared, and this is always possible when you must serve 400 people at one sitting, any fish, even salmon, can turn people away from fish forever. Too many fish haters are being generated in army chow lines and school lunch programs. Fish croquettes probably generate more than their share of food fights.

A more positive approach might exalt the healthy and economic aspects of carp with endorsement by current celebrities in entertainment and athletics. A low-profile approach might also be considered. Some popular fish dinners, such as fish and chips, are not even identified as to their actual source. Other fish, like budding movie starlets, undergo name changes. Shark is often marketed as grayfish. Tilapia's market aliases include Colorado perch, Black bass, Superfish and St. Peter's fish. Check the ingredients list on a jar of gefilte fish in your local market and you may find, as I did, that infamous name "carp."

The common carp has already gained an influential ally dedicated to improving its public image. Vern Hacker began a twenty-six-year career in fishery management by studying salmon runs in Alaska. In his present role as Supervisor of Warm Water Fish Management for the Wisconsin Department of Natural Resources, he has written a tribute to rough fish, *A Fine Kettle of Fish*. Hacker concedes that carp and other rough fish "may have the reputation of a motorcycle gang but don't let their reputation frighten you away." Carp "are excellent fighters, slugging it out on the bottom and bending the rod to the limit."

After appealing to our spirit of angling adventure, Hacker tantalizes us with recipes on how to bake, stuff, marinate, and poach carp. Chef Louis Szathmáry of the Bakery Restaurant in Chicago leads off with Carp Paprikash. Mrs. Elmer Daelke of Appleton, Wisconsin reveals her beer batter for carp. For the fisherman who lands a carp ripe with roe (eggs), Mrs. Amanda Goyke discloses how to make pickled carp roe.

Some first-time eaters of carp are turned off by too many small bones or a muddy taste. Hacker blames the carp cook for this. Carp should be scored or cut every $\frac{1}{4}$ to $\frac{3}{8}$ inches so cooking oils can soften up small, scattered "Y" bones. Removal of a prominent "mud vein" removes the muddy taste.

Wisconsin's carp promotion is not entirely altruistic. The state contracts out carp seining rights and markets carp caught by state crews. The 1978 income from the rough fish catch was $87,777. A restaurant in Omaha, Nebraska, the Joe Tess Place, relies on Wisconsin carp to meet customer demands for a 40-year-old menu standby, fried carp sandwich.

Many Americans of Chinese descent don't need to be educated about carp. Their ancestors, who helped hack a railroad bed across the snow-bound Sierra, were delighted when the carp colonized our waterways. Today, many Chinese fish markets in major American cities have tanks that swarm with live catfish and carp. A customer points to the fish he wants. The market manager dips a net into the tank and drops the selected fish on the wet, slippery concrete floor. If the customer nods his head in approval, the manager clubs the thrashing fish over the head to close the sale.

Frank Grasteit makes a career out of seining the lakes and reservoirs of the West for carp and other rough fish that he trucks live to urban markets. His main source of carp is Clear Lake, California, whose carp population was criticized nearly a hundred years ago by Dr. Jordan. For Grasteit, the inspection ritual in the fish market has its advantages. "If I had to process the carp myself, I'd have to meet a host of public health regulations." Grasteit is continually being contacted by promoters who want to export carp to Japan. "They are all confident of success but they want me to put up all the money." Grasteit prefers to diversify into catfish farming near his Clear Lake home.

If carp ever became a food rage, supply rather than demand might become the next problem. Operations you might not normally link with fish production may benefit from this predicament, including sewage treatment plants with treated effluent to spare. Wait a minute, you may say. Getting consumers to switch to carp is a formidable enough task without linking this switch to the use of treated effluent. The groundwork (or waterwork) for this potential link is already under way. Dr. Ryther and his colleagues at Woods Hole find that nutrients in effluent can generate blooms of algae that fish will eat.

Is this just an academic pipe dream? In a pilot program, the city of Oaklahoma City raised minnows and channel catfish in algae-rich treated effluent lagoons. During lagoon residency, the biomass of channel catfish jumped from 600 to 4,400 pounds. In Wisconsin, the village of Dorchester (near Wausau) donated use of one effluent pond to rear a popular sportfish, the muskie, prior to planting in recreational waters. The juvenile muskie gained more weight at a faster rate in the algae-rich lagoons than in traditional rearing ponds.

Sewage treatment operators already use fish in their lagoons to control insects. The algae-fish feeding sequence can also remove compounds from the effluent that normally require costly physical or chemical treatment. Conceivably, through fish rearing, sewage treatment plants could become municipal moneymakers. However, more work must be completed to determine what type of potentially harmful or toxic substances fish might be exposed to from a food chain in an effluent lagoon. A lagoon monitoring program would be more effective and economical than that required to monitor fish in an ocean exposed to pollution.

California, with a large farm sector and big urban markets, could become a key state in determining aquaculture's eventual success in the United States. While private catfish and trout farms do exist, the California farmer has not found aquaculture as appealing as his counterparts in the southern states. Water can cost more in California and pesticide runoff can impair its quality. If California and other semiarid states learn to recycle and reclaim rural and urban wastewater rather than relying on more interbasin water transfers, aquaculture operators might gain access to a nutrient-rich, carefully monitored water supply. Cultured carp may yet stage a comeback in the Golden State.

Hawaii has the warm marine water regime that southeast Asia cultivates so well. Hawaii is anxious to diversify its economy beyond tourism, military spending, and plantation agriculture such as sugar cane or pineapple. One limiting factor in its tuna fishery is the lack of a native bait as hardy and abundant as the anchovy, which is common off the coast of California. (In one federal fishery project, live anchovy were shipped from California to resolve this deficiency, but too many died en route.) Researchers are now trying to culture bait.

Most Hawaiian fish farmers are turning inland to raise catfish, carp, tilapia, prawns and other imported species. Freshwater prawns are cheaper to raise than marine shrimp and can be just as popular. Abandoned sugar cane fields are being recycled as pond sites.

Hawaii's fish farmers have benefited from the tumultuous social history of the islands. Importation of cheap labor to work the hot sugar cane fields brought wave upon immigrant wave of fish-eating cultures: Japanese, Chinese, Filipinos, Koreans. Their proclivity for seafood merged with that of the native Hawaiians. Thus this isolated island chain in the mid-Pacific hosts the most diverse range of tastes for aquatic products on this planet. Tamashiro's Market in Honolulu is better stocked than most commercial marine aquariums. Tuna, eel and 75 varieties of seafood on iced trays stare blankly at prospective customers that crowd the Market's narrow aisles. A piece of red meat here seems as foreign as salt shakers in a candy factory.

With local per capita consumption of aquatic products double the national average, Hawaii must import 55 percent of its seafood to meet local demand. Inland aquaculture projects promise to reduce if not eventually reverse this trend. Gross aquaculture revenues jumped from $197,000 in 1976 to almost $2 million in 1980, according to C. Richard Fassler of the state's Aquaculture Development Program. Cultured prawns are being substituted for imported shrimp in markets and restaurants. Some aquatic products are even being exported to Japan and the U.S. mainland. Other island nations dependent on food imports are watching, if not emulating, Hawaii's style of aquaculture. Hawaii has completed the first comprehensive state aquaculture plan in the United States to support this thrust towards a more self-reliant economy.

Hawaii's aquaculture thrust already spawns some happy career switches. Native Hawaiians are often relegated to jobs with limited futures. Bob Hanohano was a truck driver in Honolulu when he heard that the State of Hawaii was providing technical advice and juvenile prawns to would-be prawn farmers. Because of the limited supply and high cost of island land, most residents of Hawaiian ancestry have felt that aquaculture, while very much in their cultural tradition, is beyond their means and more the province of large corporations like Amfac and Coca Cola, which supports a pilot marine shrimp project on Oahu. Many Hawaiian families had to sell valuable coastal parcels for a song because they couldn't pay the taxes. But Hanohano's family managed to retain a coastal parcel north of Honolulu. When a sugar lease on the parcel ran out, Hanohano decided to build prawn ponds during his free time. Today, Hanohano is one of the main island suppliers of prawns. Each Saturday, Hanohano and his brothers wade waist-deep in the pond, pulling a prawn net while neighbors and goats look on. He markets Hawaiian perch too, which is the Hanohano alias for tilapia. As he stuck his hand deep into the mud bank to retrieve a burrowing prawn, Hanohano told me of his ambitious plan to build a restaurant and visitor center overlooking the ponds. He wants the center to impart the lore and the perseverance of his Hawaiian ancestors. His prawn ponds already attract 7,000 visitors a year. The only time he drives a truck is to bring his prawns to market.

To the north of Hanohano lies an old World War II runway site that now sports a maze of ponds, trenches and diked reservoirs. This watery domain is the creation of Tap Pryor, who has been trying to make a go of mariculture for over a decade. He tried to raise lobsters for Marlon Brando in Polynesia. He ran up against the same problems that have stymied so many mariculture projects. "How can you interest investors in lobster or shrimp farms instead of condos when one hurricane can demolish the whole enterprise," observes Pryor. If only saltwater animals could be raised *out of the ocean.* This seemed like wishful thinking until Pryor learned that many tropical Pacific islands, including Hawaii, are underlain by limestone aquifers that contain salt water. Such aquifers have been considered a liability until Pryor began tapping one beneath the old runway. The water, rich in nutrients, is used to generate phytoplankton in large diked ponds. The plankton-rich water is then diverted to trenches filled with oyster seed imported from California. With an all-year growing season and an optimum, controlled diet, Pryor says his oysters can grow to commercial size in six months, compared to three years in colder waters. And Pryor doesn't have to worry about oil spills, conflicts with sport fishermen and harbor authorities, wave surges and marine pollution.

While some critics contend that Hawaii's cultured products are bland in taste, I supped on one raw oyster at Pryor's project and found it to be tangy, salty and delicious. In Hamburg, Germany, customers at one large department store pay $5.50 for six Hawaii "blue diamond" oysters and a glass of champagne. The oysters are air-lifted from Pryor's project.

Why stop with just oysters? The oyster wastewater is diverted to trenches containing clams, which dine on tiny marine plants passed up by the oysters. This wastestream then goes to a trench containing seaweed. The seaweed acts as a biological filter, purifying the water before disposal back into the aquifer. Pryor plans to harvest the seaweed as feed for a commercial marine snail, the abalone, or as use as a chemical feedstock or source of biomass energy. Pryor and his technical director, Barry Goldstein, refer to this ambitious process as Systemculture.

Will these cultured oysters that never sense the movement of the tides or a boat's wake merely satisfy the food needs of an affluent clientele that uses champagne as a chaser? Pryor plans to produce 77 tons of oysters a month, an unheard-of production figure. The plankton reservoirs will be feeding 16 million oysters daily. Pryor plans to franchise Systemculture ventures throughout the Pacific basin to islands with access to saltwater aquifers. These islands desperately need an independent economy and oysters may just be the ticket. Many of these islands also have abandoned military airfields which make readymade project sites.

With this volume of production, cultured oysters might eventually stabilize, if not undercut, the price of wild oyster harvests that must contend with habitat destruction and pollution. The annual oyster harvest in Chesapeake Bay is five times less the levels produced in the 19th century. It is too early to tell if such production will materialize. But Pryor's process stresses how we are only beginning to realize the potential of aquatic culture. We will be learning as much from failures as well as successes. We can no more predict the eventual shape of aquaculture than a hunting tribe centuries ago could have anticipated that its descendents would be dining on cows rather than deer.

The Hawaiian experience suggests that one prime aquaculture site may be the backyards of our homes. Here it is easier and much less odorous to raise protein in the form of fish instead of chickens or hogs. And fish don't crow at dawn. Dr. Jeff Hunt of Windward Community College operates a series of small ponds on campus as part of his popular course, Backyard Aquaculture. Dr. K. Gopalakrishnan of Honolulu Community College has access to four different water sources at his campus aquaculture facility: sea water, brackish, tap, and sterilized. Name any aquatic animal and "Gopol" will eventually be able to show his students how to raise it on campus. Wastewater from his prawn hatchery irrigates a vegetable garden managed by botanist Joe Krahulik and his students. This academic hybrid may be the wave of the future on school campuses. To ward off the major predator, the urban vandal, such projects will have to be fenced.

Building farm ponds in the midwest, raising oysters in tropical trenches, rearing fish in treated effluent ponds, and sprucing up the image of carp may not sound as glamorous as investing in tuna clippers and ocean salmon ranching. But any national fishing strategy that ignores or downplays such policy options courts long-term failure. U.S. fishery policy is still tied to capture fisheries, to costly investment in capital-intensive, energy-intensive fishing fleets, and to high-risk mariculture projects. The Chinese, meanwhile, produce more fish at lower cost and worry less about fuel shortages, sea storms, navigation hazards, and oil spills. "Unlimited" marine stocks can no longer serve as a substitute for wise and careful fishery development. The broader dietary tastes of the Chinese, Japanese and Hawaiians promise to become a far more formidable advantage than larger fishing vessels and bigger nets. China's historic choice in fishery development no longer looks primitive.

7

A Bay to Keep

THE FRONT DOOR SLAMS SHUT. My youngest son is back from school. Muddy footprints mark his progress from the entryway to the kitchen refrigerator. I catch up with him in his room. He sips a glass of milk. "You're mucking up the carpet," I charge. Then I note the color of the mud caked on his shoes: gray. My wife often reprimands me for tracking the same color mud through the house. I lower my voice. "You've been to the bay?" He nods and tucks his shoes under his chair. "Playing?"

"No, school assignment." He waves a checklist of plants and animals.

I laugh. What a changeover. My son has one parting comment. "Dad, they don't want you to climb the bluffs any more."

Upper Newport Bay was far from being considered worthy of a school assignment when I first saw it in 1966. At that time I had no way of knowing that this bay would lead my wife and me to a courtroom.

The bay was already destined for improvement. Public officials eagerly awaited its transformation into a luxury residential marina. Its future seemed as settled as that of the Fens in Great Britain, the Zuider Zee in Holland, the Pontine Marshes in Italy, and countless mudflats that once rimmed the U.S. coast.

I can still understand, if not appreciate, the appeal of this transforming vision. Upper Newport Bay, like its other southern California counterparts, lacks the sweeping vistas of the Atlantic and Gulf of Mexico estuaries. Chesapeake Bay, for instance, washes the shores of two states, supports a commercial fishing industry, and accommodates oil tankers as well as thousands of recreation boats. One sweep of the eye can embrace Upper Newport Bay. It is about 3.5 miles long and isn't even as wide as the length of a supertanker. On a map its configuration resembles a long par 5 fairway with the dog leg to the right. Its shape derives from its geologic origin as a river-carved canyon drowned by rising sea levels.

No magnificent salmon runs pass through the bay enroute to river spawning beds. The canyon-carving river has long since shifted its course, leaving only a creek that can dry up in the summer. While the terms bay, estuary, and coastal wetland are often used interchangeably, scientists generally limit the term estuary to those bays where fresh river inflow is great enough to dilute the salt water. Marine scientist Joel Hedgpeth, revisor of *Between Pacific Tides*, classifies the bay, and others like it, as an "orphaned" estuary.

The modest bay still exudes a natural charm. It is framed almost entirely by bluffs. Homes line the bluff tops like a regiment of cavalry ready to charge forward when the upraised hand of a developer drops smartly. But at the base of the bluff, a hundred feet or so lower, the urban world above seems miles away. Clumps of willows ring with the calls of unseen birds. An aerial circus performs over the bay itself. Gangly blue herons lift off from stands of marsh grass. White terns dive-bomb the waters for anchovy and smelt.

While police sirens wail and angry dogs bark in the urban distance, you can hear tides lap at the shore. Wind rustles through the cordgrass. A bay, to me, is the introvert of the marine environment, modest in appearance, quiet in demeanor. The waves that thunder against the rocky shore or pound the sandy shore are absent here. The shore is rimmed not with bold rock forms or glistening sand grains, but with mud.

In this quiet, unassuming setting, two great plant systems converge: the fixed, rooted plants of the land and the tiny drifting plants of the ocean. Amid this quiet collision of plant systems, life flourishes in bunches: flocks of birds, beds of shellfish, schools of small, darting fish.

In this serene world overshadowed by urban tracts, my children learned to collect clams, to canoe, and to tell the difference between a stilt and a heron. The bay became our wild place, with trees and bluffs large enough to climb. Within reach of freeways, harbor marinas, and office buildings, a cultural relic was flourishing, a bay with no sewage outfall, industrial wharf, or garbage dump. More accustomed to harbors than bays in my boyhood, I learned a great deal from Upper Newport Bay about what the urban coast had lost. The same tides that lapped against the concrete shores of a harbor here revealed their full transforming power. At low tide, mudflats and marsh grass emerged as the water receded into winding channels. The sun-splashed mudflats shone as brightly as polished furniture. The shorebirds probed the mud with their long beaks and moved about on it as casually as ballet dancers on a hardwood stage. Flocks constantly arrived and departed without the aid of traffic controllers or flashing lights.

At high tide, the marsh grass, the mudflats, and the shorebirds receded as the ocean returned. Gulls and waterfowl rafted where the shorebirds had been strutting a few hours earlier. Clams extended their siphons to filter the returning tides at the risk of being nibbled by croakers or swept up by a stingray. I could canoe over the mudflats and the marsh grass. The tide-driven sea once more reclaimed its bay . . . for a few hours, anyway. Over one million cubic feet of water can move in and out of the bay each day.

As I descended into this wild place I realized I was attending an environmental wake of sorts. A media stream of unedited corporate press releases and schematics projected the bay's ultimate future: a bustling marina lined with estate homes. The bay emptied into the already transformed Newport Harbor. Here residents are liable to have two cars in the garage and two boats in the front yard slip. There are more boat dealers than auto dealers. Realtors show their clients the latest one-million-dollar listings in a Chris Craft.

Soon there would be one harbor and no bay. The wave-sheltered estuary that permited mud shores and marsh grass to flourish would be recruited to shelter power boats and yachts. A bay is the most malleable of landforms on this planet. It can be reshaped into harbors, farm fields, marinas, coastal resorts, and other productive human enterprises. The weight of human expectations was poised to fall on the bay with the finality of a piledriver.

I began to wonder how the bay had managed to escape such a fate up until now. The standard answer was that legal barriers had stood in the way. But this answer just raised more questions. Traditionally, the public owns the tidelands below the mean high tideline. However, the major landowner, the Irvine Company, claimed control not only of the bay uplands but of significant portions of the bay itself. How could this be? In the 1930s, California had granted a patent to the company to dike off the upper portion of the bay. Human expectations of the bay at that time were not as grandiose: the dike would permit salt to be evaporated in bay ponds.

A patent is not a clear title. It is still subject to public easements for fisheries and commerce, however academic dikes may render such easements.

The owner also claimed title to three islands in the bay. Islands? Why didn't I see islands while canoeing? Then it dawned on me. The "islands" were the stands of marsh grass that I could canoe over during spring tides, the twice monthly tides of maximum range. Congress had passed a law in 1850 that permitted states to grant away so-called swamp and overflowed lands above the mean high tide line. The company based its title to the islands on such a grant. The islands had even acquired names: Upper, Middle, and Shellmaker. But how can marsh islands subject to tidal submergence be considered above the high tide line? Use of the mean high tide line to divide public and private ownership derives from English custom. England, like our Atlantic coast, is exposed to uniform tides: two high tides each day of about the same height. However, tides on our Pacific coast are mixed, with one high high tide and one low high tide. The mean or average high tide line thus lies well below the tide's upper limit. Apply the English standard to a coast with mixed tides and you thrust private ownership into the active tidal regime. Historic confusion over tidal cycles was helping to seal the fate of the bay and the life it supported.

If these private bay claims were legally sound, where were those legal barriers? The lower harbor boasted over seven residential islands that were once marshes and sand bars. Why didn't the landowner go ahead and colonize his back bay islands? While maintaining that this was possible, the landowner preferred another route. The dwarf islands were big enough to block what could become a spacious navigation channel. The bluff-backed bay shore, while lengthy, was not wide enough for residental sites. The Irvine Company wanted to dredge out the fabled islands to make way for a channel. The islands could then become fill to widen the skinny bay shore. The scorned mudhole would be compressed into a luxury residential marina with a channel wider than Venice's Grand Canal. To accomplish this transformation, the landowner would have to be granted title to the public tidelands that were to be filled in. This was the legal barrier. The company's solution was a trade: it had agreed to give the fabled islands and some uplands to Orange County in exchange for the public tidelands. The company would give up 450 acres to gain 157 acres of public tidelands. The public would thus gain almost three acres for every one acre of mudflat it gave up. Who could refuse a three-for-one offer like this?

This trade was enthusiastically blessed by the local media and by public officials. It seemed like heresy, if not a waste of time, to attempt to interfere with this time-honored sequence of events. But the role of the fabled islands continued to perplex me. To justify the loss of the tidelands, the public must receive lands that were at least as valuable. Yet the islands the public would receive would be used as spoil to support private residential development that would obstruct public access. The justification for this was that the public would still get an unobstructed boat channel.

Yet I, as well as many others, already enjoyed access to the bay. The islands were no obstacle to canoeists, fishermen, clammers, bird-watchers, and swimmers. While the public already owned the shore to below the mean high tide line, the trade would permit the shore to be filled in with vertical concrete banks that would make access academic unless you were a barnacle. There would be scattered public footholds along the shore, but the park sites shared one trait. They were invariably located around storm drains and flood control channels. The site of one "major" bayfront park appeared to host virtually every tennis ball that had been hit over a fence in the surrounding watershed, along with stray waffleballs, frisbees, golf balls, and softballs. Their accumulation here suggested relatively weak natural circulation. A harbor breakwater would now abet this natural trap. The park would obviously have a built-in source of athletic gear.

The three-for-one trade seemed to be an ironic bargain. The lands the public would receive would include the islands to be used as spoil and the patent lands that were ostensibly subject to public easements for fisheries and navigation.

The logic behind this trade was becoming as fascinating as the bay itself. The public record leading up to the much heralded trade "breakthrough" proved as revealing as the visit to the park sites. One state legislative report concluded that the trade "would convert public waterways into a captive waterway primarily for the use of residential boat owners who would occupy the created area and dominate the bay." At one point I attended a local public hearing where elected officials were competing to claim credit for the trade. One young woman who had obviously spent time in preparing a typewritten statement rose to testify. She spoke of the mudhole in terms of the food chain, feeding grounds, and nutrient cycles. The public officials frowned and raised their eyebrows. She was told to limit her comments to a minute. She spoke faster. She was then hit with a barrage of questions. She lost her place in her testimony, rustled through the pages, and eventually retreated, her face tense, her testimony clutched tightly in her hands. Instead of returning to her seat, she left the hearing room.

The constituency to reclaim mud flats seemed as strong as ever. New twists had even been devised to expand this constituency. Biologists at the nearby University of California at Irvine expressed concern about the loss of natural habitat, but university administrators were in favor of the trade. The schematic plans included a university rowing course, a western Thames touted as a lure for future Olympic games. The public hearings—or promotions—exhibited one significant shortcoming. The hearings were highly organized, the technical experts well prepared, and the press releases very professional, but there was very little unsolicited citizen support. Was the trade proceeding on the momentum of the past, oblivious to the fact that public attitudes can change?

In reviewing the development of public attitudes towards wetlands and estuaries, I had discovered that most accounts of historic reclamation projects described the original bay or estuary as a malaria-ridden swamp or wasteland or, at best, a hideout for social outcasts. No one appeared to exist who would or could vouch for the natural values of an estuary. One day I was scanning an advertising brochure prepared by a large Dutch dredging company. One drawing depicted a problem faced by a sixteenth century Dutch engineer hired to reclaim the Pontine Marshes in Italy. A group of unshaven fishermen were working under cover of night to demolish dikes that the clean-shaven engineer had built during the day. One fisherman was armed with what might have been the first environmental impact report: a gun.

This sixteenth-century incident indicated that marshes did have early human champions. It wasn't until the twentieth century that the Pontine Marshes were finally reclaimed, thanks in large part to the insistence of Mussolini.

Shortly after the sixteenth-century encounter at the Pontine Marshes, British royalty retained Dutch engineers to reclaim a vast freshwater wetland called the Fens. Dikes that went up in the day came down at night. The local fishermen and fowlers realized the very root of their existence was being threatened. They complained to a local official already at odds with the English crown. Oliver Cromwell felt reclamation of the Fens represented royal arrogance at its height. The fenmen would be displaced as cavalierly as the fish and the birds. The uneducated fenmen had found a leader educated in the ways of power, and eventually became loyal soldiers in the revolution that replaced the English king with Cromwell.

It turned out to be a bitter victory for the fenmen. The urban workplaces were growing, and their populations needed more food. Reclamation of the Fens would provide farmland to meet rising food demands. As dictator, Cromwell approved the reclamation that he had opposed as a political dissenter. The Dutch engineers were rehired. Cromwell himself gained 200 drained acres. The fenmen joined the rural exodus to the industrial towns. Cried out one disillusioned and disinherited soul, "All you intended when you set us a-fighting was merely to unhorse and dismount our old riders and tyrants, that you might get up and ride in their stead."

Clearly, there was some recognition of what was being lost as estuaries were reclaimed. The unending need for more farmland, more marinas, more garbage sites, and more sewage sinks doomed this recognition. While the reclamation programs were certainly impressive engineering and economic undertakings, the estuary was being turned into a substitute for wise and efficient human practices. Fishermen and fowlers were too weak politically to reform budding urban practices, much less protect their own bays and marshes.

Upper Newport Bay had no willow-cutters, thatchers, fowlers, commercial fishermen, or squatters. Its admirers and defenders came during lunch breaks, weekends, or when school was out and the fish were running. This sort of constituency appeared to be weak, but only because it had never been organized.

An unlikely assortment of university biologists, high school teachers, fishermen, bird-watchers, and local citizens formed a group called Friends of Newport Bay that was critical of the trade. But every press release we generated was swamped by layer after layer of denunciations by the landowner, local leaders, newspaper editors, and county officials. Getting people interested in stately redwood forests or popular beaches was one thing; getting them interested in mudflats and marshes was another. Some sympathetic supporters felt this would be impossible. The media image of the bay remained intact: a swamp teeming with mosquitos, ooze, and modern-day Luddites. Our debut seemed to strengthen the push for reclamation. To reclaim the bay would reaffirm that society was not ready to step back into the dark ages and venerate natural objects.

A look at the bay itself would easily contradict the media image of a mudhole. But how to get people to the bay? A bayside road was a barrier to access. Potholes kept tow trucks and car washes in business. Only earnest lovers, bird-watchers, and dedicated fishermen would risk such an intimidating road. We decided to put on Saturday bay tours. The local press granted us a single paragraph. The guides outnumbered the audience. A green jeep driven by an Irvine Company security guard wearing a Stetson would invariably pass by. His reports to the company must have been comforting.

One day Walter Houk, an editor with *Sunset Magazine,* expressed surprising interest in our efforts. We didn't expect a popular home and garden magazine to be turned on by mud-flats. But the magazine was expanding its environmental horizons too. Photographs of the bay and the time and location of our next tour appeared in the magazine along with my phone number.

There wasn't much precedent for gearing up a wetland tour that had been advertised to millions of readers. Dr. Charles Greening, chairman of the Friends, hastily recruited more teachers and birders as guides. But the day before the tour we confronted a development beyond our control: drizzle. We decided to go ahead. Another incident, seemingly unrelated to the tour, was also in progress: the 1969 oil platform blowout off Santa Barbara.

On the morning of the tour, my bedroom phone rang. An anxious mother asked, "Is the tour still on?" I looked out the window. It was drizzling, but not hard. I said yes and hung up. The phone rang again. And again. And again.

"What's going on?" asked my wife. I told her as I hastily dressed. I grabbed my binoculars and a pile of handouts on the bay and left her to answer the phone. I realized that crowd control was going to be a problem. Cars were already lined up at the bluff top where the tours began. Families were patiently hiking up to the bluff. A yellow school bus arrived and an entire class debarked, supervised by only one teacher. The tour, which had never attracted more than forty people before, now had to handle over two hundred. As fast as we sent groups to stations along the bay, new groups would form. One school bus came from Barstow, a desert community about a hundred miles away. The green jeep with the Irvine Company security guard drove by. He had the windshield wipers going. He peered out at us with a look of astonishment. To an employee of a company that touted itself as a developer of planned communities, this was clearly an unplanned development.

Our field tours shattered the media image of the bay trade. The public could really be turned on to wetland values. A redwood forest, however beautiful and stately, tends to screen what animal life exists; but an estuary flaunts its life, from the aerial circus above to a fish jumping clear of the water. Residents who never confronted such a concentrated display of natural life now discovered that it could exist virtually at their doorstep. They bought stationery note cards decorated with bay scenes photographed by Friends member Joan Coverdale. The "mudhole" was winding up in mailboxes scattered across the nation.

Public sentiment began to shift dramatically.

The company and the county stressed that the development of the bay would emulate that in the lower harbor. This strategy backfired. The lower harbor, with 9,000 boats, already had to cope with aquatic traffic jams. The upper bay development would add at least 3,000 more. Recreational boaters unimpressed by cordgrass now saw a protected bay as an alternative to boat traffic bunched like cattle herds on the way to the great blue plains of the Pacific Ocean.

Amid such favorable shifts in public sentiment, one newspaper report decreed that the bay was more or less "dead." The asserted agent of death was tons of silt deposited in the bay by the mild-looking San Diego Creek, which drained the bay's watershed. The drizzles had turned into downpours that served to energize the silt streams. A company publicist claimed that the silt had buried much of the natural life of the bay.

The line of this reasoning was evident. Even if our claims about the bay's wealth of natural life were true, silt had destroyed this value. The bay might as well be developed. In the process, marine plants could be introduced. The "dead" bay would thus be reincarnated in a new, livelier form. Dredge and fill would be an act of mercy, if not euthanasia.

I drove down to view the biological corpse. Waterfowl still

probed the mud flats with their beaks. Fishermen still cast for croaker. Terns still dive-bombed small schools of fish. The bay seemed far from being dead. Indeed, estuaries are originally formed by the deposit of silt. Plants and animals can adapt to this process over geologic time. Eventually, silt can raise the estuary above sea level and transform it into a freshwater marsh and then a meadow. However, the time scale for this natural process involves thousands of years, not just one rainstorm.

Tules and cattails common to freshwater marshes and swamps were beginning to occupy the bay. Their presence where tides once ebbed and flowed indicated that silt loads were becoming prodigious enough to accelerate the natural time scale. Plants that seemed set in time and in space were actually retreating or advancing, as they adjusted to minute changes in elevation. Freshwater plants were being favored by the stepped-up silting process. Were we attempting to save a bay that was turning into a meadow before our very eyes? Willows were even intruding into the bay. Children now had a forest to match their wildest expectations. While we were struggling to shape the bay's future, the botanical world was engaged in its own special struggle.

A drive through the bay's watershed explained the advance of the willows. The landscape was literally hostage to bulldozers and earthmovers, deployed to replace farm fields and natural ground cover with sites for industrial parks and "fast tracts." Once content to develop a university community surrounded by productive orange groves and row crops, the Irvine Company, which was the major landowner in the bay's watershed, now wanted to develop a city of 450,000 people, preferably by the end of the century, and to reclaim the bay as a marina. The massive silt streams induced by site clearance threatened this vision of the bay's future as well as our own vision.

The heavy flows that carried silt into the bay also breached a huge bay dike. The dike had been erected by the Irvine Company to protect its solar salt evaporation ponds from the ebb and flow of the tides. With the dike breached, the tides were once more washing over mudflats after a thirty-year absence. Thus, while willows and cattails encroached on the bay margins, fish were returning to other portions of the besieged bay. Could the bay, if protected, be restored to its historic health? Could the solar ponds and the accumulated silt be removed to readmit the cleansing tides? Or would the tides end up competing with the inland siltloads for control of the bay's elevation? This raised another interesting question. How had the company protected its salt operation from past floods and siltloads? Were other man-made artifacts being displaced as the watershed was being urbanized? With the dike breached, the company closed down the solar salt operation. To the company, it made no sense to rebuild a dike that would have to give way shortly to its planned marina.

The media struggle to shape public perceptions of the bay escalated. The company and the county did concede that the "mudhole" hosted certain forms of life: sharks, sting rays, skates, and longjaw mudsuckers. This limited inventory suggested that the bay was a hideout for aquatic desperados. There were sharks in the bay, but they were not quite man-eaters. There were also halibut, barracuda, flounder, croaker, clam beds, and other forms of animal life with less tarnished reputations. Debate in the press over what constituted the predominant marine life helped to debunk the bay's traditional image as a mudhole. After all, what were sharks doing in a mudhole?

One Saturday, we had a fine sunny morning and a large public turnout for the bay tour. Bird experts set up telescopes so tour guests could get close-up views of migrating waterfowl from Canada. However, a young man was trudging knee-deep through the mudflats, banging on cans and scaring away our prize performers. Our anger turned to wonder. Why would anyone want to trudge knee-deep through mud banging metal cans? We then learned that the young man, a college student, had been hired to divert the waterfowl to a nearby pond operated by a bird-hunting club. A public now anxious to see the bay's abundant life could also see firsthand how casually this community resource could be treated. We suppressed an urge to visit the duck ponds armed with tambourines.

A state court decision at this time held that the public could gain, through historic use, prescriptive easements across private uplands to reach beach or bayfront. We felt this decision bolstered our contention that the public did not need a trade to gain effective public use of the bay. We distributed bay maps so older residents could trace their historic routes to the bay. The company's response to the court decision was to erect a wire fence around the bay. Some fence portions that strayed into the public tidelands had to be moved. The barbed wire fence disturbed local officials, including trade supporters. "We don't need the Vietnamization of the bay," complained one critic. The company switched to smooth wire and defended the fence as necessary to discourage what it considered a prime cause of bay silting: footpaths beaten by inquisitive bay visitors.

State and federal officials were now converging on the bay to see what all the commotion was about. The company preferred to bring these officials to the bay during low tide, when the marsh islands were fully exposed as obstructions to powered navigation. We would bring prospective allies and political candidates to the bay, when the fabled islands were submerged by a high tide and shaded by canoe hulls. When visitors asked where the islands were, we would point to the dark outline of the submerged marsh grass underneath a foot of water. For those who visited the bay at the behest of both contending groups, the contrast in the character of the islands must have been thought-provoking. If anything, the struggle to control the bay's future was serving to make all of us experts in consulting the tide tables and in watching the night sky to discern the stage of the moon.

8

A Fist of Mud

THE AMERICAN BAYFRONT IS RE-
plete with examples of tidelands reclaimed for Little League
ballparks, parking lots, industrial parks, and waterfront storage
sheds. Legislatures have tended to condone tideland encroach-
ments that are considered small in size or that contribute to
public goals for harbors and navigation. Should the 157 acres of
tidelands to be traded to the Irvine Company qualify as "small"?
We thought not, but we would have to persuade a judge, not
ecologists or the marine life that depended on tidelands. One
clause in the California Constitution buoyed our hopes: "All
tidelands within two miles of any incorporated city and county,
or town in this State, in fronting on the water of any harbor,
estuary, bay or inlet used for the purposes of navigation, shall be

withheld from grant or sale to private persons, partnerships, or corporations. . . ." Upper Newport Bay lay within two miles of Newport Beach, an incorporated city. In fact, it was almost surrounded by this community.

A potentially strong case was one matter; getting a lawyer was another. The advent of public interest law firms, environmental impact reports, and liberal standing-to-sue provisions was approaching, but not in time for us. Fortunately, people not worried about the bay's ecological integrity were still concerned about the trade. Title company officials wanted to be sure of their legal ability to guarantee any transfers of title involving former public tidelands. To validate the trade's constitutionality, the Irvine Company and Orange County entered into a so-called friendly lawsuit, the *County of Orange* v. *Heim*. Rather than file our own lawsuit, we could enter as intervenors in the "friendly" lawsuit. Our goal of safeguarding the public trust and protecting such a critical element of the coastal ecosystem would not be sufficient reason for the court to grant us standing to intervene. We had to seek standing as property owners whose taxes would be involved in the trade.

The county did not object to our motion to intervene; if the county had objected it would have risked adding to the image of a public agency fronting for a private developer. The Irvine Company, on the other hand, did object. Our motion was described as "an unjustified attempt . . . to intervene in this lawsuit and impose a lengthy delay upon The Irvine Company at a stage when time is of the essence." The company counsel, Robert Warren, claimed that "it is not fair for these people to work this harm upon us." The court overruled this objection. We asked that the Sierra Club be added as another intervenor. By this time, the Irvine Company lawyer was beside himself over the fate of the friendly lawsuit: "I do not take lightly the addition of more and more intervenors in the case." Judge Claude Owen concurred. "We've got to stop at some place." The intervention was thus limited to three tax-paying couples: Hal and Joan Coverdale, Frank and Fran Robinson, and myself and my wife Judy.

Getting into the court was one thing; staying in was another. In tidelands litigation, findings from hundreds of court decisions must be applied to the physical and political peculiarities of one site. Our lawyer lacked the resources to accomplish this and withdrew as our counsel. We were without a lawyer as the trial grew imminent.

The bay, which had once afforded such recreational leisure to my family, was now becoming an emotional roller coaster of ups and downs. Ironically, the departure of our original counsel persuaded the court to accept Phillip Berry, who also happened to be president of the Sierra Club at the time, as our new counsel. The ride now seemed to be veering upward.

A flood of bay maps, exhibits, and reports flowed from various legal offices to crest in the chambers of Judge Owens. Words like habitat, channelize, bird counts, bulkhead line, and tidal prisms resounded in the austere courtroom. The bay became a blue splotch of color on map exhibits.

The parties to the suit focused on the relative public benefits of a protected bay versus a developed bay. The bay wildlife entered the courtroom in a legal Noah's Ark. The court reporter had to ask witnesses to spell the scientific names of clams, birds, sharks, and skates.

To counter our wildlife celebration, the trade proponents produced a scientific expert to testify how dredge and fill projects can spare marine life. The scientist recited forms of life that existed in a marina that was once a "wild" bay; but he made one mistake. He brought all his notes and work sheets on the marina in question to the witness stand. This enabled our counsel to request that this material be made available to us. I was asked to review the material.

The life cited by the expert witness was limited mainly to fish. This approach excluded the fate of life forms most affected by dredging, the bottom (benthic) life and the abundant bird populations. The witness' own notes confirmed this omission. We produced our own volunteer expert, marine biologist Dr. Don Bright. I took the stand to confirm the existence of bay clam beds that rarely fare well when the dredge arrives. We congratulated ourselves on rebutting this strategem of the trade proponents.

The trial consumed twenty-eight days and generated 3,700 pages of transcript. Rarely has a mudhole been accorded such legal scrutiny. To convey his decision, the judge wrote an opinion forty-one pages long. To the judge, counting patent lands as part of the acreage to be "gained" by the public was not proper. The judge felt that the length of shoreline to be gained or lost should also be considered.

However, the judge, like the contending parties before him, went beyond the question of relative acreage to relative benefit. To the judge, the existing shore, while owned by the public, was of little public use. The proposed shore, even with reduced public ownership, would be of more use. The judge then invoked the expert witness produced by the trade proponents to support the claim that there would be compensating benefits for marine life too. His decision was that the trade was constitutional.

Under this reasoning, very few wetlands could ever hope to survive. The judge was reflecting the historical tradition that had doomed the inhabitants of the Fens, the Pontine Marshes, and Holland's inland seas. Wetlands had few socially redeeming values.

The roller coaster plunged downward, only to veer upwards again. The chief elected supporter of the trade had been defeated for reelection by a trade opponent. The county now voted to withdraw from the trade. The court forbade this. The case moved to the appellate level, with the county now arguing that the trade was, as we claimed, unconstitutional. The "friendly" lawsuit was becoming even more unfriendly.

Amid these rapid-fire developments, a visit to the bay became therapeutic. The celebration of life continued, from the diving terns in the sky to the jumping mullet. But the cattail and willow were still advancing. An occasional jet would shatter the bay quiet. The noise did not seem to bother the rafting birds. The jets, in their own way, were contributing to the thrust to protect the bay. The local airport used the airspace over the bay for takeoffs, and airport officials prefered to fly over natural rather than human communities.

On some weekends my family would go to rocky or sandy shores. The sound of waves crashing and the bold form of rock bluffs contrasted sharply with the quiet nature of the estuary. I began to understand better the role of bays in human affairs. The bay, by its very nature, extends itself into urban processes and expectations. Whether it is to be changed or to be protected from change, its fate is irrevocably tied up with human actions.

The courts were trying to grapple with changing public attitudes towards tidelands in other cases. In a modest bay north of the San Francisco Bay area, one owner, like the Irvine Company, held a patent to a tideland parcel he wanted to reclaim. An adjacent owner claimed that the patent was still burdened with the public trust. By the time *Marks* v. *Whitney* reached the California Supreme Court, we, along with the Irvine Company, the attorney general's office, title companies, tideland patent owners, and environmental organizations were following this case intently. If the court held that patents were not burdened with trust easements, patent owners such as the Irvine Company could more readily alter state tidelands.

The court ruled that the patent was still subject to public easements and that the state itself must determine whether any alteration would be compatible with the public trust. The court then greatly expanded the scope of the trust:

> There is a growing public recognition that one of the most important public uses of the tidelands—a use incorporated within the tidelands trust—is the preservation of those lands in their natural state, so that they may serve as ecological units for scientific study, as open space, and as environments which provide food and habitat for bird and marine life, and which favorably affect the scenery and climate of the area.

The fate of the marine ecosystem was finally gaining legal standing, however tenuous. We never anticipated this judicial appreciation of mudflats when we filed to intervene in the case of *County of Orange* v. *Heim.*

However, in another case the court held that the state could free tidelands from the public trust in certain circumstances. The court said that the state, in granting such approval, must find that the tidelands will be reclaimed "for a highly beneficial public program of harbor development," and that they are "valueless for trust purposes" and "constitute a relatively small parcel of the total acreage involved."

Once more the size of the tidelands involved in our lawsuit loomed as significant. In the above case, the tideland parcel was under 5 acres. The tidelands in our case comprised 157 acres. Was this "small" or "big"? Was the envisioned harbor a "highly beneficial public program"? Were the tidelands "valueless"?

In 1973, four years after our lawsuit began, I was pulling some weeds in the backyard when the phone rang. A *Los Angeles Times* reporter wanted to know my response to the decision by the appellate court on the trade. I asked him what the decision had been. The court had overruled the trial court and found that the trade was unconstitutional.

A party to celebrate the court decision was held. Like past parties to raise legal funds, it was called the "Back Bay Bash." The party site—a beautiful bluff-top home overlooking the bay —was a far cry from the small, informal meetings we had held four years ago. The carpets were deep pile. The walls were covered with fine paintings. The kitchen was about the size of the entire first floor of our own home. A person with field binoculars around his neck and bay mud on his shoes would have been out of place. It was a diverse group, including boaters, bird-watchers, university professors, and realtors. The bay had brought together, if only momentarily, a surprising range of interests. Some were more concerned about the public trust doctrine than about estuarine ecology *per se*. Others were more concerned about the potential influence of one landowner on public decision making than on the actual use of the bay. As the cigarette smoke and the buzz of many separate conversations escalated, I walked out to the bluff top. The waters of the bay below reflected the night lights. I could make out the breach in the dike cut by the bay's supposed death knell, the 1969 flood. The quiet of the bay below managed to reach to the very top of the bluff and to the edge of the party resonating with laughter and the clinking of iced drinks. Was the urbanization that rimmed the bluff top, and which I feared might overcome the bay, helping to save it? This modest bay, which might be considered expendable in a rural coastal region, was surrounded by people beginning to sense how easily the natural values that define the coastal environment can be lost forever.

The bay's dramatic change in social status really struck me one day when I was caught in a freeway traffic jam. A billboard depicted the virtues of a residential project by means of a bigger-than-life couple, dressed in evening clothes, sipping cocktails on a balcony. The balcony overlooked a familiar scene: the marsh islands of Upper Newport Bay. The bay as a natural entity has finally received genuine acceptance. The Irvine Company now regards the mudhole as a glamorous backdrop to attract prospective homeowners.

Later I discovered how the court reached its decision. The court noted that the "friendly lawsuit" had developed "into a truly adversary litigation of substantial proportions." The court then reduced the lawsuit's proportions considerably. To the court, the legislature must decide which trust purpose—protection or harbor development—should prevail. "It is not benefit with which we are concerned; it is constitutionality."

To the court, the controlling issue was what constituted "a relatively small parcel." To consider acreage alone would equate a bay with a chunk of real estate in the midwest. The fate of the linear shoreline must be considered as well. "As a result of the exchange and effectation of the dredging and filling plan, the public would lose approximately two-thirds of its present shoreline," declared the court. "Should we call small that which in terms of public effect is not small, we should abrogate the essential judicial function of enforcing the constitution."

If more bayfront had been left public, the trade would have prevailed. If the court ruling had been rendered earlier, such a readjustment might have been readily rearranged. But the bay had been held off the market a trifle too long. Due to dramatic shifts in public attitudes outside the courtroom, wetlands are now considered as worthy of public protection as redwood forests and sandy beaches. After being in the headlines for over five years and being viewed by thousands of people, Upper Newport Bay received a new public designation: a state ecological reserve. The fabled islands are now under the management of the California Department of Fish and Game. I can still canoe over them at high tide. The price of acquisition was far less than the cost to construct a marina. The wave-sheltered benefits of the bay remain secure for the original inhabitants. The recognition that a wetland has intrinsic value comes too late for the fishermen and fowlers of the Pontine marshes, the Fens and the Zuider Zee, but not for future generations.

Such changes in attitude are not universally appreciated. An organization called Amigos de Bolsa Chica has formed to protect a coastal wetland to the north of Upper Newport Bay. An editorial in the *Orange County Register* described this hard-working citizens group as "a strange case." After describing the group's goal as keeping wetlands "vacant, marshy and gooey," the editorial observed, "Their brain cells are totally incapable of comprehending economic reality." Ironically, the public cost to compress the wetland into a marina, a prospect the editorial writer could tolerate, would run $154 million. As you might suspect, the editorial title relied on that old bromide—"For the Birds."

Today, *County of Orange* v. *Heim* is scrutinized, quoted and cited by lawyers involved in the unending struggle to balance conflicting public and private interests in such a unique landform as the estuary. For a nation and a people so accustomed to having land use and natural resource decisions shaped in large part by a property owner, the future use of estuaries will remain a challenging task. Because estuaries are public by nature their use requires a community, a state or a nation to determine its own long-range marine goals. Demanding requirements of the public trust doctrine allow no less.

This doctrine even returns to haunt modern hotel and commercial sites seemingly beyond the tidal flux. Whether a coastal site is wet or dry *today* is not conclusive as the determination of public trust. That a landowner may have paid taxes on the seemingly dry, reclaimed land is not determinative. That an inept or conniving public official a century ago permitted a private party to claim title to tidelands is not determinative. The site's *natural* condition prior to the wholesale alienation of tideland titles in the 19th century remains determinative. Today, the term "reclaim" may apply to coastal states attempting to reassert tideland title rather than to the burial of another estuary beneath two or three feet of fill.

While the public trust doctrine can reprieve a bay, it can never ensure a healthy survival. Upper Newport Bay remains entrained in the roller-coaster nature of public decisions. I become quite conscious of this every time I hear rain start to fall. In a forest or shore, you can barely hear rain as it strikes forest leaves or the soft soil. The hard urban surface transforms this rainfall into a cacophony of patters, beats, and drips. The raindrops that patter on my roof also strike streets, parking lots, and construction sites stripped bare of vegetation. They become fine chisels, chipping away at exposed soil, and coalesce into rivulets swift and strong enough to scour away tons of soil and urban debris. The rivulets disappear down storm drains to reappear in flood control channels that converge on the bay. Its blue waters turn muddy brown, and its surface exhibits a collage of urban debris.

Freshwater greenery continues to encroach on the bay margins. Sea winds that once rustled tidal shallows now bend cattails and tules. Parts of the historic bay resemble a dirt bike track. Under cover of night, trail bike riders execute sharp turns and s-maneuvers on bay lands that have risen above the tides. In one mudflat portion, the tides run among new sprigs of cordgrass. Another marsh island is being formed well in advance of the normal geologic schedule.

The shellfish beds are still there, but my family can no longer dig in the mud for clams. Next to the sign that says the bay is an ecological reserve is one that says swimming and shellfish harvesting is banned because of the polluted runoff. The watershed has turned against its bay. This is why some 27 percent of the nation's commercial shellfish beds lie in quarantine despite growing public support to protect estuarine systems. While Upper Newport Bay contends with the discharge from only one creek, the nation's largest estuary, Chesapeake Bay, must contend with discharges from 150 creeks and rivers.

The silt streams could bury hopes of restoring the bay to its original grandeur. As the upper part of the bay continues to recede, a lingering question from the flood that disrupted the salt operations pops up again. Did the company build its salt operations without any protection from upstream floods and silting? As it now turns out, the company had built a dam just above the bay to slow the flow of storm water so silt would settle out. When the creek bed was channelized so the watershed could be urbanized, the dam was removed. Today, the California Fish and Game Department is working to reestablish a downstream silt and debris basin.

Bay defenders accustomed to monitoring bay wildlife periodically fan out through the watershed to identify careless grading practices that lead to erosion. Traditionally, many tract developers limit landscaping to their model homes. Tract developers now must prepare detailed silt control and plant restoration plans. This turns out to be no problem for the more prudent developers. The sooner they restore a graded site, the sooner they can offer a more attractive product.

Flood control officials may join in these watershed monitoring efforts. Keeping the soil in place protects the capacity of their channels to carry away storm waters. Some upstream communities plant buffer strips of vegetation along creek banks. These buffer strips turn ditchlike eyesores into scenic community assets. They also help retain and trap sediment. Bike trails on the top of channel banks form a recreational link with the bay. Such programs suggest how the harmony that once existed between a bay and its watershed can be reestablished to the benefit of both the bay and the urban residents. Once regarded as a costly nuisance, watershed controls are gradually, if grudgingly, being recognized as an economic and ecological necessity. Without such controls, upper and lower watershed areas throughout the nation will remain engaged in a macabre form of environmental warfare.

Bays and estuaries will remain prominent hostages to this warfare. So will our ambitions for a more bountiful marine harvest. As the limits of fishing technology, mariculture, and fish hatcheries become more evident, the need to maintain and restore our bays will become more pressing. By restoring an estuary we can restore an entire spectrum of marine life and related human interests.

Such opportunities can crop up unexpectedly. For example, an air force base in the San Francisco Bay area has been declared obsolete. The U.S. Fish and Wildlife Service will flood a portion of the deserted grounds to restore its original marsh character. Waterfowl and fish will be able to return to a habitat preempted for a time by fighter jets. Nearby residents appreciate the shift to flight forms that don't emit sonic booms.

Another national goal helps reinforce the wisdom of protecting our estuaries. The federal government spends millions in federal disaster control and relief measures, only to find this nation's vulnerability to natural disaster higher than ever. If we control careless urban development rather than risk disaster, we can conserve public funds as well as critical marine habitat. The residential marina planned for Upper Newport Bay would have been built on weak or soft estuarine soils prone to severe seismic shaking from a nearby active earthquake fault. When the inevitable quake strikes, the bay can survive without assistance from the government. In the lower harbor, though, residents on the earthquake-prone artificial islands may find themselves riding a geo-logic bronco.

I can get to the bay from my home today by bike rather than auto. A bike route straddles a levee adjacent to the San Diego Creek. Like a minor Arc de Triomphe, a large bridge overpass marks where the bike route enters the head of the bay. Some dikes from the salt operation still remain. I can see, if not hear, the unknowing protectors of the bay: the marsh islands, the steep-sided bluffs, and the narrow bay shore. The road, once a barrier to access, is now fit for bikes and for cars with a low center of gravity. The tow truck is no longer a standard presence. One bay activity that we gave little thought to a decade ago flourishes today. Joggers and long distance runners now tred on bay shore that would have been pre-empted by concrete bulkheads and luxury marina estates.

Horseback riders roam where the asphalt plains of a parking lot would have sprawled. Canoeists cruise on the site of a proposed landfill.

9

Dragon's Tongue
and the
Urban Coast

I BECAME ACQUAINTED WITH THE seaweed known as giant brown kelp long before I knew its name or its reputation. I was at a critical stage in life. Defending sand castles against rising tides on the southern California shore was losing its luster. That bane of adult bathers—rotting clumps of drift kelp piled up like magnified mounds of cold, leftover spaghetti, crowned by buzzing halos of flies—became my salvation. When untangled, the leathery, vinelike kelp could become a bull whip to drive an imaginary cattle herd past beach umbrellas, volleyball courts, and beer coolers. The whip could become a lariat, swirling overhead as anxious sun bathers demanded, "Watch it, kid."

While I drove cattle, my female peers would transform drift kelp into swirling hula skirts and oversized necklaces. Parental pleas to "get away from that flea-bitten mess" went unheeded.

I thought I had fully plumbed kelp's magical utility . . . until I saw another child patiently paw through a clump of drift kelp to extract some small brown bulbs. He then tossed the bulbs one by one into a flaming weiner roast. Each toss was followed by a resounding POP. I now knew the ultimate charm of kelp. It was an organic firecracker that could go POP, BANG, or BOOM depending on the type of sound track one needed. I promptly volunteered to build a beach fire for my family. When my parents departed for a brief swim, I carefully seeded the fire with kelp bulbs. That evening the blaze sounded like a firing range. My father frowned, my mother was puzzled. With the imperiousness of a genuine smart-aleck, I stepped forward, held up one last remaining bulb, and tossed it offhandedly into the crackling blaze.

If somebody had explained to me the source of kelp's supple strength, the reasons for its size, and the significance of the bulb, I probably would have been impressed, but not diverted from my own investigations. No other plant on land or shore could adapt so readily to one's play needs and not break, shatter, or splinter in the process.

My next relationship with kelp began upon my return from a Pacific island where, while in the Marine Corps, I had learned to scuba dive and explore coral reefs. The colder southern California coastal waters did not seem nearly as inviting. Wave action was more pronounced, underwater visibility more restricted. After donning a rubber wet suit and negotiating the surf with a steel tank on one's back, what could one see? Rocks? Sand? Certainly not the rainbow-hued coral reefs favored by the jet-set diving fraternity.

While I had heard references to "diving kelp," little information was available on what this meant. Some people described kelp as an underwater forest. But the drift kelp on the beach suggested a submarine jungle able to defy the sharpest machete.

Kelp fringes the rocky coast in a long, thin band beyond the surf line. It stretches out like overgrown ivy on the sea surface to form a canopy, giving a dark mahogany cast to the blue ocean waters. While the sea around the canopy is rippled by wind and waves, the surface water within the canopy is as placid as a goldfish pond. One expects to hear a frog croak or see a huge carp drift casually below. Gulls loaf on these glassy waters, waiting patiently for the next sportfishing boat to leave a wake of dead bait and half-eaten sandwiches. Driftwood and white styrofoam coffee cups bob up against the canopy.

The sense of calmness ebbs quickly on your first kelp dive. The kelp plants, which lay still and rotting on the beach, are now unfurled to their full, staggering 50- and 100-foot lengths. They sway in unison with the passing swells above. While the kelp may bend like a palm tree under hurricane winds, no sound accompanies this unrelenting motion. The silent swaying seems sinister and menacing, a *danse macabre* ready to ensnare an intruder in a deadly embrace. This eerie feeling gradually disappears. While the surface canopy above is thick and junglelike, the kelp below divides into well-spaced, arborlike columns. As you glide through this submarine arbor, you too become a part of the to and fro motion induced by swells bound for shore. The kelp now appears more stately then menacing, the motion more rhythmic than sinister, a never-ending sea waltz rather than a *danse macabre.*

After envying the ability of birds to flaunt gravity and commute freely between the humus-covered forest floor and the sunlit tree tops, I found myself imbued with the same casual freedom. With the stroke of my legs or a turn to the side, I could go wherever my curiosity led. Or, better yet, I could hover suspended in the water column like a hawk in a hot summer updraft and watch the life below parade by.

Amid the cathedrallike hush of coastal redwood forests, a visitor is often struck by the apparent lack of animal life. The redwood branches above filter out energy-giving sunlight, limiting growth of understory plants for grazing animals.

The lush kelp canopy filters sunlight, too. But the shadowy forest below literally throbs with life. Solitary kelp bass rise from the dim bottom to devour perch. A pelican may plunge out of the sky in a cascade of silvery bubbles to swallow topsmelt exposed by a canopy opening. The same silence that envelops the swaying kelp plants envelops this desperate search for food. The placid kelp canopy, populated by loafing gulls and driftwood, conceals a teeming natural marine zoo.

My first timid visit to a kelp forest lasted about 20 minutes. After renegotiating the surf, lumbering up the beachface, and unhitching my air tank, I sat down facing the sea. A grim-faced surf fisherman was untangling drift kelp from his line; I was exhilarated. I now knew you didn't need to have a coral reef to reap the scenic benefits of diving.

While its structure appears similar to land plants, giant kelp *(Macrocystis pyrifera)* is a marine alga that lacks true stems, roots, and leaves. A rootlike holdfast (haptera) attaches the plant to the bottom. The stemlike "trunk" is called a stipe. Long, leaflike blades dangle from the thin stipe; the large blades (two to three feet long) inspire one of giant kelp's nicknames: "dragon's tongue." The stipe and the blades combine to form the swaying frond. The stipes may coil around each other like wire in a cable to form well-defined columns within the submarine forest. (The well-defined space between kelp plants reminds one of the careful spacing that the desert imposes on many of its plants.)

Life within a kelp forest tends to fall within three divisions: the kelp canopy, the mid-water kelp region, and the bottom habitat. The lush kelp canopy, which can extend ten feet below the surface, is the most unstable region, exposed to the most vigorous wave action and the greatest change in temperature. Gray or white blemishes on the blades betray the presence of tiny organisms that use the blade as a substrate, or living space, in order to withstand wave action. Occasionally, a portion of the blade may appear to detach itself and casually swim away. Small finfish, which adopt kelp colors for protective camouflage, nibble the blades to ingest encrusting organisms. The juvenile finfish can gain strength and security in the canopy shelter before advancing into the blue world beyond.

Larger finfish, which sport the blue and silver colors of the open sea, cruise outside the canopy, waiting to pounce on small fish that stray beyond its protective cover. The life-converging "edge effect" common to the forest–meadow or forest–lake interface is repeated along the canopy's inshore and offshore margins.

The mid-water region, more open and less lush, reveals the shifting hues of the kelp forest. The blades above, translucent in the sunlight, may glitter like gold. The darker blades below can be bronze one moment, yellow the next. The water itself wavers between green, blue, and amber tones. You feel like you are inside a prism.

One of my favorite kelp characters may saunter through these wavering colors. The showy sheephead has a large, blunt head. What look like dog's teeth protrude from large jaws. You almost expect to hear a sheephead bark. Its bulldog features are set off in bold colors. A wide red band rings the bluish-black body of the male. The jutting lower jaw is accented in white with the careful attention to detail found in a clown's face. Curious and aggressive, a sheephead will enter a diver's bag to abscond with a large, edible marine snail called abalone. Sheephead have even been observed tenaciously hanging on to tidepool mussels above water as a wave recedes. These dedicated gastronomes can attain 36 pounds.

A fish the size of a cigar may loiter around the larger fish in the kelp forest. The señorita, with its own set of protruding teeth, can relieve larger fish of parasites. The bat ray, the giant black sea bass, and the perches will even seek out a señorita to gain cleaning service. They remain motionless and open up their gills and lips to ease the señorita's task.

The kelp bottom habitat, by far the most abundant and diverse, is much more irregular and rocky than the floor of a land forest. Like gigantic, free-form sculptures, rock outcroppings form reefs riddled with caves, crevices, and pinnacles. While dark gray in color, up close the reefs reveal orange, red, and white splotches that suggest the thick, carefree brush of a modern artist. The exuberant colors are formed by encrusting sponges.

What appears to be a flame in search of a fire may occasionally dart out of a reef crevice. The orange garibaldi can be as curious and obvious as the larger sheephead. A smaller version with iridescent blue dots may flit by. The juvenile garibaldi loses these dots as it matures.

Much of the bottom life prefers to move little or not at all. Like a starburst firecracker frozen in explosion, the red sea urchin projects a multitude of bristling spines from its round test or shell. The spines may move in unison to snare a piece of drift kelp. The smaller purple urchin crouches in crevices like a prim boutonniere tucked in a lapel.

What looks like a boulder on the reef may begin to move as deliberately as a turtle. A black, lacy fringe identifies it as the dark, rocklike shell of the abalone. The shell, up to a foot in diameter, encases a creamy flesh revered by both sheephead and divers. The abalone's muscular foot, when firmly clasped to the reef, can resist the pull of the waves and the jaws of the sheephead.

A lobster may amble out of another crevice and stroll past or over the abalone and the sponges. The California spiny lobster ("bug" to divers) lacks the large claws of the Atlantic lobster, which pleases such competing predators as sheephead, divers, and giant sea bass. (The name "giant sea bass" is no exaggeration; this kelp resident can grow to 400 pounds.)

A kelp forest is smaller in size than land forests. I can usually swim across its width in a few minutes, and its total area rarely exceeds 8 square miles. Along the 1,000-mile-long California coast, giant kelp only covers approximately 70 square miles. Yet by moving just 50 or 80 feet, from canopy to holdfast, I can observe more animal life in a matter of minutes than I might see all day in a redwood forest. These underwater forests celebrate life in all its forms and adaptations, in its cooperative as well as predatory moods.

Ironically, few members of the animal population appear to graze on the dense kelp foliage. This puzzling situation suggests a meadow teeming with deer that have no need for the meadow grasses. Just how is life in this seemingly crowded environment sustained? An understory of shade-tolerant plants provides one source of forage for grazers, including urchins and abalone. This understory includes small kelp species set on stiff stipes. Smaller algae flourish beneath the mini-kelp. A turf of brown and red algae covers the reef so completely that a diver rarely sees bare rock.

While plant systems on land include trees 100 feet high, marine plant systems, including the kelp understory, rarely extend more than a few meters above the bottom. Grazing animals in the water column itself must depend on plankton, the tiny, drifting plants and animals of the sea. The larger kelp species, particularly giant kelp, break this pattern with a vengeance. By extending its biomass into the water column, the lanky kelp expands the supply of shelter and substrate as well as the supply of food. Its value as a vertical substrate encrusted with juicy organisms may even exceed its own value as food.

Kelp may be a more important food source when the fronds decay and fall to the bottom. With this drift kelp, urchins, abalone, and other grazers have less need for living kelp. The sheephead, the spiny lobster, bat stars, and *cancer* crabs are adept enough to overcome the spines and shells of the grazers to consume their soft, edible parts and further control grazing pressures. The diving sea otter may carry a handy tool—a rock—to break open the iridescent shell of an abalone. As in the case of the mobile pastures of the sea, a dynamic system of biological checks and balances maintains the stability of the kelp forest.

By projecting its biomass into the water column above, a kelp forest sustains three times the animal life that a rock reef alone supports. How does giant kelp attain such heady heights without being ripped apart by wave surge? The holdfast grips the rocky bottom with a maze of interlocking fibers that resemble a finely-woven Indian basket. The gas-filled bulbs at the base of the blades, which I popped on the beach as a child, help buoy up the massive plant. Even so, the plant must withstand constant bending from the wave motion. Most land plants would be too brittle to perform this pretzel act. Kelp's pliable nature reflects considerable tensile strength—the ability to stretch, bend, and extend without breaking. A compound in kelp called algin helps provide this tensile strength. The supple kelp I played with on the beach was used by native Americans as fishing line and as a hand grip for wooden paddles.

Wave trains generated by storms thousands of miles away in the north Pacific can test this tensile strength. The massive plants oscillate wildly back and forth as the waves rush shoreward to collapse in booming surf. One plant may finally lose its grip on the rocky bottom and float away. Its fronds become entangled with fronds of other plants, weakening their seabed grip. This snowball effect can convulse the entire wave-wracked forest. The swells wrench up 300-pound plants with the ease of a gardener plucking up dandelions. A limp harvest of kelp floats toward the surf-battered beach. As the storm waves ebb, huge mounds of kelp are left behind.

A kelp forest after a winter storm can resemble a land forest thinned by fire or by heavy cutting. While a fir forest may recover in 30 years, and a redwood forest in 3,000 years, a kelp forest may spring back in a year's time.

How? To begin with, kelp can grow up to two feet a day. This growth rate exceeds that of all other land or sea plants, including bamboo. A single frond can race up from the shaded holdfast and reach the sunlit surface in four or five months.

Kelp's prodigious growth rate is only surpassed by its rate of decay. A month after reaching the surface, each frond begins to decay and slough off, to be replaced by another fast-growing frond. A single plant, which may live for several years, may have up to 200 fronds in various stages of growth and decay. Only the tropical rain forest can rival such productivity. With this turnover of plant material, the kelp forest can export its nutrition throughout the coastal marine system. A winter storm is often a food boom. Waves transport drift kelp many miles away into bays and rocky intertidal areas and onto the sandy shore, whose shifting substrate inhibits local algae growth. Although lacking the dignity of a fallen redwood or coastal fir, a forlorn clump of drift kelp can still sustain new life.

How does kelp secure the biological energy to sustain such growth? Land plants extract nutrients from the soil; kelp extracts them from seawater through its blades. The blades are corrugated to maximize exposure to both seawater and energy-giving sunlight. The products of photosynthesis travel down the stipe to nourish young fronds and the holdfast. Scientists call this translocation.

Special blades near the plant's base release a constant stream of spores that seek a place in the sun to grow into mature plants. Since bottom light is scarce and spore mortality is high, a blade may release billions of spores each year.

Kelp stays within 100 feet of the surface, where sunlight can still penetrate to the bottom. Its need for nutrients to sustain its growth further restricts giant kelp to areas of upwelling, where winds push surface waters away from the coast and permit cold, nutrient-rich bottom water to rise. While found in the southern hemisphere off Peru, Chile, Argentina, Australia, and South Africa, giant kelp is found only in the northern hemisphere off the Pacific coast. Although found as far north as Sitka, Alaska, giant kelp prefers coastal waters off northern Baja California and southern California. Further north, bull kelp *(Nereocystis)* dominates. A much smaller brown algae, *Laminaria,* fringes our Atlantic coast.

While limited mainly to rocky bottoms, giant kelp can grow on coarse sand bottoms and, in an area off Santa Barbara, on a mud bottom. A chain of offshore islands helps buffer the mud-anchored kelp from storm waves.

One day, when I was diving in a kelp forest, a whir like a mixmaster pierced the forest silence. I poked my head through a canopy opening. A large, bargelike vessel rigged with reciprocating knives was harvesting the kelp. This was my introduction to giant kelp as a multi-million-dollar resource that inspires dreams of seaweed plantations.

Cows on Guernsey Island once clomped through the rocky intertidal area at low tide to munch on small brown algae, and inspired a modest British industry specializing in kelp feed supplements and fertilizer. Giant kelp's size eventually inspired larger commercial visions in the image of the marine treasure chest. Brochures once proclaimed the glories of "Cattle Manamar—the Sea-Powered Feeding Supplement." ("If your livestock grazed on the seabed, you wouldn't need Manamar.") Dogs and cats could count on PetKelp, humans on Seazum. ("It makes a whale of a difference.")

PetKelp and Cattle Manamar now languish in commercial obscurity, but a recent headline brought them to mind: "Kelp Proclaimed Source of Energy." The source of this proclamation was not a supplier with a large inventory of PetKelp, but the U.S. Naval Ocean Systems Center in San Diego, California. One might think that this sponsor would be more interested in using giant kelp as a biological weapon to clog up an enemy harbor. However, the Navy, which would not want to fight a war and an energy shortage at the same time, is attempting to find out whether conversion of kelp into methane gas might form an alternative energy source. Natural ("wild") forests, however productive, could not provide enough kelp if and when bioconversion proves feasible. One possible answer, according to Dr. Howard Wilcox of the Naval Ocean Systems Center, is ocean energy farms. To extend the growing range, giant kelp would be transplanted to deeper waters and attached to an artificial substrate of submerged ropes or cable.

A pilot project funded by the Center off San Clemente Island in southern California proved encouraging enough to prompt a larger experimental project. General Electric Corporation, under contract with the Gas Research Institute and the Department of Energy, has moored an underwater module five miles off southern California. The module, which resembles a huge inverted umbrella, serves as substrate for a kelp farm. An "upwelling" pump draws inorganic nutrients for the kelp from 1,000-foot depths.

Sea storms and grazing fish have inhibited growth of the kelp. Curtains installed to contain upwelled nutrients and ward off grazers have been shredded by storms. Ironically, tapping methane gas from decomposing coastal dumps has proved to be a more feasible method of converting biomass to energy.

Is the ocean energy farm another kelp pipedream? Not necessarily. The world's gluttonous demand for energy may eventually make kelp energy-farms competitive . . . and safer and less polluting than fossil fuels or nuclear energy. Extending kelp's growing range to deeper waters might serve to expand marine habitat. Such a concept is probably far more deserving of the name sea farming or aquaculture than the raising of high-priced lobsters in pens for seafood restaurants housed in renovated fish canneries. Unlike the land farmer, the kelp farmer would not have to worry about droughts or frost. As Dr. Michael Neushul of the University of California at Santa Barbara, who helped produce the first laboratory hybrid of giant kelp, notes, "It is certainly worthwhile to explore the potential of marine plants as collectors of energy and concentrators of nutrients, since these might contribute significantly to a solar-based world food and energy production system."

While experiments with ocean energy farms continue and scientists debate whether kelp will become the "corn of the sea," kelp entrepreneurs settle for more limited commercial horizons. The barge I saw lumbering through the kelp canopy takes its limp harvest to a factory that processes kelp into a white powder called algin. The compound that helps kelp withstand wave surge possesses certain "water-loving" (hydrophilic) traits that absorb excess moisture in prepackaged foods. Today, many miles removed from the pull of swells and the nibbles of fish, algin helps maintain the icing on a cake. To maintain the foamy head on a beer, algin helps make, in the words of one proud sales representative, "tougher bubbles." Supposedly, we cannot go a day without using some form of algin, which even finds its way into plastic diapers.

Are kelp forests, like fish stocks, open to all commercial comers? No. California generally prefers to lease each kelp forest, or bed, to the highest bidder. Some similar type of limited entry might have saved the commercial fishing industry from the overcapitalization that has resulted in so many marginal fleets. With a more stable market, kelp processors can invest in mechanical harvesters and product research that exceeds the wildest dreams of halibut or cod fishermen struggling to meet insurance payments on thirty- or forty-year-old vessels. Today, two large chemical firms (Merck and Stauffer) dominate the kelp harvest. This type of corporate concentration suggests one potential problem with limited entry.

Evidence for the giant kelp's rise to notoriety can be found in unexpected places. A slender stained glass window two stories high in one California residence depicts a kelp frond that is illuminated by soft brown light. I almost expect a sheephead to hurtle toward me and check for any harvested abalone. And I really knew kelp had made it into the twentieth century while browsing through a pet supply store. The usual artifacts to decorate an aquarium were on display: pirate treasure chests, sunken shipwrecks, naval cannon, crumbling Greek ruins. The plastic marine plants, which resembled lawn trimmings, were colored green . . . except for one colored khaki brown and labeled "dragon's tongue."

Ironically, as skin divers, chemical corporations, and aquarium owners exult in its expanding social utility, giant kelp's natural existence can concern and puzzle scientists. In the late 1950s, as divers like myself were beginning to realize kelp's underwater beauty, the forests off San Diego and Los Angeles were receding. The kelp forests that once rimmed Palos Verdes Peninsula in Los Angeles were virtually gone. A dive here was a haunting one. No canopy sheltered small finfish or filtered the sunlight. A stray perch glided aimlessly by where hundreds of fish once paraded. The top-to-bottom desolation suggested defoliation by some new, horrendous marine biocide.

The urban kelp forests, which once inspired wonder and excitement, now triggered bitterness and recrimination. Sport and commercial fishermen, driven to fish rock reefs much further from shore, blamed kelp harvesters for the mysterious decline. Harvesters claimed that they were "pruning" the canopy and allowing more sunlight to reach young, struggling plants on the bottom. The harvesters, forced to travel further to reach healthy forests, blamed sewage pollution. Outfall operators, who claimed their sewage was only "fertilizing" the coastal ocean, suggested that fishermen might be removing animals that controlled populations of kelp grazers. This was no mere finger pointing for the sheer, cantankerous joy of it. Each special interest feared that its particular marine activities might be curtailed.

The embarrassed trustee of the kelp forests could not resolve the cycle of recrimination. The state of California could not even explain the kelp recession. This lack of knowledge surfaced *after* the state had approved kelp harvesting, massive urban coastal sewage disposal, and intensive harvesting of kelp-associated marine life. The state knew how to exploit but not necessarily how to maintain its million-dollar seaweed.

Marine scientists, called in belatedly to halt the decline of salmon, Pacific sardines, and Pacific mackerel, were now hastily recruited to solve the kelp recession. However, they first had to learn more about the natural history of kelp because of lack of prior funding interest. A scuba-diving biologist with ten years of experience in exploring California's kelp forests was scheduled to play a prominent investigative role. But pioneer underwater naturalist Conrad Limbaugh died in a diving accident in 1960. A steady stream of kelp blades, stipes, and juvenile plants began flowing into the Scripps Institution of Oceanography at San Diego, where Limbaugh had been chief diving officer. One natural cause for the recession was identified: an abnormal warm-water period that retarded kelp's growth. (The kelp canopy sloughs off when water temperatures exceed 68°F.) But previous warm-water periods had not triggered such a severe, persistent decline.

Were human beings partially responsible? In the lab, kelp was placed in seawater laced with sewage. This mixture in some cases appeared to enhance kelp growth. Meanwhile, a scuba-diving biologist was roaming through the ghost forest. To Dr. Wheeler North, something was out of place in the ghost forests. One particular animal abounded. Urchins remained even though there was no kelp—living or drift—to graze on. It was like cattle thriving on a dusty pasture. What were the urchins subsisting on? North suspected sewage. By remaining in a stream of particulate sewage, the urchins could prevent kelp from recovering even when cooler waters returned.

Could the ghost forests be revived if urchins—now regarded as "spiny locusts" in the press—were eliminated? Volunteer divers descended with hammers to crush urchins, but this approach was not fast enough. One day, a miniature snowstorm descended on urchins in a receded kelp forest off San Diego. The snow consisted of caustic lime. Young kelp plants soon began sprouting up among the dead urchins. Would urchins migrate in to devour the reviving kelp? The kelp grew fast enough to satiate urchin appetites with drift kelp. As the kelp returned, so did abalone, sheephead, scuba divers, and kelp harvesters.

More than liming was needed to revive the barren Palos Verdes area. Biologist Ken Wilson of the California Department of Fish and Game would pry up plants whole from healthy beds, place them in burlap bags aboard a vessel, and then lace the holdfasts to anchor chains on the Palos Verdes bottom. Grazers nibbled away at an initial transplant. Over 1,000 plants were imported to one site to satiate the nibblers. Dr. North, who had moved from Scripps to the California Institute of Technology, learned to transplant young plants cultured in the laboratory.

Under the care of the underwater rangers, kelp off Palos Verdes expanded from 1.42 acres in 1974 to 593 acres by 1980. The area now provides transplants for other restoration sites, including Los Angeles Harbor. This success helped inspire the ocean energy farms idea; Dr. North is chief scientist with the current test project. The urban kelp revival has a personal meaning for Dr. Neushul, the marine botanist working on kelp hybrids. He first became interested in kelp as a boy growing up in the Palos Verdes area during the early 1940s, when the local kelp covered over 1,000 acres.

Ironically, scientists are unable to pinpoint the chain of events behind either the kelp's revival or its decline. As cooler waters and more vigorous upwelling returned, some beds recovered without the aid of a single transplant or liming. Urban sewage remains a prime suspect in the original decline. Some scientists agree with Dr. North's theory of sewage as urchin nourishment. Others feel that the sewage particles also reduce energy-giving light penetration. By accumulating on the bottom, the particles may also snuff out young plants. Kelp now grows near coastal outfalls that have reduced their particulate sewage load to comply with federal regulations. Outfall discharges of DDT have also been reduced, particularly at the Los Angeles County Whites Point outfall off Palos Verdes (the largest single sewage discharge in California). DDT, which has already been linked to the reproductive failure of brown pelicans, also could be toxic to kelp spores, according to Dr. Alan Mearns, who is now a marine pollution expert with NOAA.

Perhaps the most intriguing question in the kelp equation is the continuing imbalance between kelp grazers and their predators. Fur hunters purged the urchin-loving sea otter from southern California waters in the early nineteenth century, long before the severe kelp recession. The most intensive kelp harvest occurred during World War II, when entire kelp plants were yanked up to provide a wartime source of potash. But kelp continued to thrive. Los Angeles County opted for wastewater disposal rather than reclamation in 1937 and constructed the Whites Point outfall. By the early 1940s, as industrial and municipal sewage loads spiraled, an urban kelp decline was noted, to be followed by the warm waters of the late 1950s and the severe decline.

A marine ecologist, Dr. Paul Dayton of Scripps, has nominated another potential agent of change. In the early and mid-1950s, with the advent of scuba diving, divers seeking game zeroed in on the showy sheephead, whose curiosity makes it easy prey, and the spiny lobster, which was already being trapped by commercial fishermen. Thus, not one but three urchin predators were missing or being selectively removed when the waters warmed in the late 1950s.

An indirect control was being reduced too. When the otter was exterminated, a favorite otter meal—the abalone—could move out from protected crevices to compete with urchins for living space and for drift kelp. But the abalone, with the advent of both hard-hat and scuba diving, is under increased harvesting pressure. Thus four direct or indirect controls on urchin populations have been reduced or eliminated. An abalone moratorium exists along the Los Angeles–Orange County shore as California attempts to restore populations with laboratory-raised juveniles. Recovery of lobster populations, even with stiff regulations, is complicated by an illegal market in undersize lobsters, or "shorts." A lobster takes nine years to mature to legal size; fishermen have been caught with up to 3,000 shorts. (Scientists link a population explosion of urchins on the eastern coast of Canada and the United States to human predation on the American lobster. The liberated urchins graze down beds of a small brown kelp, *Laminaria*. Restoration of lobster populations here may determine whether the *Laminaria* beds can be restored as well.)

What happens when an urchin predator recovers? Along the central California coast, the resurgent otter is reasserting its appetite for both urchins and abalone. Abalone fishermen want to curb this natural competition; human defenders of the otter want to curb the fishermen. As their range expands along the central California coast, the controversial otters harvest Pismo clam beds by using one clam as a rock to crack open the shell of another. An enraged political alliance of clammers and abalone divers may halt expansion long before otters can return to southern California kelp beds.

Meanwhile, off Santa Barbara, some 150 miles south of the current otter range, sea urchins are no longer ridiculed as "spiny locusts." They are being harvested for profitable export to Japan. Will this harvest reduce kelp grazing pressures and enlarge kelp forests? There are two species of urchins. The smaller purple urchin is more common in shallow waters, including intertidal areas; the larger red urchin flourishes in subtidal waters. The red is the favored commercial species. Will the purple move into subtidal waters to replace the harvested red? And will the purple's appetite for kelp balance the red's? Scientists are now trying to ascertain this. The purple, with its much smaller spines, cannot replace the red's important function as a protective spine shelter for juvenile urchins, abalone, and some small fish. (One pretty sight in a kelp forest is the retreat of a small fish into the radiating spine canopy of a red.) Since 1971, the red urchin catch has jumped from 200 pounds annually to 9 million pounds. That's a lot of spiny locusts. A kelp harvester has been asked to cease liming urchins in one kelp bed because fishermen want to remove the urchins themselves.

Harvesters lime to maximize the kelp harvest, about 200,000 wet tons annually in California. Kelp is imported from Baja California to keep abreast of demand and offset periodic declines in the California supply attributed to poor upwelling years. The revival of urban kelp beds has helped restore the supply.

As pressures to cut more kelp intensify and as divers collect understory plants with valuable gel properties, some scientists question how beneficial the pruning effect is. While land plants receive nutrients from the soil below, kelp receives its nutrients from the canopy above. Do repeated cuttings inhibit growth and weaken the holdfast, making it more vulnerable to the tug of waves? Do repeated cuttings affect the juvenile fish that depend on the canopy for shelter? The California Fish and Game Department is attempting to resolve these questions. California limits the depth of each cut to four feet; frequency of cutting is not regulated.

Like redwood forests onshore, the kelp forests offshore are even being accorded special status. One scenic kelp forest near my home is now classified as a Marine Life Refuge and an Area of Special Biological Significance. That's a big step in social recognition for the monster seaweed of my boyhood days. A delightful green wedge of steep canyons and coastal hills backs up this kelp-fringed coast. The same landowner who wanted to channelize Upper Newport Bay recently proposed to build tier upon tier of view estates built on manufactured slopes for 38,000 residents. One possible side-effect of this development was an extensive silt and stormwater runoff that could mock the kelp forest's refuge status. Community groups are now promoting their own alternative, a land-sea park predicated on natural coastal values, including intact hills. The luxury urban development would contribute to the need for a 14-mile-long hillside freeway whose configuration would resemble a roller coaster ride. Its cost—$10 million a mile—makes park acquisition look cheap. Development has already been scaled back to make room for a state coastal park. Community groups, with the support of local congressmen, are working to create an Orange Coast National Park.

The fate of the giant kelp personifies the changing public image of seaweeds. Once regarded as a nuisance by everybody except young children on the beach, then subjected to unwitting exploitation, the monster seaweed now emerges as a key ecological element that must be maintained if we expect to reap the full human benefits of the living oceans. As in the case of the mobile pastures of the sea, prudent use can prevent costly ecological backlashes. Restore a depleted big game fish and you restore its stock alone. Restore a marine plant or algae community and you help retrieve a whole spectrum of marine life, from the diving seabirds above to the gangly lobster below, as well as helping to revive the fortunes of commercial fishermen, sport anglers, skin divers, and seaweed harvesters.

The fate of the kelp forests has triggered interest in the fate of other stressed marine plant and algae communities throughout the world. Nations trying to restore depleted fish stocks in the Mediterranean are now expanding their perspective to include another beach nuisance, sea grass. In the sea, sea grass (poseidonia) beds provide shelter, food, and nursery grounds. "The conservation and vitality of the poseidonia beds are critical to the sea bottom ecosystem of the entire continental shelf," declares one report prepared for the United Nations Environment Programme.

Hawaii may eat through some of its seaweed resources. Native Hawaiians had no onions, peppers or tomatoes to spice up an otherwise uniform diet of poi (pounded taro) and fish. Limu —seaweeds—that were drafted to fill this nutritional void provided key vitamins too. Hawaii's immigrant groups stepped up the demand for edible seaweeds. Today, one popular seaweed, the crisp-tasting, red-colored ogo, can fetch $3 a pound. Local supplies have been stressed by mounting market demand, silt runoff and habitat destruction. A reef runway at the Honolulu jetport obliterated one popular seaweed patch. Jerry Kaluhiwa, formerly a commercial fisherman, wants to grow edible seaweed in cages. He interested Bob Nakata of the Heeia-kea Community Association in the project and has received a grant. Kaluhiwa and a staff of water-oriented teen-agers must first clear project sites of an occupational hazard, broken bottles. Then they must convince commercial collectors to leave their nursery beds alone.

Dr. Maxwell Doty of the University of Hawaii is becoming the Johnny Appleseed of the Pacific Basin. He teaches Filipino and Polynesian coastal communities to raise a red algae, *Eucheuma*, on nets set in coral atolls. *Eucheuma* buyers show up from Europe and the United States. A *Eucheuma* extract keeps the chocolate in chocolate milk in suspension.

Other coastal regions are learning to monitor the condition of their native seaweeds. It is a lot easier to prevent damage in the first place. The conclusion to man's unbalancing of the kelp ecosystem is far from over, as the economic and ecological problems raised by the recovered otter herd indicate.

As policy conflicts swirl around the "dragon's tongue," it is a relief to dive kelp and regain the fascination and wonder of my first dives. While some of my favorite creatures are no longer so abundant, most of the values remain intact. The canopy above sieves the sunlight into wavering beams of amber, bronze, and green. The blades dangle like golden pennants. The coiled stipes rise like stately solar towers five stories or more high. Quick death in the form of darting bass and plunging pelicans rides this fertile water column like a busy elevator. The colossal plants sway quietly. I hope the future will have room for both ocean energy farms and wild kelp forests.

Onshore, my younger son builds fewer sand castles and rummages through more clumps of drift kelp. As he untangles a kelp stipe, I want to tell him how that clump can form forests in the sea. As he ponders the stipe that dangles from his hand, I decide to move away. Another cattle drive is about to begin. The values I cherish he'll discover for himself.

10

The Dance
on the Shore

ANKIND'S MAJOR MARINE AC-
tivity is not fishing, drilling for oil, or making war. These are all
secondary to the person who comes to the sea to relax and be
refreshed.

Seaside pilgrims come mainly from just one part of the world
—the industrial nations. But their intense desire for sea and shore
can influence the economy, lifestyle, and ecology of nations and
tiny islands throughout the watery planet.

This intense migration is, in many respects, a relatively
recent phenomenon. As late as the seventeenth and eighteenth
centuries, bathing in the sea was considered unhealthy in Europe.
Great Britain, perhaps the world's foremost maritime nation,

once prohibited swimming in natural bodies of water by statute. Even sunbathing is relatively new.

If these attitudes persisted today, there would be no Miami Beaches, Atlantic Cities, suntan manufacturers, swimsuit designers, and jet holiday trips. The seashore would remain as it has been throughout most of history, a place to fish, to dock, or to make war.

Why have these attitudes changed so dramatically? The leisure-time turn to the sea appears to be linked to the industrial revolution. This revolution created a technology that made possible mass migrations to the sea—by railroad, steamship, and eventually the automobile and the jet airplane. More people than ever before had the money and time to pursue leisure. Congestion in industrial cities made the solitude of the seashore that much more inviting.

But the roots of man's attraction to the shore, as a resort, are far older than the Industrial Revolution; they reach into ancient Rome.

While many ancient cities had risen and fallen before, Rome had some special distinctions. It was populous even by modern standards—almost a million people. Rome spilled over with people from exhausted farmlands, played-out mines, denuded forestlands, defeated provinces, and depressed colonies. Wave upon wave of immigrants swarmed into the city. The press for space led to high-rise tenements and to height limit debates. Augustus set one limit at 70 feet, and Trajan lowered it to 60.

To sustain its swelling population, Rome depended on engineers. Sea and land routes radiated out from Rome like arms on an octopus to keep the city fed, sheltered, and entertained. Rome's Coliseum could accommodate 255,000 screaming spectators eager to display the thumbs down signal. Great aqueducts tapped wilderness watersheds to slake the city's thirst. Huge drains transported sewage to the Tiber River. On the magnificent stone highways, carts would haul food into Rome while other carts hauled away the city's garbage.

Rome had to cope with problems that are familiar to us

today—congestion, overcrowding, filth, and pollution. Heavy vehicles were banned from the city center so citizens could sleep at night. To one resident, the stench, the heat, and the noise shattered the beguiling illusion of an imperial city reflecting man's building genius. To the satirist Juvenal, Rome was "the great sewer." Take a walk on the city's streets with Juvenal:

> We have to fight our way
> Through a wave in front, and behind we are pressed by
>   a huge mob
> Shoving our hips; an elbow hits us here and a pole
> There, now we are smashed by a beam, now biffed by a
>   barrel.
> Our legs are thick with mud, our feet are crushed by large
> Ubiquitous shoes, a soldier's hobnail rests on our toe.

If you didn't wear the purple toga of power you might sup on pike "born on the banks of the Tiber, fat with the gush of the sewage drain, and well accustomed to scavenge the sewage pipes." After your repast, you had to remember to bolt the door and bar the windows against nighttime assassins. With the run on iron to padlock Roman houses, Juvenal feared that "we will have little left for hoes and mattocks and plowshares." With your pike digested, your home padlocked, and your body weary from urban strolls, you might have been ready for some sleep. Warned Juvenal:

> Here in town the sick die from insomnia mostly.
> Undigested food, on a stomach burning with ulcers,
> Brings on listlessness, but who can sleep in a flophouse?
> Who but the rich can afford sleep and a garden apartment?
> The oaths of stalled cattle drovers would break the sleep
>   of a deaf man or a lazy walrus.

The solution to sleepless nights and hair-raising days?

> Tear yourself away from the circus and buy a country
>   cottage
> For no more than a year's rent of your super-slum in
>   Rome. . . .

Live with spade in hand, the boss of a neat garden.
After all, it is something, even in a lonely corner,
To make yourself the landlord of a single lizard.

Juvenal's retreat to the country was in accord with Rome's roots in its agricultural past. Legislators such as Cato maintained a rural farm to retain a sense of the soil. But the urban Roman, while paying lip service to this pastoral past, was prepared to pioneer a new recreational outlet. He wanted release, but not over a hoe or in a farm cottage.

To fend off Rome's staggering growth, officials encouraged people to settle along the coast and to develop ports to handle food imports and to fend off pirates. But Rome's affluent class needed neither government incentives nor encouragement by travel agents to commute 100 miles south to "the Bay of Luxury."

The irregular, 5,400-mile-long coast of Italy hosts any number of charming coves and bays. The Bay of Naples still stands out among these. Here the water seems a deeper blue, the bluffs more majestic, the curve of the bay more sweeping. The end points of this 50-mile-long crescent bay are two stately headlands. The rocky bluffs are riddled with cool caves and spacious grottos lapped by tongues of blue sea water. From the bluffs, the eyes entertain one enchanting vista after another: the blue Mediterranean, Capri Island, vessels under way, Mount Vesuvius thrusting skyward. The islands lack the modest profile of coral atolls; they rise sheer and bold as a clenched fist. As the sun circles overhead, the colors of land and sea shift, inviting reexamination like a kaleidoscope. Even under moonlight, the bold landforms retain their visual identity and yet merge into a graceful symmetry.

The Greeks had come here before establishing a colony at Cumae. They came not for recreation but to till the fertile volcanic soil on the coastal plains. Grain, fruit orchards, and olive trees flourished in these soils. Vineyards dotted the volcanic slopes. The soils inspired a Roman poet, Vergil:

This soil will weave your elms with joyous vines
And yield our olive crop, and it will prove
When cultivated, gracious to the herd,
Submissive to the plowshare's curving blade.

The first batch of Roman officials to colonize the bay were more interested in harvesting quiet and solitude. Here Cicero wrote *Academica.* During writing breaks, Cicero enjoyed trying to rank the various bay views.

This delight in the natural world did not extend to accommodations. The urban Romans eschewed camping, backpacking, and communal dwellings like inns or hotels. They wanted privacy after the forced intimacy of Rome. The bay became enveloped in a second home boom unmatched in human annals. The maritime villa made its debut on the global shore. The first villas were modest. Some might boast fine gardens or imposing statuary. Some would have fishponds. Salt water fish were prized over fresh water ones. Ponds were filled with bay water regulated by gates. One owner spent more to tunnel through a mountain to tap sea water than on his villa.

The larger and more congested Rome became, the more the Bay of Naples prospered. The dusty, rutted road from Rome discouraged traffic. The solution: a special road built with the finest Roman engineering skills. The Via Domitiana established the bay as Rome's premier resort region. Roman aqueducts swept by Greek temples and tombs.

At this stage, one Roman realized that you could obtain fame and fortune without making stirring speeches in the Forum or conquering another tribe in Gaul. C. Sergius Orata expanded on the fishpond concept. He supplied Lake Lucrine with a bay channel to breed and supply a favorite of the epicures: oysters. He also built and traded in coastal villas. To make his villas more attractive, he built fine and ornate baths. When Orata repurchased one villa and found that its seller failed to disclose an encumbrance, he could retain a leading legal light of the day, Licinius Crassus, who owned a villa himself. To villa scholar John

D'Arms, Orata "was the first Campanian speculator to cater to the leisure of the great grandees; he prospered."

Cumae, with its now servile Greeks, became an intellectuals' and artists' colony. Here Cicero and other Roman officials would imbibe Hellenic culture. Budding young Roman writers also came. Vergil wrote,

> Now we set sail for the havens of bliss whereby
> attending the learned lectures of Siro we will free our
> lives from all anxiety.

A collection of villas entirely separate from prior colonies sprang up at Baiae, Rome's first full-fledged coastal resort. It straddled a bay headland and the shores of oyster-rich Lake Lucrine. Its lifestyle would be scorned by Cicero, deplored by Saint Jerome, and denounced by Saint Augustine.

The value of the coastal villas began to exceed that of the inland villas once prized for their farm income. The coastal villa owner enjoyed rapid appreciation without even having to own a great deal of property. The sea view came free with the villa site. A rocky coastal niche could be transformed into a luxurious property because of the wealth, stress, and dreams generated by a huge city a hundred miles away.

With the imperial age, competition for good villa sites took a feverish turn. Some emperors would level aging villas and rebuild more gloriously. Others would extend their villas into the sea on supporting piers. The villas often had two dining rooms with solar exposure appropriate for winter and for summer. The energy merchants of the day were architects. Without proper solar exposure, it might take 300 pounds of wood per day to heat a villa during the winter.

Villas became multilevel affairs, terraced on the bay bluffs. A Roman engineering advance expedited the villa craze—fast-setting hydraulic cement. Villas could curve, loop, and ramble along the bluff topography.

With the villa walls and roofs in place, artists would grace the vaulted ceilings and the bath with painted cupids and lions. Porticos would be draped with curtains. Rose-colored awnings would suffuse rooms in a pinkish glow. One villa portico was draped in nets of hemp so birds inside would not escape.

Marine life was not only recruited for table fare. Step into one villa and you might step on an alabaster dolphin with gemstone eyes while an octopus loomed at you from the wall. Look into a reflecting pond or bath and you might think you were looking into an aquarium. The mosaic artists infused motion into their fish by curving their tails and arching their backs. With the water brightened by the sun and ruffled by sea breezes, the stone fish would turn into wriggling, shimmering life.

Tiberius appropriated the Isle of Capri for his villa, which he built on the island's highest point. It sprawled over 30,000 square meters and contained four large cisterns. Villa materials had to be transported 1,000 feet above the sea coast.

Baths became as big as swimming pools and as ornate as temples. Gold rings were attached to prize pets in the fishponds. The sea was tapped more intensively to supply jaded stomachs. Wrote Petronius in the *Satyricon:*

> Gluttons of genius, the belly inventive,
> Scouring Sicilian waters for the parrot-fish, the scare,
> And the wrasse borne swimming to the table, still alive;
> The oysters from Lucrino torn, the fabulous, the rare,
> Jogging jaded hunger with the fillip of expense.

To ward off déjà vu, villa owners could carouse in trimarans, sup on oysters and peacock on a barge, or sip wine and watch the Greek mimes in Cumae. One did not even have to set foot on the shore to enjoy it. You could sleep over the surge of the sea in a room set on piers and fish from your bedroom window. And there were always the beloved baths. Wrote Seneca, "Today we call baths louse-holes if they are not designed to attract the sun all day through picture windows, unless men can bathe and acquire a suntan simultaneously, and unless they have a view over

---

the countryside and the sea from their pools." Villa rooms would be added just to gain a new view of the volcano or the blue Mediterranean below.

The competition for space became more hectic. Strabo spoke of Baiae "with one mansion on top of another." The entire bay "gives the appearance of a single city." If you were hiking the shore and happened to look into one of the caves, you might be in for a surprise: a sumptuous party. The caves' cool environment made for a nice banquet hall during the hot summer, particularly if the cave floor could be marbled and the cave walls decorated with murals celebrating Neptune and heroic naval warriors.

Emperor Gaius wearied of having to travel around the bay to get from party to party. He spanned the bay with a double row of vessels to support a wood road heaped with earth. Suited up in military costume astride his horse, Gaius would dash from one end to the other, followed by cavalry. Sometimes he would trade in his charger for a chariot. The causeway was lined with torches so coastal residents could see Gaius on the go during the night. With this exercise in naval construction, Gaius considered himself in league with Darius and Xerxes.

If Baiae pioneered in the development of the flashy seaside resort, it also spawned the harbingers of moral outrage and social concern. Baiae sent the stoic Seneca up the wall: "A pleasure resort . . . with adulterous women sailing by, multitudinous craft painted with various colors, roses drifting over the lake, midnight wrangles of serenaders." Seneca thereupon issued the sort of castigation that only enhanced Baiae's popularity. "Let the wise man therefore not go to Baiae, the home of vice. Inside its walls, license is triumphant."

Observers more sympathetic to revelry had their own cause for concern. The more popular Baiae became, the more it cost to holiday there, whether one wanted another plate of oysters or another villa addition. Lamented Martial:

Oh give me back the gloomy baths of yore;
Why bathe in luxury and sup no more.

Horace and Cicero were more concerned about the fate of the natives. Some villa owners began speculating in farmlands in the Campania, displacing the small farmers. Cicero opposed this: "Will you allow the one most beautiful estate of the Roman people, the source of your wealth, an adornment in peacetime, a support in war, the basis of your revenues, the granary of your legions, the relief of your grain supply—will you allow all this to perish?" The answer was a resounding yes. Who needed the Campania when you could import grain and corn from Egypt to fill bellies in Rome?

Horace rebuked one villa owner for displacing small farmers. "Man and wife are driven forth bearing in their arms their household goods and ragged children." Without ever having set eyes on the highrises of Hawaii or Miami, Horace was able to sense the transforming power of coastal leisure. He rejected this transformation:

> Amid your very columns you are nursing trees,
> And you praise the mansion which looks out on distant
> fields.
> You may drive out Nature with a pitchfork,
> Yet she will ever hurry back,
> And ere you know it, will burst through your foolish
> contempt
> In triumph.

Seneca and Horace were no more successful than periodic earthquakes and volcanic eruptions in stemming such growth. The seaside resort as urban playground was becoming embedded in the human experience. Only the lack of skeletal steel kept Baiae from reaching skyward before Miami Beach did. The great sewer had spawned its own frenetic sanctuary.

The moralizers and the villa grandees shared an ironic bond. Seneca and Horace despised the villa opulence while praising nature and Rome's pastoral past. The villa owners in turn were spending fortunes to reproduce pastoral scenes within their own villa walls. Nero acquired 200 acres for a villa with pastures, zoos, mini-forests, and a lake designed to represent the ocean. Nero had anticipated Walt Disney by 1900 years. The site was right in the middle of crowded, congested Rome. To secure this site, Nero evicted thousands of Roman citizens. This may have been the first exercise in urban renewal. "All Rome is transformed to a villa!" sneered one unimpressed observer. Nero's own announced goal was uncharacteristically humble: "Now, at last, I can live like a human being."

Today, much of Baiae is surveyed by skin divers willing to risk swimming in waters polluted by modern Naples. The style of human energy it catered to went into hibernation during the so-called Dark Ages. There were no harried urban conglomerations to spawn affluent coastal pilgrims. There were no more Via Domitianas to offer safe and convenient shore access. Even a noble seeking out the shore would need a retinue of bodyguards.

The seaside as a sanctuary receded from the European scene. Bathing, in both fresh and salt water, fell into disrepute. It was considered immoral because of its association with Roman high life. In the sixteenth century, university students at Cambridge, England, were not allowed to cool off in rivers, lakes, or ponds. Those who dared to dip risked flogging on the first offense, expulsion on the second. Later, students could swim without fear of flogging, but sea bathing remained unpopular. It was considered unhealthy to steep oneself in "saline effluvia."

Inland bathing, particularly in mineral springs, was considered fine medicine. Some springs turned into fashionable spas, frequented by royalty and the new merchant class. For shelter, they preferred hotels rather than individual villas. Richard Nash, an entrepreneur with Oratalike insight into human needs and vanity, began to organize the town of Bath for his own profit-making purposes. He sensed that spa visitors coveted pleasure as much as health. Installing himself as master of ceremonies, he began leading visitors on an unending chain of dances, meals, readings, and dips. Generals as well as dukes would submit docilely to the regimentation they meted out to their maids and orderlies back home. An artist was available to immortalize spa patrons in oils. Of his subjects, Thomas Gainsborough wrote:

"They have but one part worth looking at, and that is their Purse." For a change of pace, Gainsborough would paint seascapes and fisherfolk.

In 1752, a fashionable London physician identified an antidote against "the consumption which greatly afflicts our Island, and in the cure of which, our Physicians find the greatest difficulty." The agent was seawater. Dr. Richard Russell's *A Dissertation on the Use of Sea Water* quickly went through four editions. Another seaward migration was cresting. As one poet noted:

> Then all, with ails in heart and lungs,
> In liver or in spine, rush'd coastward to be cured like
>   tongues,
> By dipping into brine.

This rush was intriguing in view of the prescribed use of seawater: to drink it. Patients, particularly children, could cut the salty medicine with milk, port wine, or beef tea. This would seem like a good way to cultivate a distaste for the seashore.

Some physicians did invest sea bathing with therapeutic value—but only in the winter, when the water was cold and thought to be free of saline effluvia.

What an introduction to the seashore! Drink from the sea and, if you must bathe, do so in the winter. Yet sea spas began capturing trade from inland spas. Cities were becoming as crowded, congested, and unsanitary as Rome. The industrial revolution was on the horizon. Wealth was spreading beyond the landed gentry to a rising merchant class that demanded entertainment. As Samuel Cowper put it:

> Gay widow, virgin, wife,
> Ingenious to diversify dull life,
> In coaches, chaises, caravans, and hoys,
> Fly to the coast for daily, nightly joys,
> And all, impatient of dry land, agree
> With one consent, to rush into the sea.

The Russell prescription was becoming a passport to coastal leisure. Some free spirits sea dipped in the summer without any apparent ill effects. An English painting in 1735 shows both sexes frolicking off Scarborough in their birthday suits.

For people alienated from a rural past and, to a degree, from physical activity, the shore was becoming a sensory delight. Here was a place to walk barefoot, to stretch limbs cramped in coaches and drawing rooms, to breath sea breezes, and above all, to see natural vistas. Nature itself, once regarded as dark and evil, was now seen in terms familiar to Horace and Vergil. To Cowper,

> The ocean exhibits, fathomless and broad,
> Much of the power and majesty of God.

Charlotte Brontë was overcome by tears when she visited the shore for the first time. Later she wrote, "The idea of seeing the SEA—of being near it—watching its changes by sunrise, sunset —moonlight—and noonday—and calm—perhaps in storm—fills and satisfies my mind."

Government officials wondered how this popular new activity might be taxed. The Earl of Chesterfield, taking the sea air at Scarborough, wrote: "As bathing in the sea is becoming the general practice of both sexes; and as the kings of England have always been allowed to be masters of the sea, every person so bathing shall be gauged, and pay so much per foot square as their cubicle bulk amounts to." This excise, which might have abetted the cause of slimness and good diet, was never enacted. It would have been interesting to administer. Tax clerks might have announced to onlookers the weight of each duke and duchess. Onlookers might have engaged in side bets on the correct weight, while others engaged in gossip or portraiture. Those being weighed would probably not have even worn a stitch of cloth. Swimming wardrobes were still in the future.

Urban investors now realized that dreary seaports, fishing hamlets, and vacant coastal heaths could be transformed into paying propositions. Coastal pilgrims were not inclined to build their own accommodations. The way was open to erect lodgings with dining places. The quality of shelter and table seemed designed to subvert seaside popularity. Macaulay remarked that the quality of hotel fare at Brighton was "a dinner on yesterday's pease-soup, and the day before yesterday's cutlets." Another Brighton visitor eulogized his dinner as "a brace of soles that perished from original inability to flounder into the ark and the fossil remains of a dead sirloin of beef." An American visitor, an uncertain fork in hand, meditated over "a meat pie which weighs upon your conscience." Nathaniel Hawthorne surmised that the staff of the seaside resort was "united in a joint and individual purpose to fleece" the traveler. Local contractors were becoming as adept as villa owners in altering the natural setting. Satirist Osbert Lancaster scorned local contractors whose "combined essays . . . have done more to ruin the beauty and romance of Wales" than war itself.

Entrepreneurial opportunities extended to the very tideline, if not beyond. Many beach visitors were not as schooled in leisure and the arts as royalty. Few could swim. Fewer seemed inclined to learn. They preferred to stroll the beach and walk along the boat piers. Concession shops started sprouting up on the piers. Soon piers were being built to cater entirely to tourists rather than boats.

Rentals of all sorts proliferated: carriages, cabs, carts, horses, donkeys, sedan chairs. The resort was becoming an urban fairyland, momentarily shorn of smokestacks, class conflict, and assembly lines. Rather than listening to lectures about thrift and productivity, one could sup on confections or indulge in bingo. Everyone's money was equal.

The fact that some visitors, including children, persisted in bathing presented a problem in the Victorian Age. Because many men still swam in the buff, bathing became segregated. Women shifted from the buff to a surplus of clothing. But this was only the first defense against accidental exposure. Some women, draped in yards of cloth, would go down to the sea in a wooden bathing machine or chariot pulled by a horse or muscular matrons. The matron might extend an awning ("modesty hoop") over the woman as she slipped into the seawater. The matron might even carry the woman off the machine, dunk her, and then return the wetted bundle to the machine. These matrons were known as dippers. By regulation, vessels could not approach within 200 yards of bathing machines except to save a human life. (The Victorian authorities did not have to deal with scuba divers and snorkelers.) Public wardens would stalk the beaches to arrest persons who undressed in the open air. Some municipalities derived revenue from renting bathing huts and tents.

From our vantage point, the bathing machine is an easy target of ridicule. But it helps stress how sea bathing has often been an alien experience for most. On a typical beach, you can observe a thick band of people on the beach proper, many of whom will avoid the water. There is a thinner band in the shallow water. Only a few swim beyond the waves. The people in the bathing machine had no easy access to swimming pools, swimming rafts, or swim flippers. The matron was as much a lifeguard as a guardian of Victorian morals. The surfeit of clothing was not necessarily discomforting. The women prized a pale white complexion with pink cheeks (milk and roses) rather than a suntan. Some were arthritic, seeking to have their pain eased momentarily by the dip. They did not want their emaciated limbs to be on public display.

For exercise, most beach visitors would walk endless miles on the promenade, the pier, or the sand flats at low tide. Hawthorne noted that "the visitors perambulate to and fro without any imaginable object." These visitors were, in their own unique way, pioneering our way to the sea. The seaside, as well as a natural adventure, was becoming a social adventure separate from the mechanized existence in the dark shadows of the industrial city. Nature and the city were switching roles. The latter was becoming dark and evil.

The growth of the English seaside resorts in the nineteenth century was phenomenal even by today's standards. In 1783, the Prince of Wales visited Brighton and gave it a royal aura. By the end of that century, Brighton's population had more than doubled from 3,000 to 7,000 people. By 1831, the population reached 40,634. Even greater growth lay ahead. In 1859, when the railroads had reached the coast, as many as 73,000 people visited Brighton in a week's time.

Technological change was abetted by social change. At first, many factory owners did not believe in holidays even for themselves. The people who might have benefited most from a seaside respite, the industrial workers, were literally prisoners of the mine, the factory, and the assembly line. Seaside resorts did not seek greater market volume. Some resorts initially rejected railroad connections as being too crass. No media campaigns stressed the virtues of a vacation. In time some factory owners saw holidays as a means of coping with slack periods. Others felt periodic holidays would refresh and recharge workers. While gaining more acceptance, holidays were usually unpaid and were limited to the occasional religious "holy day" (the root words for holiday), such as Christmas or Easter.

While the most popular month for the coast had no major religious significance, more and more people thought August was as worthy as Christmas or Easter for time off. By 1871, Parliament passed the Bank Holiday Law, mandating a series of holidays including the first extended weekend in August. While aimed mainly at clerks in commercial cities, the bill's impact spread. Retail shops and public buildings also closed down.

Holidays with pay and two-week vacations, which would open up the world to mass tourism, still lay ahead. Churches, which feared holidays would lure away their flocks, set up church summer camps on the coast. They offered singing and family entertainment while monitoring bathing customs and night activity. The more fundamentalist groups had a baptismal area close by.

The newly liberated pleasure seekers could relax at home, go to local attractions, or travel into the countryside. But the seaside already had the basic necessities and conveniences. There were not only the natural attractions of sea and air, but the commercial entertainments. Indeed, the seaside resorts were achieving popularity prior to the advent of today's recreational activities and technologies—surfboarding, swim fins, riding waves on rafts, snorkeling, volleyball, Frisbee, marina development, and sun-bathing. The seaside became a somewhat static backdrop for festive public celebrations. Everyone was invited and could participate as much or as little as he or she desired. Unlike the mountains or the countryside, the seaside had the right combination of space and basic facilities to cater to people by the thousands. No religious observance was needed to trigger a festive mood. The shining sun, warm temperatures, and crashing waves were sufficient. The original motive for a seaside visit was now shifting from health to pleasure and excitement. Medical claims for saltwater bathing gave way to more emphasis on clean air. Another seaside commodity—sunshine—was also being touted. People could enjoy themselves merely by watching other people dance, by walking down the promenade, or by riding a donkey by the seaside. Musical bands with barrel organs, brass bands, bagpipes, and French horns proliferated. Somebody decided to compose songs honoring the seaside. Now the human voice could abet the brassy blare:

> For I am offully fond of the Sea-side!
> If I'd only my w'y I would de-cide
> To dwell evermore
> By the murmuring shore
> With the billows a-blustering be-side!

The urban rush to the seaside, peaking in August, resulted in severe resort overloads. Out-of-season rates and staggered vacations began to extend the vacation season. Seaside communities were opting for tourism over traditional fishing economies. Municipalities competed to attract tourists. Blackpool began investing in piers, concert halls, and a seven-mile-long promenade to outshine its coastal rivals. Public gardens sprang up along the waterfronts of many coastal towns. One community proudly announced its investment in a significant sanitary advance—an outfall.

Some London artists prized the seaside both as a place to

work and as a place to relax away from the noise and din of London garrets. James McNeill Whistler and some of his friends began to frequent St. Ives on the Cornwall coast. Their presence attracted other members of the art world. Just as Cumae flourished along the Bay of Luxury, the artists' colony was becoming part of the British coastal scene. In the next century, coastal art colonies would find new niches in North America.

Artists began opening up the marine perspective with the boldness of the maritime explorers of the fifteenth and sixteenth centuries. Once merely a static backdrop to historic naval battle scenes, the sea began emerging as a vital, dynamic natural force worthy of being the sole subject of the canvas. Waves once represented with the tameness of finely combed hair now seemed to burst from the canvases of William Turner in England, Winslow Homer in the United States, and Hokusai in Japan. Constable, Whistler, and Germany's Casper David Friedrich were enchanted by another aspect of the sea: its immense, calming solitude in the brightness of the sun or the reflections of shimmering night lights. Persons hundreds of miles away from the sea were being drawn toward it by these compelling sights.

With the worker on the domestic shore, British royalty and the upper classes scouted for less plebeian areas. They began to fan out through Europe, which was untouched by seaside mania. Some would frequent inland mineral springs and spas in Germany. Others would hike the Swiss Alps. A more ethereal group began infiltrating the Mediterranean basin. Poets like Byron, Shelley, and Browning trooped through the ruins of Venice, Rome, and Naples, in turn repulsed or mesmerized by the social decay. To Byron, Venice was "thou sea Sodom." The Mediterranean presented an escape from a society that required young women to go down to the sea in bathing machines. Through the writings of these British expatriates, the Mediterranean reemerged in the world consciousness, not as a world power but as an escape to pleasure.

For Shelley, the Mediterranean was a refuge from the noise and din of the industrial revolution:

Earth and ocean seem
To sleep in one another's arms, and dream
Of waves, flowers, clouds, woods, rocks, and all that we
Read in their smiles, and call reality.

Italy at first took little notice of the dreamy expatriates. The Italians did not realize that they were looking at the vanguard of an economy that would be able to offset trade deficits for food imports.

Some restless British tourists began to pass through the French Mediterranean coast en route to the Italian ruins. To A. C. Swinburne, this coastal region was a "grimy, parboiled country without trees, water, grass fields . . . and such females with hunched bodies and crooked necks carrying tons on their heads and looking like death taken seasick." For others, the sparkling blue presence of the Mediterranean cast the same spell that once entranced Roman senators. The French Riviera was being colonized as a refuge from the Brightons of the British shore.

The independent state of Monaco was almost bankrupt due to tax fights over olive oil and fruit. It resorted to a coastal use British resorts shunned: gambling. With Monte Carlo, Monaco was back in the black. This coastal enterprise engendered Seneca-like seals of disapproval that delighted resort owners. Wrote one French writer, "Innocent bathers are enticed into the labyrinth of evil, this cathedral of vice, the casino of Monaco." To another observer, the casino was a "large house of sin blazing, flaming and shining by the shore like the habitation of some romantic witch." The casino owner knew how to diffuse such vitriol. He helped France pay off its foreign indemnity after the Franco-Prussian War.

European aristocrats in the twilight of their power hastened each winter to the French Riviera, reviving the art of the palatial marine villa. Prince Tcherkovsky kept a staff of forty-eight gardeners. They had to rearrange each flower in his garden nightly so he would not be bored by a day-old garden upon awakening in the morning. If Brighton was demonstrating the popular appeal of the domestic seaside, Cannes and Monte Carlo were demonstrating the fabulous returns possible from exotic distant seashores, where labor was cheap and ununionized, at least at the beginning.

At first the French Riviera flourished only during the winter. In summer, the Mediterranean was left to the natives and the maids. Through a chance invitation from Cole Porter, two twentieth-century American expatriates, Gerald and Sara Murphy, began to host an artists' colony on the Riviera during the summer. They moved the site of sociability from the hotel patio and the villa garden to the beach proper. They preferred "beach attire," from comfortable swimsuits to casual sportswear including white duck pants. These new coastal pioneers assiduously courted suntans as a sign of robust health and outdoor vitality. The seaside innovations by the Murphys were well publicized by F. Scott Fitzgerald in *Tender Is the Night.*

After centuries of avoiding sea bathing and the sun, Europeans and North Americans now spend millions to cultivate two-week tans at the risk of sunburn and peeling skin. The Depression temporarily stalled the rise of the coastal Rivieras. But the people of the industrial nations had found their major refuge from industrial and urban life, the domestic and foreign seaside. This sanctuary was and remains shot through with paradoxes: the quest for privacy versus social activities, the emphasis on landward rather than marine activities, the loss of natural charms to resort construction, the duel quest for simplicity and for convenience, the oppressive inflation that raises the cost of paradise and displaces the original residents. Horace and Juvenal would have found the buildings and technology strange, but not the people.

The resort trends pioneered in Baiae and in Great Britain have bloomed in the twentieth century. The jet brings once remote Pacific and Caribbean islands within the orbit of global tourism. Wet-suit technology and recreational boating can make the coastal season last year-round. The affluent can commute between tropical winter beaches and temperate summer beaches nearer home. The pastoral seascapes of Whistler and Constable have been supplanted by Reginald Marsh's limb-entangled scenes of the New York urban beach.

The urban populations that once commuted from harbor cities and inland communities are now liable to work and live on the shore. Industry moves to the suburban shore to find attractive sites to recruit engineers and executives weary of older, aging cities. Retired couples follow the same seaward path. While populations decline in inland urban and rural areas, they sky-rocket along the coast. In the United States, the population is shifting from the industrial east and the midwest to the Gulf and Pacific coasts. California, with few natural bays and limited coastal plains, has literally grown on top of its coastline. Florida's original resort communities have grown into full-fledged conurbations.

Today, a day at the beach is one of the most prevalent shared human experiences in a world divided by competition for more tangible resources. Ironically, the global investment in marine recreation and tourism, from the Brightons of the northern hemisphere to the Tahitis and Jamaicas of the tropical seas to the Aegean islands in the Mediterranean, exceeds the global investment in marine fishing and mining. As in the case of the commercial fishing industry, the natural processes that maintain this investment are often ignored. We have come to love the sea but not necessarily to respect it.

II

A Stage that Shifts

A BEACH MAY APPEAR FLAT AND inert, but it is a living, moving, powerful thing. The sand may come from a thousand miles away, move on tomorrow and cover other beaches while new sand arrives. The constant turnover gives the living beach a toughness unmatched in nature.

Each summer hundreds of millions of people come to tramp, run, and camp on the world's beaches. The beaches accommodate them in numbers that would destroy alpine meadows and damage even rocky desert canyons. Yet the durable beach is a most humane ground cover. As the Romans at Baiae and the British at Brighton discovered, a beach is the ocean's welcome mat.

After laying down countless grass infields, asphalt playgrounds, and astroturf gridirons, we still cannot match a beach's friendly durability. The beach can host leaping, running, and diving volleyball players one moment and then become a quiet solarium for the bikini brigade. For the very young children of the world, tottering about on shaky legs, the beach can be a reassuring experience. A landform that shakes off hurricanes is gentle to a baby's bare feet. Maybe our fondness for the beach springs from this first gentle encounter.

The delighted cries of the young join with the sounds of blaring transistor radios to suffuse the urban beach with noise. Yet, in the middle of this high-decibel, high-density world, a student may prepare for an exam while a dedicated swinger sleeps one off. Does the sound of the surf buffer the noise and shelter this uncanny solitude? I wish I could understand this quality better. Relocate the noise and the people in any other environment—natural or man-made—and you might be confronted with a riot. With this acoustic quality, the ocean's welcome mat becomes the world's downtown of coastal leisure.

Today, when I go down to the beach, I may excavate the sand with a tablespoon and place some in a plastic bag. I may ask my students and my friends to do the same when they vacation at a beach. Only the very young at the beach accept my peculiar obsession with sand. It is, after all, very easy to take the ocean's welcome mat for granted.

When I run my hand through the sand, I now realize I am handling broken rock particles, finer than gravel and coarser than silt. The main mineral is quartz, which consists of tiny bright crystals; the second is dark-colored feldspar. There are also bits of magnetite, ilmenite zircon, mica—even tiny specks of gold and other gems too minute to mine. Where do these bright smithereens come from? Where are they tumbled and milled in volumes sufficient to form beaches five miles long and dunes two stories high?

Scientists identify three main sources: (1) rocky masses eroded from coastal bluffs, (2) sediments deposited by rivers in the ocean, and (3) offshore deposits of sand.

Beaches on Cape Cod, Long Island and Sandy Hook, New Jersey, for example, get their sand from coastal bluffs eroded by wave action. Along our Pacific Coast, the main source is river sediments, including those transported by the great "sand rivers" of southern California. Often dry during the summer, these rivers resemble sandboxes, filling up with quartz-rich sediment eroded from pine-covered mountain ranges. A beach can reach as far away as distant mountain peaks to collect its sand.

A beach may lie many miles from a river mouth or a coastal bluff. How does the sand reach it? If you've ever had to call your children to return to the spot on the beach where they first entered the surf, you've noticed the longshore current. Waves that appear to strike the beach head on actually strike at an angle, and this generates the longshore current. This current, which pulls you downcoast when you swim, transports sand from coastal bluffs or river mouths to sustain beaches many miles away. Stand in the surf zone and you may feel small particles pepper your legs. These are sand grains entrained by the current.

This current performs another valuable service. Sediment from a coastal bluff or river discharge contains silt as well as sand. So why don't we have mud beaches? The turbulent surf zone sorts out the sediments. Silt particles, being lighter and less durable, are carried out beyond the surf zone to settle on the seabed. Tougher sand grains can withstand this turbulence and remain within the surf zone to be carried along by the longshore current.

The longshore current runs parallel to the land; its direction varies with the winds and the angle of the coast. But the dominant direction on both our Atlantic and Pacific coasts is toward the south (because the prevailing winds are northerly). Sand from Carolina beaches eventually reaches Florida beaches. Whole beachloads of Oregon sand can wind up in California. Approximately 300,000 cubic yards of sand move past Santa Barbara annually.

This current also displaces older grains and carries them downcoast to supply another beach. Beaches seem inert, but they are only way stations for the moving sand grains. Beaches are as fluid as the waves that wash up against the beachface.

Given this endless stream of sand, why don't the beaches balloon out like overfed humans? Because sand is being continually diverted away from the conveyor belt. We carry a tiny amount away in our shoes and bathing suits. Sea winds skim much more landward to form dunes. Swift currents in tidal inlets suck more into quiet bays. Along the California coast, huge submarine canyons close to shore trap tons of sand.

So beaches are poised in a dynamic equilibrium. They need a never-ending supply of new sand to replace sand lost to dunes and to submarine canyons. A sand grain becomes a geologic nomad, forever condemned to roam our coastal rim at the bidding of winds, ocean waves, and harbor dredges.

Besides moving along the shore, the nomadic grains may shuttle back and forth between the beach and the surf zone. At times, a portion of the beach may even migrate seaward. The turbulence generated by storm waves moves the sand seaward to build up submerged sand bars. More gentle waves return sand from the submerged bars to the beachface, the sloping portion of the beach normally exposed to wave uprush and backwash (the sheet of return flow). We often see only half of the total beach system. The other half lies submerged in the form of sand bars that parallel the shore.

Although these bars are often below the surface, you can see their influence on waves. A wave may break only to reform into another, smaller wave. The wave breaks first as it moves across the outer bar. The surf reforms into another wave over a trough or depression between the outer and inner bars. (The longshore current running parallel to the shore may scour out these troughs.) The reformed wave then breaks again on the inner bar. Off southeast Cape Cod Bay, a series of bars extends over a mile seaward. Here a wave may break and reform several times before lapping up against the shore.

Beaches contract in winter and expand in summer. Imagine if this situation were reversed! Our summer beaches would be narrower and even more packed with barefoot families. Fortunately, the violent storm waves are more frequent during winter. The more gentle waves of summer can restore the battered beach in time to accommodate the human migration to the shore.

While the processes that form beaches are similar, the actual forms that beaches take can vary dramatically. I first learned to build sand castles on the beaches of the Pacific shore that slope seaward from the foot of coastal bluffs or cliffs. While a delightful natural playground, these bluff-backed beaches were never very far removed from the urban world. On the bluffs above, the stern urban countenance of Los Angeles would glower down at us in the form of glass-walled cocktail lounges, high-rise apartments, and storm drains that drooled with street runoff. Rental telescopes, lenses glinting in the sun, would peer down at us too, obviously looking for more than tankers on the horizon.

I was just getting ready to graduate from sand castles to surfing when my family moved to Chicago. When summer came, I was disconsolate, a would-be surfer without surf. Then my dad announced we would vacation at the nearest available oceanfront, the Atlantic. Would the Atlantic shore measure up to the California shore?

I still remember my first excited sight of the Atlantic shore. Instead of driving down a steep bluff, we crossed an old bridge that creaked underneath our car. The beach was separated from the mainland by a long, narrow bay. The beach itself was long and narrow. I could run across its width without stopping for a breath. No bluffs impeded my passage, only soft sand hills twenty or thirty feet high. "Those are called dunes," my mother informed me. Dunes by the ocean? I thought they belonged in deserts. The beach itself did not look much higher than the waves cresting offshore. One good-sized wave looked like it could demolish the beach and our vacation plans.

Was I disappointed in this modest-appearing beach? No sir. I had entered a new world. Like a moat protecting a natural kingdom, the bay separated us from the urban world on the mainland. No cliff-top cocktail lounges or rental telescopes

---

A Stage that Shifts

peered down at me, only the blue sky and soaring gulls. I was on a barrier island.

However thin and squat, the island met all the exacting requirements of my boyhood imagination. In the morning, I would run upwind along the beach to inflate a white mattress cover used to raft the waves. Boogie boards (styrofoam belly-boards) still lay in the future. As the mattress cover began to lose air and sag, I would shift my activities to the sand dunes. Unlike the steep Pacific bluffs, I could climb, jump, and roll down dunes. Or I could slink around one dune to scout out enemy cavalry. Or I could simply recline on a dune, let the sun dry off my skin and my swim trunks, and watch clouds glide across the sky like huge white blimps. Two weeks later, as we crossed the bridge to reenter the real world, I asked my dad when we could return. I now realized that all beaches did not need bluffs to exist. The Atlantic shore had measured up to the Pacific.

Over 300 barrier islands border our Atlantic and Gulf coasts. Many of our most popular urban beaches and resorts are located on barrier islands: Jones Beach on Long Island, Virginia Beach, Atlantic City, Miami Beach, Daytona Beach, Ocean City, Maryland. The Texas barrier islands, up to five miles wide and over 100 miles long, are the longest and widest of the barrier islands. Historically, barrier beaches and islands protected the low-lying Netherlands from storm waves. Why are barrier islands so common to these coasts while bluff-backed beaches dominate our Pacific coast? Barrier beaches and islands are associated with low-lying coastal plains exposed to long-term changes in sea level. When the sea level drops, sand may be deposited over the exposed seabed. When the sea level gradually rises, waves may entrain these sand deposits and build up the barrier islands along the coast. These islands can retreat or advance as the sea level rises and falls. Tree stumps actually stick out of the sand on some barrier islands, reminders of an age when the land extended much further seaward.

Bluff-backed beaches are associated with young (geologically speaking) mountain coasts of the world. Where waves attack a cliff composed of uniformly weak or unconsolidated materials, a wave-straightened coastline results. Where waves attack more resistant cliffs, an irregular coastline results. Scenic examples of the latter include La Jolla and Laguna Beach in southern California, the Big Sur area along central California, and the Maine coast.

Tucked within the folds of these rugged coasts are cove or pocket beaches. Projecting headlands shelter the crescent-shaped cove and the ocean appears to come to a halt. Tiny wavelets lap the sand like ripples in a pond. Small in size, the cove beach is possibly the most charming of all beach forms.

I once thought that beaches possessed the color range of highway concrete. Then, along a coastal road south of Hilo, Hawaii, I saw a beach, wetted by the surf, glazed by the sun, that was black. Not dull black or off-black but shiny, glossy tuxedo black, like polished marble. Volcanos that rise high enough into the tropical sky to wear a snow mantle sustain these stunning black beaches. The volcanos spew forth red-hot masses of lava that cascade into the Pacific amid huge clouds of steam. The waves gradually mill the lava down into glistening black grains. Some lava flows contain olivine rocks that produce green beaches downcoast of the black beaches.

You don't always need an active volcano for basic beach decor. Step on beaches along the coast of northern California, Oregon, and Washington and you expect clouds of soot to engulf you. But the charcoal-colored sands are firm underfoot. The parent rock for this sand is dark-colored volcanic rock in coastal mountain watersheds. Quartz-rich granitic rock gives beaches in southern California their light color.

The dazzling white beaches along the Florida Gulf Coast look as if they are poured from a salt shaker. Run your hand through these snow-white grains and you will feel bits of shell. The beach literally tinkles with the sound of shell debris. In tropical waters, coral and skeletons of tiny marine animals provide sand that can range in color from orange to white. Beaches are not particular about the color or source of grains as long as they can withstand the tumble of the waves. This is one reason I am such an avid collector of sand. By comparing beach sands, I can better appreciate the diverse nature of beaches. One beach in northern California is composed of rusting cans, courtesy of an old coastal dump. There is a comic quality about this tin can beach but, as will become apparent later, the last laugh may be on us.

Beaches have signs or signals by which you can divine their relative safety. Beaches with a gentle slope are generally safer. Waves breaking directly on a steep beachface can generate a backwash strong enough to sweep you off your feet. Check the grain size as well. Gently sloping beaches contain medium to fine sand grains; steeper beaches, coarse grains. Texas beaches contain very fine grains called powder or flour sand. The white grains can adhere to your body and transform you into a ghostly apparition fit for a Hallowe'en party. Fine-grained beaches can pack down into surfaces so firm that Daytona Beach can host auto races. Coarse-grained beaches, being less firm, can be difficult to walk on. They swallow your feet after each step. Coarse grains are associated with steep beachfaces. The more vigorous wave action here tends to remove smaller grains to quieter waters offshore or downcoast.

Next, scan the waves for signs of a rip current. Water may pile up and flow seaward through a narrow channel cut through a submerged sand bar. This confined rip current can be strong enough to carry you out beyond the surf zone, where it dissipates. Rather than attempting to swim back to shore against this current, you should swim to either side of the narrow current and then return to shore. This response demands a high degree of swimming confidence. Fortunately, bathers can recognize a rip before entering the surf. Lighter-colored, sand-laden plumes of water that extend seaward and fan out beyond the surf zone mark a rip. I don't rely on billboards that proclaim the "World's Safest Beach" when assessing surf conditions.

During early morning walks on a falling tide, I have discovered another delightful beach trait. The sloping beachface—

stamped the day before by footprints, scarred by stray Frisbees, punctured by umbrella poles—stretches out smooth as a freshly ironed sheet, a trillion sand grains impeccably in place. The receding surf can fashion delicate collages on this sand canvas with the most modest of materials: stray pebbles, bits of shell, and seaweed. Fine, wavy lines that run roughly parallel to the shore may be embossed on the beachface. These fine lines criss-cross each other like unraveling twine. Each line is composed of a tiny ridge of sand grains and shell bits deposited by the feather edge of the wave uprush, or swash. Swash marks, formed during a falling tide, leave a fine, looping calligraphy embossed on the sand canvas.

Small obstacles—pebbles, shell bits, even the feeding appendages of burrowing sand crabs—may divide the thin sheet of return flow, the backwash. This divided flow can leave streaks of darker-colored sand that form a series of inverted Vs, like a geometric design dye-stamped on fine cloth. You almost expect to get ink on your feet.

Water trapped in the sand during high tide may seep down the beachface and cut tiny channels. The channels will branch into smaller channels, like the root system of a tree. The braided channels are called rill marks. Their intricate patterns can resemble miniature forests or leaf designs on cut crystal.

The upper beach may contain small sand domes no larger than my hand. One finger tap can collapse these domes. Do these delicate domes shelter a burrowing beach animal whose gift for sand architecture is at the mercy of our footsteps? Fortunately not. Air can fill the spaces between sand grains as they dry out, then a later swash that sinks into the sand can trap the air. The air migrates upwards and puffs out a large bubble that lifts the damp sand surface into a low, well-defined dome. A walk on the beach can be like browsing through an outdoor art gallery where exhibits change daily under the stroke of the waves.

The beach is for listening as well as seeing. Sometimes I ignore the roar of the breaking wave for a moment and listen closely as the swash rushes up the beachface and covers my feet.

I hear a fizz, like carbonate from soda pop. Escaping air trapped during the wave's collapse causes the fizzing sound.

I look seaward as more blue waves crest and crash into the frothing mass of white water. This churning white front flattens into swash thin as cellophane. The swash creeps up the beachface, pauses, and then recedes. Within a day, a thousand more waves will rise and fall, reshaping and reworking our most dynamic and resilient landform.

Did civilization have to wait on the emergence of oceanographic institutes to understand and appreciate the beach's fluid, shifting character? Not at all. Many coastal societies, from the Mediterranean basin to Polynesia, were very aware of it. Their homes and settlements were built well back of the active beach zone to compensate for seasonal shifts and storm surges. They could not rely on federal disaster relief.

This sort of caution can ebb as the commercial value of the beach skyrockets. Today, luxury hotels and entire coastal resorts encroach on the beach zone. This seaside intimacy generates its own unusual forms.

12

No Dancing

ONE SUMMER DAY, I TOOK MY family to one of the favorite beaches of my boyhood. The California sun was shining and the waves were up. But no surfers were riding out to meet the waves. No Frisbee players were in evidence. No volleyball teams were locked in sunny combat. Even the pigeons were missing.

Instead of riding waves or tanning their bodies, people were filling burlap bags with sand and piling them against beachfront patios to blunt a swelling surf. The beach, which once buffered beachfront homes and hosted thousands of beach visitors, was missing. We left our rafts and beach towels in the car and helped fill sandbags. When we finally took a dip in the surf, it was to revive our aching muscles.

A community severed from its beach can be a tragic sight. The sounds of the crowded beach—the blaring radios, the shouts of children, the thump of the spiked volleyball—are replaced by the harsh, dirgelike rumble of cobbles. The beachfront homes once envied by tourists find themselves in a battle zone. Surf that once beat on the sandy shore now beats on patios, leaving cobbles, shells, and driftwood in its churning wake. This was my first personal encounter with a perplexing global problem: beach erosion.

A Chinese dictum set down in 240 B.C. reads: "Nothing under the heaven is softer or more yielding than water; but when it attacks things hard and resistant there is not one of them that can prevail." No coastal structures are immune from this relentless aquatic attack. South Cape May, New Jersey, has lost one-fourth of its land area, including two Roman Catholic convents, a lighthouse, and a Coast Guard radar station.

The usual beachfront controversies—Should dogs be leashed? Should alcohol be banned? Is there enough or too much public access?—now sound almost banal. The usual irritants—sand too hot to walk on or sand in a hot dog—have an ironic ring. On many beaches sand enough to sour a hot dog would now be a blessing.

With its understanding of beach processes, science can expose many of the forces behind beach erosion. Geologically speaking, coastlines often move seaward or retreat landward because of glacial processes that raise or lower the sea level. These long-term movements occur centimeter by centimeter over the ages and explain why ancient beaches exist inland and submerged beaches exist on the continental shelf. However, this gradual rearrangement of the earth does little to explain how beaches a football field wide can disappear over a two-year period, as did the Surfside-Sunset beach just south of Los Angeles. Such swift changes can only be explained by the works of man.

During World War II, a jetty was built up the coast from this beach. Soon thereafter, owners above the jetty saw their beach widen. Recalled one resident, "I nearly died of thirst getting to the surf." At the same time, the harbor protected by the jetty was filling with sand instead of water. The jetty was effectively damming up the sand transport. The other portion of the missing beach lay inland, trapped behind dams along the San Gabriel River. At last count, over a dozen California beaches were suffering from various degrees of sand starvation due to such diet suppressors as dams, jetties, and breakwaters.

Beaches may become sand-depleted by other causes, too. Many celebrated beachfronts in New Jersey, for example, began starving back in the nineteenth century, before breakwaters and other shore improvement projects became so fashionable. Land developers and resort promoters there built Atlantic City, Cape May, Ocean City, and Stone Harbor on "barrier beaches." These barrier beaches, by absorbing the punishment of 25-foot waves, buffer the mainland from hurricanes and winter storms. Hence their name. Unfortunately, while they are quite suitable as public beaches, nature never intended these islands to be colonized by high-rise resorts. Developers were asking people to reside on a natural seawall. Historically, these beaches, when battered by hurricanes, have been replenished with the aid of sand from the dunes. However, developers often leveled these stockpiles of sand to accommodate subdivisions. Today residents often find their homes besieged by sand drifts and sandstorms. The offshore winds responsible for forming dunes still blow what little sand is left.

Recently, New Jersey has been improving its tidal channels with jetties to accommodate marinas, with much the same downcoast results as in California. The New Jersey shore ranks as one of the world's most unstable.

Scientific insight into beach erosion would seem to bode well for erosion control. Historically, however, people tend to view the ocean, rather than their own coastal artifices, as the real troublemaker. This is not an unnatural impression, given the surf's dramatic appearance and sonorous sound. Noted one well-

---

known shore control engineer, Andries Vierlingh, "Your foe Oceanus does not sleep by day or night, but comes suddenly like a roaring lion, seeking to devour the whole land. To have kept your country is a great victory won." Vierlingh lived in the Netherlands during the sixteenth century, which helps explain his wary regard of Oceanus.

However, this martial cant still survives. The Corps of Engineers, charged with "the improvement and protection of beaches along the shores of the United States," is more than ready to execute its mission. "Our campaign against the encroachment of the sea must be waged with the same care that we would take against any other enemy threatening our boundaries," comments a Corps brochure.

Under the spell of this bias, it is only natural to build massive seawalls to repulse the enemy. However, a seawall's steep gradient fosters a severe backwash. The backwash can undermine whatever beach remains and, eventually, the seawall itself. The beach recovery is ostensibly sacrificed to protect upland property. However, a seawall is often too short to block storm waves but just high enough to prevent overtopping water from draining back into the ocean. All this protection is costly, requires constant maintenance, and hardly lasts as long as a natural beach, which costs nothing.

Another popular sea defense work, the groin, juts out from shore to hoard the offshore sand transport for a starving beach. When nothing happens, the groin's design is often blamed. As a result, groins come in a variety of shapes and are made from many different materials, including concrete, sheet metal piling, oyster shells, and wire fence. Despite this design virtuosity, groins can be found wanting. Users would make more headway by questioning the groin's basic utility. If the sand transport is cut off from its supply of sand, a groin is no more helpful to a thin beach than a fork to a starving man. If there is still some sand to stop, the groin will stop it—for the upcoast beach. Some groins may shunt sand out to deeper water beyond the reach of the beach and the longshore current. Downcoast beaches will erode that much faster. Downcoast owners may then erect their own groins to compete for what is left. Today, over 300 groins in various stages of storm-battered decay protrude from the New Jersey shore. Some groins at shrinking South Cape May now serve as underwater reefs. From an airplane, the shoreline resembles a steeplechase run.

After construction of some 42 groins and 37 different seawalls, Hawaii's celebrated Waikiki Beach continues to erode. Seawalls that encroach on the beach zone are considered to be the main cause.

British shore expert W.W. Williams ascribes the remarkable popularity of groins and seawalls (in the face of their failure) to the "period of responsibility factor—building a structure which in the long term may be a waste of money and effort, but which is likely to survive for the vital span of thirty years, and so seemingly do credit to its authors during their periods of responsibility if not for the rest of their lives."

Today, sea defenses are virtually synonymous with any extensive human presence on the shore. Russia's deputy minister of the Maritime Fleet, G. Pyasetskiy, refers to the shores of the Black Sea as being "shackled in concrete." The persistence of beach erosion despite man's concrete contributions to the shorescape encourages alternative strategies to the fortification approach. "In coastal engineering, progress has not been our most important product," concedes Neill E. Parker of the Corps' Coastal Engineering Research Center in Virginia.

The Corps now tries to control the human impact on beach processes rather than control the ocean itself. Since the Corps, often under pressure from local interests, designs or approves many beach-eroding jetties, this is appropriate. The idea is to pour sand onto the shore instead of concrete into seawalls. It is a method more in line with scientific insight and yet more demanding of engineering finesse than groin building. Would-be beach builders can haul in millions of cubic meters of sand only to see the artificial beach vanish faster than the original beach. This can happen, for example, when beaches are restored with sand grains smaller in size than the original grains.

Grains greater in size than the original ones can also be a problem. Oceanside once possessed one of southern California's most spacious beaches. Harbor jetties at Camp Pendleton Marine Corps Base and at a pleasure marina severely eroded this asset. Sand trapped in the marina harbor was dredged up to restore the beach. Unexpectedly, the dredge sucked up a tremendous number of fist-sized stones as well. The sand eroded away quickly, leaving the stones. City authorities were prepared to bulldoze the stony beach into the ocean until it was pointed out that the stones served in effect as a seawall to retard shore erosion. Today much of the Oceanside Beach looks like it is made out of corrugated iron.

Sometimes the grain size is right, but the sand fails to reach the beach. The Corps dumped 600,000 cubic yards of sand off Long Branch, New Jersey, and waited for nearshore currents to nourish starving beaches. Nothing happened. The mystified Corps checked the offshore sandpile. It was virtually intact. The water depth—38 feet—exceeded the normal range of nearshore currents. Such attempts to control beach erosion have been likened to building an airplane without much knowledge of the nature of air.

Beach builders understandably turn to the research community, which has its own peculiar problems. Knowledge of beach phenomena stems from empirical observation. Scientists would like to be more scientific, but installing a speedometer, a weight scale, and a sand grain counter on the sand transport is difficult. Many researchers turn landward and build ingenious models of the shore in wave tanks to test theories. But it is difficult to duplicate tides and rip currents. Also, as Dr. Douglas Inman of the Scripps Institution of Oceanography notes, it is very risky to scale up data from a wave tank to a beach ten miles long.

The need to instrument the surf zone becomes all the more important. A principal agent of beach erosion can be helpful. By measuring the rate of beach accretion upcoast of the Santa Barbara, California, breakwater and the rate of erosion downcoast, scientists have estimated the annual sand transport as approximately 300,000 cubic yards. Similar measurements at the Port Hueneme jetty revealed an annual transport of almost a million cubic yards.

To analyze beach processes without installing jetties, scientists inject the sand transport with radioactive tracers, fluorescent sand, weighted croquet balls, perforated ping-pong balls, and other undercover agents. Downcoast retrieval of these agents provides insight into the speed and direction of the sand transport. (It also provides for some remarkable double takes on the shore. The sight of grown men in swim trunks patiently dumping bags of sand on the beach inspires wondering glances among bathers. Downcoast, wonderment turns to questioning frowns when a man with an empty sand bag tells the curious, "I am collecting green sand.")

Manual sorting and counting of fluorescent sand grains amidst countless millions of normal grains poses obvious problems. Florida beach investigator D.G. Teleki's automatic fluorescent particle counter can process 55,000 particles per second and discriminate between four tracer grain colors. Working with electronic engineer W.A. Koontz, Dr. Inman has devised "mini-digital wave staffs" that monitor the surf zone and feed data to computers onshore. Such instantaneous measurements can expose the surf zone to full scientific view. They have important implications for another area in great need of precise techniques: the distributive patterns of outfall discharges. Dr. Inman even measures wave energy lost through heat and surf noise in order to identify the net budget of wave energy in the nearshore environment.

Even with more accurate nearshore sand-specifications to rely on, beach builders must still locate and transport tremendous amounts of sand. An inexpensive, properly sized and ready source may be within a stone's throw of a starving beach. Upcoast harbors that trap downcoast beaches are happy to be relieved of such navigational hazards. Sand bypassing by means of hydraulic dredges is reviving Surfside-Sunset Beach and many others along the Pacific and Atlantic coasts. An ancient beach found stranded half a mile inland served to revive Doheny Beach in southern California. With sand imported from different sources, the famed Waikiki shore along Honolulu can resemble a crazy quilt of colors. This simplifies giving directions. I overheard one young lady say that she was staying at the hotel "with the orange beach." Her friend said he was staying at the hotel "with the white beach." They were standing on a tan-colored beach. About the only color missing was black, but this may only be temporary. Waikiki, which already imports sand from other islands, may eventually try to tap the black beaches on the big island of Hawaii. Concerned about Waikiki's voracious appetite for sand, the state of Hawaii now bans mining of sand on stable beaches.

To keep up with beach and dune building, the Corps of Engineers goes to sea to uncover suitable offshore sand deposits isolated by geological processes, lusty tidal channels, or exceptional storm waves. New Jersey's fickle beachfront may be shored up by a sand shoal containing an estimated 40 million cubic yards of sand. Promising shoals also exist off the coast of Florida.

Gratified by these discoveries, the Corps is now encouraging the dredging industry to leave quieter waters for the open sea to mine submerged sand. However, the industry is not noted for its sense of innovation. "On the premise that a profession is known by its literature, dredging might well be eliminated," John Huston of Huston Engineers in Texas has observed in the *Journal of Harbors and Waterways*.

Dredges traditionally are restricted to protected harbor waters and to navigation channel maintenance, which explains their nickname, "mud mills." To make mud mills seaworthy, it has been suggested that they be equipped with tractor treads and a snorkel so they can operate on the seabed and below rough surface seas. People interested in mining offshore placer deposits of gold are keenly interested in Corps efforts to make dredges seaworthy. In time, tailings from offshore mining efforts may even be drafted to restore beaches.

Beach nourishment programs are no panacea. And their success can be misleading. They depend on an unlimited supply of sand. (Surfside-Sunset Beach is now on its sixth artificial beach.) Harbor shoals, offshore deposits, and ancient beaches cannot provide that. Many beaches depend on sand sediments carried to the ocean by rivers and streams. Contemporary civilization rapidly impounds this supply. Over 50 percent of southern California's watershed is dammed. Soon the figure will rise to 75 percent.

The sand and gravel industry is competing for diminishing sand sources to meet building construction demands. Marine mining expert Dr. John Mero considers that such extraction will be a financial dark horse in ocean exploitation. The industry already extracts sand conveniently impounded behind dams. Sand once carried to the coast by dammed-up stream flows may accumulate in flood control channels. Coastal regions sometimes dredge out this sand and sell it for a profit, even though their own coastline may be short of sand. California is trying to implement a sand rights concept that would require river sand to be placed on the beach where it belongs in the first place. To Dr. Inman, the specter of a sand shortage is the most serious problem in shore stabilization.

The artificial nourishment approach poses a special problem for the barrier islands of the Atlantic Coast. Here sea level is rising a foot or more each century. This may not sound substantial until you realize the low-lying nature of the barrier islands, particularly if the dunes have been bulldozed. A one-foot rise in the sea level could extend storm surges 500 feet and more inland. To attempt to stabilize an urban barrier island with a seawall or a new beach is to expose it to a greater frequency of punishing storm surges. The shore itself may become too steep to hold imported sand. Original or synthetic dunes may be undercut and toppled by the rising sea levels.

Natural barrier islands adjust to rising sea levels by "rolling over" and retreating landward over time. The National Park Service is now shifting from structural devices to a strategy of submission in its barrier island parks.

Most coastal communities prefer to stay put even though they can turn into municipal invalids. At Sea Bright, New Jersey, beach residents live in the shadow of a towering sea wall decorated with huge painted flowers and aerosol graffiti glorifying the pelvic zone. Their homes might as well back up against a prison wall. Sun porches straddle the top of the wall like guard towers. The porches bear proud No Trespassing signs, as if trespassing is the main problem faced by Sea Bright. No beach remains, only the rubble of previously destroyed sea walls and groins. To Duke University geologist Orrin Pilkey, Sea Bright has reached a point of no return. "If you remove the sea wall and let nature take its course, Sea Bright will disappear. The beach wants to be hundreds of feet behind where the sea wall is."

Public funds for shore improvement far exceed public funds to remedy the harsh consequences of these improvements. Port Hueneme's tribulations are enlightening in this respect. The erosive harbor jetty was built with local public funds in 1939. By 1942, with erosive consequences very much in evidence, Port Hueneme did not even have a harbor to show for its shoreline misery. The Navy had condemned the harbor for a Seabee training base. The community, left with the responsibility of stemming ocean tides, extended a seawall down the coast until it was over a mile long.

The community was trying to finance the seawall as its tax base was literally washing out to sea. The shore was receding up to 900 feet. Whole city blocks disappeared, along with a railroad track. Property values were dropping. There was no tidal insurance to be had.

Neither money, sand, nor equipment seemed to be available to rebuild Port Hueneme's beach. Amid civic gloom, a promising solution materialized. Why not build a marina along the eroded shorefront to protect the shore and revive civic fortunes? The marina certainly would not be bothered by any sand shoaling. "We were financially prepared to live without sand," recalls city official Walter Moranda.

At this point, federal officials told Port Hueneme to hold everything. Erosion was extending 6 miles downcoast and threatening a federal facility, Point Mugu navy missile base.

Public funds now were suddenly available for beach nourishment. All that was needed was sand and a feeder beach. The Corps of Engineers expropriated the marina idea and moved it upcoast to a point where a marina breakwater would trap sand before it sluiced into Hueneme Submarine Canyon. The trapped sand is now bypassed to a feeder beach below the canyon and the harbor jetty. The beach is Port Hueneme's, and it is rebuilt every two years.

With its shorefront more or less stable, Port Hueneme can redevelop its deteriorated shore properties. The rebuilt outfall lies beneath some 30 feet of sand to compensate for periodic erosion. "I think it's fair to say that the harbor jetty set back Port Hueneme's growth several years," says Moranda.

After installing countless seawalls and artificial beaches, the federal government finds the goal of a safe and stabilized American shore more and more elusive. A Corps study finds that action to halt significant erosion along 2,700 miles of American shore will cost an estimated $1.8 billion, plus $73 million in annual maintenance. At the same time, after reviewing what happened to $15 million worth of Corps beach erosion control projects, the General Accounting Office observed, "At present, no structural solution has been devised which will ensure the permanent preservation of the nation's shoreline and coastal areas."

This no-win situation becomes all the more galling when one realizes that disaster-prone development on barrier islands is often encouraged by federal grants for infrastructure—bridges, sewer plants, roads, airports. Thus Congress itself is providing cradle to the grave subsidies for careless coastal development, from roads to disaster relief.

One federal grant will rebuild a bridge wiped out by a

hurricane to serve 1,200 residents on Alabama's hurricane-prone Dauphin Island. Cost of the bridge: $32 million. This works out to a $26,000 federal subsidy per resident, while major cities must cut back on urban transit projects. Island ferry service would be a cheaper alternative and less vulnerable to the next hurricane.

Senators Dale Bumpers (D.-AR), and John Chafee (R.-RI) and Congressman Philip Burton (D.-CA), member of the House Committee on Interior and Insular Affairs, want Congress to eliminate federal infrastructure grants to remaining undeveloped islands. Bills to accomplish this have been supported by such diverse groups as the National Taxpayers Union and Friends of the Earth. Laurance Rockefeller, chair of the Barrier Islands Coalition, charges that present federal policy "is burning a hole in the taxpayer's pocket at the same time as it endangers human life and impairs vital natural systems." There is also support for more federal acquisition of these undeveloped islands. One federal study estimates that developed barrier islands will soak up some $11.2 billion in various federal grants over the next twenty years—five to six times more than the figure needed to acquire the remaining undeveloped barrier islands and thus cut the growing federal disaster liability. Federal budget constraints may limit acquisition efforts.

Given the commercial popularity of the shore, coastal developers would probably still find it profitable to encroach on the beach zone even without federal grants.

In some coastal states, including California, Oregon, and Florida, new construction must be set back from the active beach zone, and dunes must be preserved. The natural vegetation line indicates the upper limit of the extreme high tides and storm surf. (Driftwood and heavier urban debris may be piled up here too.) This vegetation line is often used to identify the edge of the active beach zone and to establish proper construction setbacks. A strategy of submission can benefit existing communities as well. Unlike some of its cluttered urban counterparts, the shorefront at Hilo, Hawaii, is spacious and open, populated by picnickers and fishermen. Was a far-sighted planner or civic organization responsible for such a hospitable shorefront? Not quite. The initial agent of change was a train of devastating seismic sea waves (tsunamis or tidal waves) generated by a submarine earthquake in 1960. After losing sixty-one lives and millions of dollars in property damage, Hilo relocated its shorefront commercial and residential district to higher ground.

The shorefront now serves as an open space safety buffer. Reborn out of tragedy, Hilo's shorefront is one of the nation's most scenic . . . and a graceful reminder that coastal communities do not need to rebuild for a return engagement with disaster. We cannot build the seawalls long enough or the artificial dunes high enough to disaster-proof the American shore.

Such coastal initiatives promise to conserve both beaches and the public purse. Given the tremendous economic gain to be made by subdividing the beach zone, these measures require considerable public support to be implemented. So do measures to maintain sand transport in critical coastal watersheds. Whether the American public's obvious desire for beach recreation will translate into political action to protect beaches remains to be seen. The costly legacy of barrier island development will be an instructive reminder of what happens when we take the sandy shore for granted. Italy is having enough trouble with just one Venice; we have built a whole series of Venices along our shore. What goes on in front of and, for that matter, behind the modest beach vegetation line will tell just how well we are learning to respect critical beach processes.

The pressure to develop beach tourism in developing nations and tropical islands could trigger a new round of beach erosion. For a small island, loss of the shore may be a prelude to the loss of the land itself. Restoring a beach backed by a bluff or a continent is one thing; restoring a beach backed by a coral atoll or a small coastal plain is another.

The solution to a sand shortage will require funding as well as scientific and technical ingenuity. Will we have to install expensive sand sluiceways on dams and release precious water to transport that sand to the ocean? Dr. Inman has suggested the possible recycling of the sand transport: breakwaters upcoast of submarine canyons would trap sand, and pipelines would pump the trapped sand back up to a feeder beach. Energy costs could be high.

Obstacles to natural sand transport will increase. There are plans to install artificial islands, offshore airports, and high-speed causeways in the nearshore. Creating artificial means for sand to bypass these impediments can moderate interference with sand transport. At the same time, however, some of these projects may shunt sand into deep water.

Sand transport can become a transnational issue. Some 1,000 square miles of coastal watershed tributary to the California coast lie in Mexico's Baja California. Historically, a border area has supplied sand to San Diego's Imperial Beach. A Mexican dam is now disrupting the sand flow, and Imperial Beach has been receding. In the Mediterranean, the sand transport system transcends the borders of Egypt, Israel, and Lebanon. A groin race to rival that of the New Jersey shore could occur here unless the three nations can manage the sand–ocean interface on a multilateral basis.

The enigma of adequate beach management arises when I visit a popular summer beach where the sands are still present. It is a delight to watch the beach come alive with activity. Unlike our predecessors at Brighton or Baiae, we are much more adept and skilled in the beach arts, from catching a Frisbee between our legs to spiking a volleyball or riding a wave. But we still have to learn the ultimate skill, sustaining the beach itself. I think we realize, as never before, the need for this skill, but not the amount of careful effort and planning that it entails.

13

The Aquatic Boomerang

SOME OF AMERICA'S FINEST RIV-
ers merge here. But no water skiers, spawning salmon, or canoeists are to be seen. Work clothes rather than French-cut bikinis
are in fashion. The point of merger is the concrete confines of
sewage disposal plants in our coastal cities. The name of the
riverine blend is raw sewage. It departs as treated effluent, to be
dumped in coastal waters traversed by whales, nuclear subs, and
Liberian oil tankers. The mouth for this polyglot discharge is a
concrete outfall.

During a drought, many natural rivers run low or dry. But
not coastal outfalls. Drought or no drought, the plants prepare
diverted river flows for ocean disposal. This is the ultimate in
conventional, water-borne disposal, esteemed by professional so-

cieties, extolled by Schools of Sanitary Engineering, and funded by the Environmental Protection Agency (EPA).

Ironically, we are turning to systems once regarded as backward or primitive to help rescue us from the costly shortcomings of disposal at sea. This change in attitude has come about because we are in a real pickle. We are investing more and more public money in large, central sewage disposal plants so they will not pollute our rivers, lakes, bays, and coastal waters. But this investment can be jeopardized by ever-escalating sewage loads from regional water transfers. In short, we are running out of treatment capacity, sewage sinks, and wilderness watersheds. If this bind is not bad enough, imported water systems can deprive the wastewater systems of a much-needed source of revenue: water reclamation. We have developed two very large, centralized systems that can work at extraordinary cross-purposes.

How did we get ourselves into such a predicament? With the best of historical intentions. In the nineteenth century and the early twentieth century, centralized water and wastewater systems were considered critical in safeguarding growing urban areas from potential diseases posed by individual or decentralized systems, whether it be local wells, outhouses, septic tanks, or rooftop cisterns. Ancient Rome had to rely on gravity feed to make its stone aqueducts and sewers work. Two nineteenth-century advances—the steam pump and the cast-iron pipe—facilitated the shift to long-distance transportation of water and sewage. Water could now be pumped over hills to reach distant cities or coastal outfalls. Given the health epidemics of that era, one question was neglected: could decentralized systems be better operated or maintained? The only good outhouse, to paraphrase another saying of the day, was an outhouse razed. The urban shift to water-borne disposal, from toilet flush to outfall discharge, was well underway.

Even sewage farming—the land application of municipal effluent to crops or pasture—went down the proverbial outfall. Plant nutrients in domestic sewage were valued by European farmers as early as the sixteenth century. Cheap synthetic fertiliz-

---

ers and imported Peruvian guano were still in the future. Communities became interested in land application of sewage in the nineteenth century. In 1865, one British commission stated that "land application was the only way to avoid river pollution and make a profit." Some towns cancelled sewage agreements with farmers to start city-owned operations. Sewage farms as large as 300 acres served cities with 50,000 people. Edinburgh was a pioneer in sewage utilization. Paris and Berlin followed suit. In 1899, most of the 143 sewage treatment systems in the United States and Canada used land treatment. But community growth could outstrip system capacity. Raw sewage bypasses became common, particularly during cold weather. Rather than acquire more land to expand capacity, the communities switched to water-borne disposal, which seemed cheaper at the time. The old sewage farms were paved over and sewered.

The need to recruit local water bodies as sewage sinks added impetus to the urban drive to import water from remote wilderness watersheds. Booming coastal cities on the Atlantic seaboard extended their water pipes to out-of-state watersheds. Boston reached out to the Connecticut River, New York City to the Delaware. A semiarid coastal city on the Pacific Coast, Los Angeles, would develop the most extended water reach—into Owens Valley over 400 miles away. Although originally intended to supplement local sources, imported water became the predominant source as urban growth boomed. Local surface and subsurface water supplies became too polluted.

As urban areas grew, water and wastewater systems became more centralized, at both technical and political levels, culminating in massive federal water and sewer programs. Yet each system still retains a separate political identity. With one turn of the water faucet or toilet handle, the flow shifts from the jurisdiction of the water department to the jurisdiction of the sewage or sanitation department. No matter that the flow may merely graze a coffee cup or dinner plate. It is raw sewage. It must receive the same pretreatment and outfall discharge as high-strength industrial wastes.

These systems, highly centralized yet separate, can persist for reasons other than historic health concerns. Onsite systems meet the immediate needs of the individual or the existing community. But try hooking up a suburban tract to the nearest cistern or septic tank. With a central system, you merely extend the water and sewer pipes and you can play land developer.

Not surprisingly, suburban land developers are fond of central systems. This perspective can take a novel twist. Governing boards exist that exclude from representation the very people they tax. This situation seems somewhat inconsistent with the idea behind the Boston Tea Party. Yet, to be elected to some water district boards, you must own land. Furthermore, the more you own, the more votes you get—one vote for each dollar of assessed value. Some water board directors receive more votes than state governors.

Why have the courts tolerated a property qualification on the vote? Only one class of citizens, farm owners, is generally involved. However, this judicial tolerance assumes farmers intend to farm forever. Large landowners on the suburban fringe may prefer to urbanize. With a landowner-controlled water district, the landowner can float general obligation bonds to water and sewer his property. No regional sewer plant to hook into? Float more bonds to build a sewer plant. No money to operate the plant? Impose sewer and water rates on incoming residents. With this ability to fund private development through public funds, landowners don't need to fiddle with onsite systems.

As a general rule, the larger the water or sewer system, the larger the fee for consultants and contractors. Septic tanks, sewage farming, or well systems have a tough time competing against central systems in this regard. Another influential sector of society can thus find special virtues in central systems.

Such systems are also popular in industrialized socialist and communist nations. They fit in well with the centralized engineering practices of any industrial society, ideology aside.

These systems thus enjoy a tremendous degree of unquestioned acceptance. However, so-called primitive or backward systems still manage to persist, even in urban regions. Melbourne, Australia, has irrigated cattle pastures with its wastewater for decades. The city's bay is spared large sewage loads. Cattle sales help offset treatment costs. A million tons of produce annually, from tomatoes to hot peppers, grow on farmland irrigated by Mexico City's wastewater. This wastewater reuse system also irrigates world-famous Chapultepec Park.

Nations that find resource self-sufficiency a political as well as climatic necessity also employ water reclamation. Israel and South Africa are two examples.

In the United States, land application survived primarily in the arid southwest, short of both water and water bodies to serve as sewage sinks. California and Texas, so reliant on central systems, have a long history of wastewater land application systems. Early in this century, Los Angeles engaged in sewage farming. The windblown sand dunes that once comprised Golden Gate Park were made to bloom with San Francisco wastewater. The same source still irrigates fuchsias and New Zealand ferns and fills ponds used by goldfish and recreational boaters.

Because of its historic use and relative success, land application remains as a perennial alternative to water transfers and sewage disposal. Four decades ago, Ray Goudey informed the civic leaders of metropolitan Los Angeles, where he worked as a sanitary engineer, that it would be cheaper to reuse wastewater rather than tap another wilderness watershed. His political superiors preferred to lengthen the aqueducts and the outfalls. The Los Angeles City outfall must rank as the world's largest manmade marine artifact, a modern competitor to Alexandria's fabled lighthouse and the Colossus at Rhodes. Stand this outfall on end and it would shadow Mount Everest. It is seven-and-a-half miles long. Perhaps some day a poet in a scuba tank will grace this structure with a Byronic ode.

In the 1950s, officials with the Sanitation Districts of Los Angeles County wanted to shift from large disposal plants to smaller reclamation plants dispersed throughout the service area. Would the Metropolitan Water District of Southern California

(MWD) be interested in a local source of water to irrigate farms and recharge groundwater basins? MWD was upset. MWD regarded sewage salvage as an unwelcome diversion from the main task at hand, approval of more water transfers. To MWD, the destiny of sewage plants was to dispose of imported water.

The fact that water reclamation uses less energy than water transfers was not significant in the fuel-rich 1950s. Moreover, it was cheaper to use water bodies, including the ocean, for sewage disposal than to use urban land for wastewater application. Parks alone cannot soak up urban sewage production. Nutrients in treated effluent can help fertilize soils, but cheap synthetic fertilizers were now available. (From 1930 to the early 1970s, no major sanitary engineering text even bothered to include a section on land treatment.)

Water-borne disposal is also more adept at transferring the consequences of inadequate sewage treatment—including odors—downriver and downwind than land treatments. Despite its reputation for pollution, water-borne disposal has thrived because it has seemed cheaper (more "cost-effective") than land application. Thus the nutrients that would have fertilized our farms and parks served to trigger algal blooms and pollute our most cherished water bodies. With its polluting prowess now evident, water-borne disposal inspires the federal Clean Water Program and the massive EPA sewer grants program, today the nation's largest public works program. Washington has intervened into local affairs to an extent never foreseen by the original promoters of central systems.

In 1974 I was retained as a consultant to the California Coastal Commission. With water more scarce and sewage pollution more common, I thought the time was ripe for water reclamation. I recommended that MWD and the Los Angeles sanitation districts enter into a joint powers agreement to develop reclamation. The Commission liked this proposal, but MWD was upset once again. MWD branded reclamation as "premature" and the joint powers agreement as "particularly inappropriate." MWD sensed something sinister was afoot—that the proposal "has been made to prohibit southern California from obtaining water from the State Water Project" (a project to divert water from central and northern California). Sewage plants must learn to keep their place. The coastal outfalls must continue to divert more wastewater to the ocean than most California rivers discharge.

Under its grant program, EPA seeks to upgrade disposal through "regionalization." Smaller disposal plants are consolidated into one central or super plant to achieve that nirvana of public administrators, economy of scale. Larger plants are supposed to be more efficient, better equipped, and better staffed. EPA can fund 75 percent of plant construction and can impose sanctions against communities that prefer not to regionalize.

Combine federal sewer grants with federal highway, water, and flood control grants and you have the basic infrastructure necessary to urbanize farms, ranches, and vacant lots on the suburban fringe. Land developers and their water districts become well acquainted with EPA's funding programs. In fast-growing Orange County in southern California, large corporate land developers such as Philip Morris (Mission Viejo) and Avco (Laguna Niguel) float multi-million-dollar bonds and lobby for state and federal water and sewer grants.

This urbanizing impetus can antagonize rural residents who find themselves being taxed for a service they don't want and which destroys their very lifestyle. Proposals to regionalize can generate the same heated community disputes as freeway route hearings. California's Humboldt Bay region has been engaged in such a dispute for a decade.

In these disputes, some residents invariably question whether a central plant will improve treatment. Initially, these critics were regarded as septic tank buffs eager to protect their right to pollute the nearest lake or bay. A major sewage spill in San Francisco Bay has served to moderate this attitude and, at the same time, has brought wholesale reliance on water-borne disposal into question. In 1979, billions of gallons of marginally treated sewage laced with ammonia, bacteria, chlorine, and floating matter gushed into the bay's south end, where circulation is sluggish. The sewage shock load depressed oxygen levels. An estimated eight tons of shrimp were lost. The spill lasted for thirty-six days.

This massive sewage spill was generated by a plant EPA has considered to be a model in its grant program. The $150 million San Jose–Santa Clara Water Pollution Control Plant covers some 1,700 acres close by the south end of the bay. With its concrete structures, spacious grassy malls, and reflecting pond, the complex exudes the quiet serenity of a deluxe cemetery fit for celebrity burials.

In the plant, microscopic bacteria break down and remove impurities in sewage. This is known as the activated sludge system, which is considered more efficient than wastewater lagooning but can also be more complicated. A change in the strain of bacteria occurred. A new, larger strain clogged the system. This is called "bulk sludging." The plant had to bypass partially treated sewage. The spill was on.

The disruption of a $150 million facility by a change in bacteria suggests how demanding the new generation of central plants can be. They require the same careful technical attention as a modern mechanized brewery or winery. It took a month to regain operational stability. Plant officials had to call in a private consulting firm.

In the wake of the spill, San Jose discovered that it had to spend over $800,000 on new staff members—including a training instructor—and on engineers hired to study plant reliability. What happened to the purported regionalization benefit of a better-trained and better-qualified staff?

While EPA funds much of the plant construction, local jurisdictions must fund operation and maintenance (O&M in the trade). These costs can trigger substantial budget increases. I received an early warning of this when my wife waved a local utility bill and declared, "Do you know we now pay more for sewage than for water?" The residents of Greenville, Maine, are very aware of this trend. They closed up their septic tanks, hooked into a new EPA-funded sewage system, and saw their sewage bills run over $200 a year. The $3 million system does not work, some residents refuse to pay their bills, and EPA is designing a new $3 million facility.

Some communities can find training instructors expendable until a plant disruption occurs. As EPA Administrator Douglas Costle observed in 1979, "O&M costs are rising rapidly due to inflationary trends in the cost of manpower, energy, and chemicals, and the increasing complexity of the plants themselves."

At the time of the spill, some thirty plant positions were vacant. Why would San Jose, part of a metropolitan region with California's highest median income, understaff its plant? Early in 1979, a city salary freeze was in effect, caused in part by Proposition 13. One sanitary engineer who left in February returned to the plant in September as a key member of the private consulting team. The central plants, by expanding the demand for technical manpower, can generate recruitment binds and brain pirating not unlike that in the San Jose electronics industry.

The plant was not even prepared to notify authorities properly about the spill. The spill was flowing for over a week before a dismayed shrimp fisherman called it to official attention. Why were authorities left with perplexed fishermen as a pollution monitoring system? In language strikingly similar to that used by operators of the Three Mile Island nuclear plant during its hiatus, San Jose officials said they thought the problem was only "temporary" and "under control." To plant officials, the main problem was not so much late notification as media "exaggeration" of the spill.

If not promptly notified, health officials cannot immediately assess potential health threats and prevent people from swimming or even harvesting potentially toxic marine life. Marine life can decompose rapidly and deprive investigators of evidence to assess a spill's impact. California fish and game official Mike Rugg placed fathead minnows in a water sample from the stricken area. All died within six to forty minutes.

Court sanctions, including fines of up to $25,000 a day, can be imposed for discharge violations and for failure to report such violations. The former superintendent for the Little Rock, Arkansas, treatment plant received a suspended prison sentence in 1978 for submitting false reports on plant performance to EPA. The former superintendent of the wastewater treatment plant in New Albany, Indiana, was fined $1,500 for filing false discharge compliance reports. The attorney general of California has filed a civil action against the City of San Jose for discharge violations that could result in a record $300,000 fine. (Such fines go into a state cleanup and abatement fund for pollution incidents caused by unknown parties.) One commercial fishing firm has filed a claim against the city for loss of income due to the interrupted shrimp fishery.

Will stepped-up court action ensure better operation of regional plants? Perl .ips. However, false reporting reflects tremendous pressures on plant superintendents caught between the technical demands of large plants and limited O&M funds. These costs will eventually exceed construction costs. In terms of municipal budget demands, sewage may run second only to schools.

Is regionalization resulting in federally funded plants that cities are unprepared or unqualified to operate? As Costle conceded to Congress, "one-half of the inspected plants . . . failed to meet their original design standards and about 25 percent have severe or chronic operation and maintenance problems." A random sample by the General Accounting Office of 242 plants showed an even more dismal picture—87 percent of the plants were in violation of their discharge permit.

As the San Jose spill dramatized, one large spill from a central plant can match, if not exceed, pollution damage from a series of the smaller, supposedly inefficient plants. Potential single point shock loads from central plants haunt this nation's bays, rivers, and coastal waters. The San Jose spill, according to the Regional Water Quality Control Board, "unreasonably affected and prevented full enjoyment of commercial and sport fishing, marine and freshwater habitat, boating, esthetic and other beneficial bay uses." Dedicated community efforts to restore the bay for urban recreation can now hinge on the reliability of a plant whose complex processes can be jinxed by bacteria, and whose site serves to maximize damage from a bypass. One prominent hostage to this predicament is the San Francisco Bay National Wildlife Refuge, which flanks the disposal plant. In August, 1980, oxygen levels in nearby tidal sloughs plummeted again when the plant suffered another bulk sludging upset.

Some troubled plants may become obsolete before they become reliable. The San Jose plant is fast approaching its design flow capacity of 143 million gallons daily. Aging sewer lines and poor joints permit groundwater to infiltrate the system and augment wasteloads. (Raw sewage can decompose and corrode pipes en route to the central plant.) Estimated cost to upgrade 300 miles of sewer line: $15 million. O&M does not come cheap.

There is more to these spiraling wasteloads than aging sewers. Known as the Prune Capitol in 1950, San Jose will soon pass San Francisco to become the Bay Area's largest city and the third largest on the Pacific Coast. Federal grants, including sewer grants, help pave "the way to San Jose." Central sewage systems can thus be more successful in inducing growth than attaining reliability. EPA's Costle concedes "the grants program has contributed to the underwriting of suburban 'sprawl' in some metropolitan areas." As the smog overhead indicates, the $150 million plant is not alone in suffering from urban overload. "You leave your heart in San Francisco and your lungs in San Jose," goes one local saying.

Another federal underwriter may add to the miseries of EPA's model plant by the bay. Some 1.6 million pounds of explosives are blasting a seven-mile-long tunnel through nearby smog-shrouded hills. The tunnel will help divert water from a wilderness watershed, the Trinity, to the former Prune Capitol of the World. With assorted dams, canals, high-pressure pipelines and energy-guzzling pumps, the San Felipe Project will cost $200 million. The financial angel: another federal agency, the Water and Power Resources Service (formerly the U.S. Bureau of Reclamation).

It may seem strange that one federal water agency can shepherd a project that exceeds the treatment capacity of a facility funded by another federal water agency, but this is the logical outcome of managing water and wastewater as two separate systems. The central plants, despite their modern appearance, are primitive in concept. They continue to treat sewage as a waste rather than a resource. If reclaimed, effluent from the San Jose plant could reduce the need for massive new water diversion schemes while providing revenues to offset o&m costs. Ironically enough, the Water and Power Resources Service rejected a request by EPA for a year's delay on the San Felipe Project to study water reclamation alternatives.

Such carefree water transfers upriver now pose as much of a threat to our aquatic heritage as polluting outfalls downriver and downcoast. Massive water transfers from Atlantic and Gulf watersheds can alter salinity levels downstream, affecting movements of shad and striped bass and the habitats of oysters and clams. Such water transfers on the Pacific coast can dehydrate spawning streams for salmon and steelhead trout.

Tidewaters from San Francisco Bay and river flows fed by Sierra snowmelts meet in the productive marsh mazes of the California Delta. A substantial portion of the river flows may be diverted hundreds of miles south to southern California, finally reaching the ocean via an outfall. A multi-million-dollar project called the Peripheral Canal would accomplish this feat. In the process, the sensitive aquatic interface in the Delta and San Francisco Bay could be disrupted, impairing a Delta existence based on fishing and farming.

In Russia, rivers that bring nutrients to the Black Sea and the Azov Sea have been diverted for canal and reservoir projects. As a result, two seas once rich in herring, mackerel, sturgeon and bream are nearly lifeless, according to Dr. David Tolmazin of the

Ukrainian Academy of Sciences. To restore the seas, Russia must engage in the same costly programs that the disrupted Great Lakes ecosystem requires.

The 1980 National Estuarine Conference in San Antonio, Texas, sponsored by the U.S. Fish and Wildlife Service, issued a summary concluding that "no more than 25% to 30% of the historical river flow can be diverted without disastrous ecological consequences to the receiving estuary." The conference summary recommended that EPA establish a standard to ensure that current and proposed water diversion projects do not sacrifice downstream estuaries. This proposed standard could conflict with the efforts of Secretary of the Interior Watt to solicit new water-diversion projects from western governors.

The star-crossed San Jose plant provides us with one more catch-22. A nearby industrial area is willing to buy the plant's treated effluent. The hangup is the funding for lines to transport the effluent, which must be kept separate from potable drinking water lines. One potential funding source is EPA. However, as a general rule, EPA will only fund projects in which reclamation is needed to meet federal water quality standards. The plant's improved level of treatment, when operating properly, meets these standards. Thus water-borne disposal continues to survive and thrive amid droughts, public funding cutbacks, spiraling O&M costs, and periodic disruptions.

In the wake of one drought, California Governor Jerry Brown announced an ambitious state water reclamation program that is now jeopardized by the same EPA funding constraint. State and local jurisdictions can rely on their own funds . . . or lobby for federal water transfers like the $200 million, tunnel-blasting San Felipe project.

EPA now finds itself caught in similar policy binds. Congress is less enthusiastic about funding conventional disposal plants that turn out to be surprise polluters. The General Accounting Office (GAO) is urging EPA to shift from conventional or "structural" projects to nonstructural measures, including low-flow toilets and showerheads to reduce wasteloads. One obstacle GAO cites is "architectural and engineering firms' tendency to favor large projects, since their fee is tied directly to a project's cost."

While Congress and GAO admonish EPA to be more thrifty, cities and urban states lobby for more grants. The Gulf Coast States and California seek sewer grants to keep abreast of growth. Older Atlantic regions, which are losing population, seek EPA grants to replace aging sewers. Some pipes in Manchester, New Hampshire, date back to the Civil War era. Sewage systems may be the best-preserved part of our urban past. The estimated cost of upgrading sewer lines in eleven New England states is $4.5 billion.

While EPA urges its municipal clients to be more frugal, EPA's enforcement arm may cite them for violating federal water quality standards. EPA's dual role as standards enforcer and as paymaster for plant construction promises to become schizophrenic. Illinois is suing EPA for withholding grants the state claims it needs to meet EPA water standards. If a court sides with Illinois, watch for Congress to amend the Clean Water Act to avert a fifty-state assault on the federal treasury. EPA's estimated cost for the construction and repair of municipal disposal plants and sewers through the year 2000 is $106.2 billion. The estimated cost of controlling stormwater runoff is another $62 billion.

Amid this fiscal crossfire, and with the ambitious goals of the Clean Water Act at stake, EPA as well as state water officials are becoming more tolerant of alternatives to costly central disposal plants.

14

Detours Around
the Outfalls

THE CORN FIELDS LIE BEYOND A
water storage pond favored by whistling swans. The corn, ripe
and plump, will provide another $1 million harvest. The farmer
is Michigan's Muskegon County, and the 5,000-acre farm is part
of its wastewater system.

The county received pollution notices instead of money
when Lake Michigan received the wastewater. A lakefront occu-
pant, Scott Paper, was ready to depart rather than have its operations curtailed by pollution injunctions. Lakefront boating and
fishing firms were ready to depart for bluer waters. The county,
with a population of 190,000, was being done in by its own
sewage.

Rather than build a super sewer plant, the county decided
to try land application. After being aerated in lagoons, effluent

is sprayed on the fields. Besides income, the corn fields provide the equivalent of tertiary water treatment. The nutrients that once triggered algal blooms help speed growth of the corn. The crop-soil filter decomposes organic matter and filters out suspended matter. A nineteenth-century sewage farmer from Britain would feel at home in the Muskegon corn fields.

Scott Paper is still around, benefitting from one of the nation's lowest sewer rates. So are the boat dealers. The lakefront is blue again. EPA, which helped fund the capital costs, has memorialized the Muskegon experience in a color brochure. The Muskegon project is only one of a surprising range of alternatives available once the super sewer plant syndrome is overcome. These alternatives can lead to an unexpected dividend—a more self-reliant community.

Even septic tanks can enjoy official favor. Under California legislation encouraged by architect Sim Van der Ryn and State Senator Peter Behr, septic tank districts can be formed to ensure that individual tanks operate properly. To avoid the pollution fines and the need for a sewage plant, Stinson Beach north of San Francisco has established such a district. Some forty-seven failed tank systems have been voluntarily repaired by owners at an average cost of $1,400, according to San Francisco Regional Water Quality Board official Lester Feldman. The district has temporarily cut off water service to owners tardy in uprating defective tanks. The district is funded by a user charge ($104 per home annually) and a state demonstration grant. The state has also approved a $100,000 loan for homeowner repairs.

Another onsite wastewater system may return to official favor. In the late 1960s and early 1970s, summer resort lakes in Scandinavia were being transformed into polluted, algae-clogged ponds. The culprits were septic tanks, subject to excessive seepage in poor soil conditions. Sweden, Finland, and Norway frantically sought ways to phase out septic tanks. Some private firms studied the use of compost toilets that use no water. One firm devised an improved, odor-free, fly-tight model made out of fiberglass that passed health tests for the presence of disease-causing bacteria and viruses. Over 5,000 units of the Carousel Toilet have been installed in Norway. The benefits include reduced water consumption and utility bills, cleaner lakes, and humus for flower gardens. Ski resorts are participating in the revival of compost toilets.

These units are now being manufactured in the self-styled surfing capitol of California—Huntington Beach—and being installed in Oregon, Washington, and Maine. The unit only handles toilet waste, not graywater from kitchen and shower units. A septic tank unit half the size of a regular tank can handle graywater and avoid the use of the nearest hillside as a surface leach field.

Other onsite water reclamation systems are being revived, too. During a recent drought that required water rationing, residents of the Monterey, California region realized they were wasting 18,000 acre feet of water—more than their total annual water usage—to the Pacific Ocean each year. This is local rainfall carried away by the region's elaborate storm drain system, from gutters on rooftops to concrete drains under the streets. William Woodworth, a director of the Monterey Peninsula Water Management District, is leading a drive to capture this wasted water through use of cisterns. Rather than buckets or large rooftop tanks, pipe cisterns made of lightweight plastic can replace gutter downspouts. With eight pipe cisterns, Woodworth collects 1,000 gallons of rainwater each winter to water his grass, plants and trees in the summer. Needless to say, this onsite system requires less energy than a water import system and loses less water to evaporation and leaks. Rainwater is better quality than imported water, which can accumulate high levels of dissolved solids and salts that corrode water appliances. A house with a roof area of 2,000 square feet can capture 1,247 gallons of water in cisterns with just one inch of rainfall. One potential problem: rainwater turned acidic by sulfurous air pollution.

Cisterns and rooftop ponding can also reduce storm runoff that pollutes local waters. The General Accounting Office (GAO) recommends rooftop ponding as one alternative to expensive runoff control measures. Industrial and commercial structures with flat roofs can store up to six inches of water for cooling, fire prevention, and washing. Roofs must be maintained properly to avoid overloading. The Skyline urban renewal project in Denver, Colorado, uses both rooftop storage and plaza ponding to reduce stormwater runoff in its eighty-acre project. California now extends tax credits to property owners who install cisterns.

While onsite systems are returning to favor, water reclamation is staging a comeback in suburban and urban areas. Ironically, many innovative advances in reclamation have been developed by those small "inefficient" plants that manage to avoid the taxing embrace of regional sewage authorities. For example, the town of Arcata, in the Humboldt Bay region of northern California, nurtures salmon and trout smolts (juveniles) in wastewater treatment lagoons.

Can centralized plants shift from disposal to reclamation? Being situated downhill or downgrade to take advantage of gravity sewage feed, they must pump reclaimed water uphill to users, thus raising energy costs. Why not decentralize and locate smaller plants uphill? The Sanitation Districts of Los Angeles County built reclamation plants for groundwater discharge in its upper service area. However, neighborhood opposition shot down a similar proposal in the San Jose area. Other regional sewage authorities feel financially committed to a central plant and its massive trunk sewer lines.

The reproductive needs of ducks may help transform such lowland sites into a benefit. While loss of saltwater wetlands has been slowed by tighter public controls, restoration of freshwater wetlands is lagging. Many ducks that feed in estuaries require freshwater habitat for their newborn. In the shadow of an industrial area and freeway on San Francisco Bay, a restored freshwater wetland now shelters ducks of all ages. The source of fresh water is the Mountain View Sanitation District. The district was faced with the cost to pipe treated effluent to a bay outfall to meet dilution standards. The state approved the wetlands alternative as a mitigation measure that enhances the environment. Mosquito fish take care of mosquitos. To better mix water in the pond, wind power is enlisted to turn an underwater propeller. The mixing keeps dissolved oxygen high and algal blooms low. The project originally cost $130,000, and maintenance costs $20,000 yearly. The estimated cost of the pipeline alternative was $2 million plus.

The beleaguered San Jose plant lies next to lowlands prone to both flooding and severe seismic shaking. Rather than urbanize these disaster-prone lands, they could be restored as freshwater wetlands too. San Jose State University biology Professor Tom Harvey, the Sierra Club, and the San Francisco Bay National Wildlife Refuge have urged the San Jose plant to participate in such a project. If they do, the city destined to be the largest in the bay region would also have the safest and most spacious bayfront.

Groundwater pumping can deplete coastal aquifers and allow ocean water to intrude. Ergo, another lowland reclamation opportunity. Palo Alto, California, uses its treated effluent for groundwater recharge to resist saline intrusion. So does the Camp Pendleton Marine Base near San Diego. Reclaimed water is also being used for this purpose in Texas, Arizona, and Florida.

Lubbock, Texas, on a windswept, arid plain far from oceans and free-flowing rivers, enjoys more aquatic recreation than cities whose waterways suffer from pollution and water diversion projects. The city's reclaimed effluent sustains a chain of four recreation lakes that swarm with bass and catfish. A canyon that once served as an industrial back alley and urban dump hosts the lake chain, along with fishing piers, sandstone waterfalls, foot bridges, pine stands and raft races. Lubbock had a headstart in skillful water reuse. For over 40 years, a local farmer has used the city's treated effluent to irrigate up to 5,000 acres of farmland.

David Argo of the Orange County Water District in southern California manages a plant that transforms effluent into water safe enough to be injected into coastal groundwater basins and extracted later for use. Reclaimed water can have a high salt content that exceeds state standards. Through a process called reverse osmosis (RO), the district can desalt treated effluent. Argo finds that the actual cost of imported water exceeds the cost of water produced by his "Water Factory 21." More energy is required to import water. However, because state and federal grants subsidize imported water projects, the water can be sold below actual cost. "It's going to take action at the governor's level to reform these types of pricing problems," says Argo. (The EPA funding limit on reclaimed water lines has temporarily derailed Argo's plan to expand into landscape irrigation.)

Industry is finding reclaimed water attractive. Some industrial water uses, such as cooling, do not require drinking water. Bethlehem Steel uses Baltimore's secondary effluent. Bethlehem saves some money while the wasteload on Chesapeake Bay is reduced somewhat. Kaiser Steel in Fontana, California, recycles its process waters. Such industrial reuse could become as critical, if not as glamorous, as irrigating Golden Gate Park or corn fields. Nationwide, gross water withdrawals for manufacturing and for power plant cooling exceed those for municipal consumption by more than ten times.

The community of Hercules, located along San Pablo Bay, California, has been faced with a familiar choice: hook into a large central sewage system or forego future growth. To regain some control over its civic destiny, Hercules is testing the "Solar Aquacell" developed by Solar Aquasystems of Encinitas, California. In this system, raw sewage first percolates upward through a bed of biologically active sludge. This stage is anaerobic (functions without oxygen). Risk of oxygen depletion from primary effluent shock loads is avoided. Methane gas produced in this stage can be sold to offset the cost of the system. The wastewater then enters lagoons where water hyacinths help remove remaining contaminants, lead, mercury, and cadmium. Hyacinth crops can be composted and used to condition soil or feed livestock, depending on the uptake level of heavy metals and potentially toxic compounds.

This system requires no chemicals, outside energy sources, or mazes of concrete treatment tanks. It is cheaper to construct and operate than conventional systems. Hercules, with a lucrative tax base stemming from the presence of an oil refinery, can fund the system without federal or state grants. If the system proves efficient and reliable, treated effluent will irrigate an extensive community greenbelt. Current capacity—350,000 gallons daily —could be scaled up to 2 million gallons.

Will the use of aquatic plants and animals in wastewater treatment make aquaculture a flourishing urban enterprise, or is this taking biological treatment too far? Fish control plant growth in one wastewater lagoon system. The plant eaters are then sold to food fish dealers to offset treatment costs. This system is not used by some backward hamlet deep in the recesses of Africa or Asia; it serves the city of Munich, Germany. The fish is carp, considered a delicacy fit for holiday occasions in Europe. Given such options, commercial water wonderlands of the future may reside next to urban sewage plants.

Is the solar aquacell concept strictly for use by small communities? San Diego is developing a one-million-gallon-a-day aquacell system. According to San Diego Water Department director R.D. King, the department also has the longest continually operating RO unit in the world. King plans to merge the new wastewater aquaculture unit with the RO unit to reduce energy needs further and to desalt the final effluent. The water will then be blended with other potable sources in a lake. EPA is assisting this project with a $2.5 million grant. The fact that San Diego combined its sewer and water services into one department two decades ago helps inspire such a broad perspective.

While promising, the shift to reclamation demands more careful planning than disposal. Without such foresight, reclamation districts can pollute too.

The Irvine Ranch Water District handles both water and sewer services for a fast-growing area in central Orange County. It has opted for land application of treated effluent rather than ocean disposal. While irrigation demands drop in the winter, sewage production remains constant. In the winter, surplus reclaimed water must be stored in a reservoir system originally designed for farming needs. Storm runoff competes for limited storage capacity. So do siltloads from careless construction site clearing. Storage in one reservoir has been cut back because its earth fill dam must be upgraded to meet state seismic standards. The district requires repeated emergency waivers to discharge reclaimed water into surface streams. One dam has had uncontrolled spillway flows two out of the last three years. The flows cut into a channel bank and ruptured a water line. The repair cost of $68,000 was billed to federal disaster relief. The emergency discharges tend to deflate a district claim that its reclamation system results in zero discharge.

The district has other headaches. In summer, reclaimed water is applied to farmland. On occasion, the water's high salt content can pollute groundwater and violate state standards. Some reclaimed water infiltrates the district sewer lines, so that the treatment plant must recycle salt as well as water.

The reclaimed water lines mainly serve agriculture, which pays a much lower water rate than urban users such as schools, community greenbelt associations, and public parks. The district is now trying to extend more lines to urban users who must irrigate with costly drinking water.

The district was originally controlled by the major landowner, an agricultural concern turned land developer, the Irvine Company. In 1979, Orange County Judge Edward Wallin found that the district's formation violated the one-man, one-vote principle and ordered a prompt transition to publicly elected directors. The suit was brought by the City of Irvine and a community organization, Irvine Tomorrow, whose counsel was the Center for Law in the Public Interest. The rise of reclamation can shake up the water establishment in many surprising ways.

As planning for reclamation improves, funding will remain a major obstacle. But even here there can be surprises. MWD, which disdained the ambitious reclamation plan of Los Angeles County sanitation officials three decades ago and rejected my recommendation seven years ago, has finally begun to study reclamation. It has even entered into a joint powers agreement with, of all people, the Los Angeles County sanitation officials. ("I thought we'd have to camouflage a sewage plant as an alpine lake before MWD would visit us," one sanitary official told me.) The study has found that present reclaimed water use of 50,000 acre feet a year could be increased eightfold to 400,000 acre feet. This could save on energy required to pump imported water over mountain ranges. Some 700,000 barrels of oil a year could be saved, according to project study director Wiley Horne.

Horne foresees that such energy savings could fund reclamation systems, including Argo's derailed plan to irrigate public parks. Indeed, by opting for more reclamation, southern California could regain more economic and political control over its own affairs. The frantic need to lobby federal and state agencies could be reduced.

Urban regions that ignore reclamation risk another problem. Some state constitutions prohibit wasteful use of water. The courts consider this constitutional admonition when judging whether urban regions can divert more water from rural areas. Reclamation dramatically expands water-efficient use ... and the legal liability of regions that ignore this opportunity. Semirural regions resent more than ever having their aquatic ecology drained to preserve car washes, fairways, plaza fountains, seven-gallon toilet flushes, and other one-shot water uses in a coastal megalopolis.

Will alternative water and wastewater systems become the wave to catch in the future? While economic and environmental factors are more favorable for such systems, the human attachment to old ways, even in the United States, cannot be underestimated. Events that cannot be readily predicted—major droughts, the state of public financing, new technical advances, the state of the economy—will have a major bearing. If alternative systems do take hold, some very exciting prospects may emerge. Land application would increase the value of conserving urban open space, whether as parks or as income-producing farms, forests, or aquaculture enterprises. And studies are underway regarding the export of coastal urban effluent in California by land outfall to inland farm regions. Land outfalls may offer a nutrient-rich product that is cheaper than state or federal project water. EPA reports that there are now over 3,000 land treatment systems in the United States that treat 3 million gallons of wastewater per day.

Some semirural areas are facing growth moratoriums because of bans on sewer hookups pending commitment to large regional sewage authorities. The ability of alternative systems to overcome growth constraints on a limited basis may transform land developers into appropriate technology buffs. It's true that public agencies must monitor alternative systems more closely than conventional disposal systems. (Arcata, pioneering in wastewater aquaculture, has been cited by state officials for accidental sewage spills into Humboldt Bay.) Otherwise, alternative systems can be manipulated as another dodge around water quality standards. Land treatment sites must be expanded to meet community growth or else they will duplicate the fate of the nineteenth-century sewage farms.

Large coastal urban areas, from New York City to Los Angeles, are the greatest fiscal victims of a throwaway economy, whether it be water or solids. A costly and losing urban battle to dispose of waste production ensues. Reuse promises a way out of this economic and political quagmire. For many communities, a shift from water-borne disposal to land application can make them more self-sufficient, both economically and politically.

By being so dependent on large central water systems, urban regions make themselves vulnerable to a whole range of hazards hundreds of miles away. Pollution, flash floods, or electrical faults can curtail delivery of imported water. In a recent publication, *Emergencies in Water Delivery,* Professors Roland Schinzinger and Henry Fagin of the University of California at Irvine find water districts ill prepared to deal with such events. Water reclamation could help cushion their impact. In urban regions vulnerable to water shortages—natural or man-made—to ignore reclamation is to play Russian roulette with climatic cycles. With reclamation plants, the New York–New Jersey area could have watered parks, gardens, school grounds, and highway medians with reclaimed water rather than drinking water during water-short 1980.

Tropical islands that find it hard to keep both residents and tourists in water and ice cubes can benefit from alternative systems. The Virgin Islands, which barges water from Puerto Rico on occasion, now reclaims effluent once dumped into coastal waters. Despite tourist ads that feature honeymoon couples splashing in waterfall-fed ponds, Hawaii is reaching the bottom of the well. It is learning to apply reclaimed effluent to sugarcane fields and golf courses. (Some golfers complain that reclaimed water makes the rough grow too fast.)

Aid programs to less-developed countries can encourage reclamation. Why not help these nations leapfrog over environmental mistakes? A reclamation plant may not be as glamorous as a dam; but even Egypt, for example, now realizes that the Aswân High Dam is by no means an unmitigated blessing.

The World Bank estimates that two billion people on this planet lack access to safe water and proper sanitation. The cost to remedy this with large centralized systems, from dams to sewers, could run $300 billion. This scale of funding is never going to materialize as all nations, rich and poor, cope with budget deficits. Reliance on more innovative and simple onsite systems, from cisterns to compost toilets, may improve water supply and sanitation at far less cost.

Reclamation may even outstrip weather modification, iceberg towing, seawater conversion, and other high-tech promotions as our most feasible new water source. One trouble with seawater conversion is that the oceans, unlike rivers and lakes, are too low: demineralize ocean water and you still have to pump it uphill before somebody can drink it or flush it.

Reclamation, of course, is no more of a panacea than 100-mile-long aqueducts or 7-mile-long outfalls. There is a bottom to the well, even on the watery planet. We must conserve and reclaim. EPA now requires grant applicants to prepare flow reduction plans, as GAO urges. One conservation incentive is a sewer user fee pegged to volume of use. In many jurisdictions, a retired couple and a supermarket will pay the same flat sewer rate, regardless of the relative wear and tear each user places on the system.

Alternative systems could tie in well with the move to other decentralized systems, including onsite energy systems. If onsite systems, including cisterns and composting toilets, are perfected in rural areas, watch for urban homeowners, tired of soaring water and sewer rates, to install similar units. If this occurs, watch for water and sewer utilities to complain that they are losing their rate and tax base. This economic concern may be cloaked with predictions of a public health threat if homeowners are permitted to manage their own water and wastewater.

Some large water districts may even wind up funding onsite systems. By helping to postpone the need for costly new centralized projects, onsite cisterns and compost toilets may be considered just as worthy of public funding as dams and huge sewer plants. The Los Angeles Department of Water and Power provides its customers with low-interest loans to install flow restrictors, drip irrigation systems and landscape irrigation timers and sensors.

The move to alternative systems could benefit the environmental movement. While successful in identifying problems of centralized technology, from atomic energy to supertankers, the movement is blamed for creating rather than solving problems. Applied ecological concepts, including recycling, promise to identify the movement with low-cost, problem-solving projects. These projects can make the individual and the community more, not less, self-reliant. Promoters of nuclear plant complexes, bigger dams, and synfuel flings can also lay claim to such virtues, but they have difficulties when they campaign for federal subsidies and for waivers from federal health and environmental standards at the same time. Water hyacinths, rooftop cisterns, and sewage salvage may seem unlikely economic and political liberators, but that may well be their role. It is interesting to speculate on what might have happened if, eighty years ago, coastal cities had opted for more reuse. Sewage treatment today might be associated with irrigation of coastal parks, pastures, and money-making urban farms rather than seven-mile-long ocean outfalls, unreliable multi-million-dollar plants, shellfish quarantines, and soaring public budgets.

15

Contrary Winds

ONCE HE SPOTTED THE SPANISH
galleon in his spyglass, the English captain would order his sailing
force to stay below the marine horizon. He would wait for favorable winds to maximize surprise and minimize response. Vessels
victimized by this tactic litter the seabeds of the world, where
they now attract marine treasure hunters.

Today, a far different force lies below the marine horizon off
the beaches of Cape Cod, the wetlands of the Gulf coast, the
coral reefs of Hawaii, the headlands of California, and the island
nations of the Pacific Ocean. This modern force has its own
unique cover: the glamorous schematics and four-color glossy
magazine ads that depict the ocean as a resource bonanza for a

world running out of land resources. But once this force material-izes above the horizon in the form of an iron archipelago of oil rigs or a swift fleet of fishing vessels, another prospect may emerge. Oil spills can preempt summer tourism. The open coast can be preempted by tank fields as dense as barnacles on a ship's hull. Dockside explosions can shatter thousands of windows for miles around. An abundant coastal biomass that sustained local fishermen for decades can recede under pressure from more "effi-cient" fishing techniques.

By the time a coastal region decides it doesn't like such an industrial marine armada, it may confront another harsh reality: loss of control over its own destiny. Such massive environmental and social change can be sanctified by laws and policies rooted in maritime history. An economic safeguard pioneered by Vene-tian shipowners, based on the idea of shared risk and limited liability, haunts coastal regions in the shadow of tanker traffic. Control over energy siting and related safety and environmental hazards can shift from coastal states to the federal government. Coastal regions, regardless of size or political clout, find them-selves caught up in national political juggling acts to balance population, energy, and resource demands.

The most sensitive portion of the coastal environment lies within state jurisdiction; the most lucrative—just from sheer geographic size—within federal jurisdiction. The federal govern-ment has a strong incentive to favor accelerated exploitation of the outer continental shelf (ocs). Unlike resource development on private land, the federal government gains substantial reve-nues and royalties from ocs leases as the owner, not just as a taxing authority. Any act by a coastal state that serves to reduce, however minutely, the value of ocs resources can be summarily nullified. Louisiana firemen and police must protect facilities that handle both federal ocs gas piped ashore and state-produced gas. The state can tax the latter but not the former. Federal authori-ties consider the federal gas a form of interstate commerce and thus more or less immune from state regulation or taxes. Louisi-ana is currently challenging this disparity in the courts.

Rapid exploitation of the ocs and the overlying waters can also contribute to a more favorable balance of trade. Fish, oil, and mineral imports can be reduced. (This has been and remains a traditional rationale for risking depletion of coastal fish stocks.) However, such development can hasten the rate of depletion and foster even greater trade deficits. Meanwhile, a coastal state's own favorable balance of trade, based on food fisheries and tourists attracted by a high-quality marine environment, may be in shambles.

To reap such illusive marine windfalls, the federal government can be quite receptive to industrial pleas for tax credits, investment guarantees, and construction subsidies. The United States subsidizes construction of American-built oil tankers and fishing vessels. (Domestic fishermen are prohibited by law from importing cheaper foreign vessels, thanks to the domestic shipbuilding lobby.) The federal government has a broad stake in intensive marine development to gain revenue, recoup subsidy investment, and attain a favorable balance of trade.

The federal bias reveals itself best in the fate of the Marine Protection, Research, and Sanctuaries Act. Under this act, the secretary of commerce can establish marine sanctuaries to protect natural values. Sanctuary status does not create a pure type of reserve; the act focuses on development of a comprehensive intergovernmental plan to ensure that exploitive uses are compatible with sanctuary values. Federal agencies are required to practice the type of broad planning that Congress wants coastal states to practice under the Coastal Zone Management Act.

The Marine Protection, Research and Sanctuaries Act was passed in 1972. By 1979, a grand total of two marine sanctuaries had been established. One is the site of a sunken Civil War ironclad, the *Monitor,* off North Carolina; the other, a coral reef off Key Largo, Florida. Is the American coastal environment so bereft of natural values that half of the existing sanctuary system consists of a man-made artifact that sank?

The Georges Bank off New England is the most productive fishing area in the entire North Atlantic, including the Grand

Banks and the North Sea. Its annual yield of 500 million pounds may increase if current efforts to restore depleted stocks succeed.

Fishing communities like Chatham, New Bedford, Gloucester, and Provincetown depend on the Bank. The catch has a high value. While 70 percent of the Gulf of Mexico catch goes into fishmeal and other industrial uses, some 78 percent of the Bank catch, from cod to lobster, goes directly for human consumption. Community groups have nominated the Georges Bank for sanctuary status. The prospects for such an event are not bright.

For its first oil lease on the United States' North Atlantic continental shelf, the Department of the Interior leased some 660,000 acres of Georges Bank to oil drillers. What about concerns over spill impacts on the part of commercial fishermen, the Massachusetts attorney general, and the Cape Cod resort area? The final environmental statement by the Interior Department notes, "The *Argo Merchant* oil spill did not have any appreciable effects on the seasonal tourist economy of Cape Cod." No wonder. The spill occurred off-season (in December) and favorable wind and wave conditions minimized beach exposure. Coastal spill exposure will be intensified by the need for tankers to transport oil from the Bank, which is too far from shore for a pipeline.

To the dismay of congressmen from oil-impacted states, federal agencies lack even the capability to adequately monitor and detect environmental changes once intensive marine oil development and attendant "accidents" occur. After the *Argo Merchant* spill, Congressman Studds wondered how federal agencies were assessing possible damage to Georges Bank. "We found the most remarkable bunch of Federal scrambled eggs I have ever seen in my life," Studds told his fellow congressmen. "We had the EPA and the Interior fighting each other about who was responsible—neither was doing anything, of course. And the long-range studies and monitoring were not done, at least as far as I know—and certainly were not actually funded."

Since fish eggs and larva are most susceptable to oil spills and their degree of survival does not show up in adult stocks until a year or two after a spill, such long-term studies are critical. To conclude that a spill is not damaging without such studies is about as wise as judging that a pesticide is safe after a person who is sprayed with it still manages to walk away.

And how do existing regulations handle drilling fluids or "muds"? These fluids, consisting of wet clays mixed with various chemicals, serve to lubricate drilling pipes and to maintain pressure to prevent blowouts. The muds, dumped off the platform along with drill cuttings, can cover the seabed one to two feet deep 100 yards out from the platform. There is concern that such dumping can suffocate bottom life and expose fish to toxic compounds. (Biocides, for instance, are used to control bacterial growth in the drilling pipe.) Interior officials conclude that the fluids pose no threat, but two other federal agencies, EPA and the National Oceanic and Atmospheric Administration, claim tests used to arrive at such a conclusion have serious defects. EPA contends that Interior does not know all the chemical components in the muds because some are kept proprietary by oil firms. The Interior Department can be somewhat proprietary about its own drilling fluid research. Observes EPA's Dr. Richards, "There is very little drilling fluid research information that has been peer reviewed. Therefore, I would hesitate to put much confidence in studies that were done with very little distribution or review."

Drillers are supposed to ensure that discarded drilling muds are not toxic to marine life, based on responses of selected organisms. These bioassays, to the dismay of respected marine scientists like Dr. Joel W. Hedgpeth and Dr. John Mohr, professor emeritus of the University of Southern California, rely on brine shrimp, sticklebacks, mosquito fish and other organisms that can survive in environmental extremes much greater than that encountered by organisms in the colder depths of drilling sites. Such hardy, estuarine-type organisms can have a higher tolerance to toxic compounds, too.

Some energy officials lose patience with concerns over drilling fluids and assessment efforts. They proudly point out that, while oil development has expanded in the Gulf of Mexico since 1970, the annual fish catch remains the same. This comforting statistic is often buttressed by color slides of fish congregating around an oil platform when the camera's lens is not obscured by dumped drilling muds. But as Dr. Suzanne Bolton, a biologist with EPA, told congressmen, "ten times the number of commercial boats" are now needed to maintain the 1970 level of catch. This fact only heightens the concerns of those fishermen who must depend on Georges Bank for a living.

Federal agencies willing to challenge the tilt towards marine exploitation may be trumped by other federal agencies themselves. For example, in approving a large refinery at Portsmouth, Virginia, in 1979, then–Secretary of the Army Clifford Alexander said, "I believe that the refinery and the Chesapeake Bay resources can coexist free of disastrous implications." In supporting the secretary's decision, Virginia Governor John Dalton cited the refinery as "a prime example of the costly delays and policy frustrations caused by over-regulation of energy development."

Such confident statements conjure up the image of a carefully selected site being obstructed by an elite band of ecology buffs indulging in Doomsday fantasies and nit-picking environmental reports, tying up the courts and otherwise paralyzing the American political system. In reality, the refinery proposed by the Hampton Roads Energy Corporation (owned by oil entrepreneur John Evans and by Cox Enterprises, an Atlanta-based newspaper publisher) was opposed not only by major environmental organizations like the National Wildlife Federation but by three federal agencies. The bay shoreline, including tributaries, measures 8,100 miles. The site selected manages to maximize spill threats to critical spawning areas for two major bay resources, oysters and blue crabs. To the Interior Department, "Hampton Roads is one of the worst locations in the United States for an oil refinery." To EPA the site "should be one of the last areas to be considered for such an activity." To the Commerce Department, the refinery "poses a significant risk of substantial harm, including many lost jobs, to the Maryland and Virginia fishing industries and thus, to the economies of those states."

"The costly delays and policy frustrations" stem from the efforts by the project sponsor to denigrate such high-level concern. The original project application for the 620-acre site sounded as innocuous as a zoning request for a corner gas station. A public hearing attended by 1,000 people exposed the gravity of the project. The applicant then minimized threat of tanker groundings in one key area "due to the soft mud bottom and absence of rocks." The bottom, observed the Commerce Department, is "composed of hard sand and some rock" augmented by numerous anchorages and two bridge tunnel systems. The project sponsor now claims that oil spills will be minimized by "future improvements in either the technical or the regulatory climate," without providing bothersome detail on economic or political feasibility. The Commerce Department notes that the major cause of tanker spills "is human error which neither the industry nor government has been able to eliminate through technical or regulatory mechanisms."

While no corporation would ever invest in a product based on unspecified "future improvements," Secretary Alexander relied on this hope in claiming that the refinery can coexist with oysters, blue crabs, and the bay's $200 million a year commercial and sport fishery. Human error may be the major cause of tanker spills, but it is such wishful decisions that expose America's marine heritage to the consequences of human error. Two months after the Secretary's decision, a Malaysian tanker rammed a Navy oiler close to the refinery site. Because the point of impact was aft of the oiler's tanks, no oil escaped.

EPA urges that deepwater oil leases off California be deferred until failure probabilities and impacts from untried deepwater oil technology can be better assessed. Unimpressed, the Bureau of Land Management observes, "Technology will not advance if deepwater tracts are not offered for development. Deepwater technology would stagnate if the 300-meter limit proposed by EPA were adopted." California's continental borderland thus qualifies as both a shallow-water oil patch and an industrial guinea pig for deepwater oil technology and, presumably, spill control.

Onshore residents as well as marine ecosystems can become hostage to this haste to exploit. If not effectively forecast and controlled, air pollution emissions from tankers, platforms, and refineries can contribute to failure of coastal urban regions like Los Angeles, Jersey City and Norfolk, Va. to achieve compliance with federal air standards. EPA can cut off federal funds to urban regions that fail to meet air standards.

The federal-state cooperation that manages to survive the federal rush seaward often exudes a stage-managed air. The Interior Department proclaims a massive offshore oil lease sale that sends local officials climbing up the nearest sea wall. Interior then "slashes" the size of the sale. Local officials congratulate themselves for hanging tough. The oil industry, meanwhile, continues to enlarge its marine presence and to expand the federal fiscal appetite for OCS revenues. Inevitably, the "slashed" area reappears in the next oil lease sale. In one of his first public acts, Interior Secretary James Watt proposed to reinstate four offshore oil leasing tracts that outgoing Secretary Cecil Andrus had deleted as being too environmentally risky. The Watt resubmission was protested by a senior Republican congressman, Don Clausen, whose district abuts some of the leases, and by Governor Jerry Brown, concerned that the marginal oil potential of the tracts does not justify jeopardizing the well-documented natural values of the Pt. Reyes–Big Sur coast. Watt classified this response as "shrill". The Watt approach seems to contradict President Reagan's avowed campaign promise of working more closely with state and local governments.

Watt next decided to disband the Interior's Heritage Conservation and Recreation Service, which helps cities renew urban waterfronts with offshore oil revenues, and placed a freeze on national park acquisitions authorized by Congress. This act serves to jeopardize federal pledges to help create major coastal-urban parks, including the Santa Monica Mountains National Recreation Area north of Los Angeles. This cannot be considered a very prudent economy move, since properties scheduled to be acquired rise in value 20–40% a year, according to Ruth Kilday of the Santa Monica Parks staff. The funding power of the $1 billion available for national parks acquisition will thus be eroded by inflation during the freeze. "At this rate, the only thing we will be sharing with the federal government is oil spills," noted one perplexed California state official.

Unrestrained, the federal marine perspective can favor growth of a national economy and political constituency in its own industrial image. While coastal states, tourist interests, and the marine recreation sector campaign against the prospect of federal preemption of coastal energy siting, the growing marine oil sector, with its support industries and unions, lobbies for preemption. Standard Oil of Ohio (Sohio) boasted that Long Beach, California voters had approved its proposed oil terminal facility in a community referendum. However, in the referendum campaign Sohio outspent community groups concerned about terminal air pollution by $800,000 to $17,000. Sohio later pulled out of the project. While unable to ante up such lush campaign donations, federal agencies can find ways to participate in state and community elections. Federal nuclear agencies distributed free pro-nuclear literature throughout California when a measure to restrict nuclear expansion, including coastal siting, was on the state ballot. The measure (pre–Three Mile Island) was defeated.

The federal Fishery Conservation and Management Act of 1976 preempted state regulation of most coastal marine species. Thus, while extending its seaward jurisdiction to control foreign fishing, the federal government drastically reduced state fishery control. Regional fishery councils and the Department of Commerce are now in charge.

The temptation to exploit without adequate assessment can re-occur here too. As Chapters 2 and 3 point out, the new management system has been tardy in living up to Congress's mandate to prevent overfishing and to manage stocks on a multi-species basis. California has acted to reduce federally-approved catch quotas on a forage fish, the anchovy, while Florida is taking a tougher stand on use of wire traps that trigger incidental fish kills. These coastal states are trying to retain some effective control over the future of their coastal marine ecosystem.

Coastal states that go to court to challenge careless or risky federal marine decisions risk being impaled on a sharp legal trident. The prongs consist of supremacy, federal preemption, and interstate commerce. Under the supremacy clause of the Constitution, state laws that clearly conflict with federal laws must yield. Where federal regulation in a particular area implies a legislative intent to preempt this area, the doctrine of federal preemption can nullify state regulations in the same area. Under the Constitution's commerce clause, the federal government can preempt interstate commerce regulation. In a modern urban coastal complex, you or your activity would literally have to stand still to survive as intrastate commerce.

Combine this legal trident—truly fit for a modern-day Neptune—with the currently fashionable doctrine of judicial restraint, and you have a legal breakwater that will repulse state legal challenges no matter how strongly based on substantive concerns about urban safety, risk-creating activities, and irreversible damage to marine ecosystems. A federal judge who overturned a portion of California's nuclear safety regulations relied on the doctrine of federal preemption. The U.S. Supreme Court relied on the same doctrine to limit the state of Washington's control over tanker traffic in that state's most critical waterway, Puget Sound. The federal government can encroach on state jurisdiction while being insulated from state attempts to encroach on—or share in—federal marine jurisdiction, however grave the potential coastal impacts. Evidence needed to prove damage can be undercut by the federal failure to adequately assess and monitor intensive marine development.

What about that new era of federalism, to be ushered in by high-toned concepts such as consistency and shared jurisdiction? To soften up these concepts prior to judicial challenges, all sorts of innovative riders and clarifying phrases can be devised. Federal actions are to be consistent with coastal state programs "to the maximum extent possible." National security needs or the latest energy crisis can be invoked to transform "maximum" to "minimum." Consistency roars like a paper lion. Coastal states generally prefer that ocs oil be transported by pipe onshore rather than loaded onto tankers, a riskier but cheaper process. Exxon has opted for the latter process to serve twenty-eight wells in the Santa Barbara channel. Federal authorities support Exxon's version of consistency. A federal judge has ruled that Exxon's tanker loading facility is exempt from the Deepwater Port Act and thus not subject to state veto. In time, the federal government may choose to preempt coastal energy siting or develop its own iron archipelago of off-shore sites. And the fenmen thought they had it rough.

Massachusetts Attorney General Francis Bellotti and Boston's Conservation Law Foundation filed a court challenge to Interior's leasing program on Georges Bank. In a subsequent settlement, Interior agreed to use the "best available and safest technology" and the Commerce Department agreed to reconsider Georges Bank for sanctuary status. The former provision, while certainly noteworthy, contends with the fact that a spill containment system for the high seas that wash across Georges Bank simply does not exist. The latter provision may be rendered academic by the uncertain future of the sanctuary program. As part of the settlement, the plaintiffs had to agree to no longer challenge leasing on the Bank in court.

Did the founders of this nation intend that the U.S. Constitution should shield such political sleight of hand? Is our vaunted system of federalism—which is supposed to bring government closer to the people and avoid central decision-making—a modern-day illusion? This brings us to the origin of federal supremacy and the other legal time bombs that were planted when the U.S. Constitution replaced the original Articles of Confederation. Promoters of the Constitution (federalists) were largely conservative merchants, such as Alexander Hamilton. These men wanted a strong national government, the preservation of the sanctity of contracts, and free trade, in the British mode, unhindered by state or local regulations. Uniformity of regulations in matters of commerce was ranked next to saintliness. For the federalists, the Constitution furthered particular economic goals. The antifederalists, the small-is-beautiful constituency of the day, preferred an agrarian democracy and decentralized government. The federalists prevailed, in part by portraying decentralized governance as narrow in outlook, economically illiterate, and divisive, an image later states-rights advocates would all too successfully live up to.

As long as resource development was restricted to the land, much of it privately held, state and local governments could shape their own economic and political destiny through land-use decisions. Today, the seaward economic thrust serves to reinforce federal supremacy at the expense of coastal regions. Coastal regions themselves can contribute to federal encroachment. By relying on centralized water and sewer systems, coastal states can become dependent on federal grants. By permitting careless or hazardous land development, coastal states can become dependent on federal disaster relief and structural control projects. By remaining on a hydrocarbon high while protesting coastal energy projects, coastal regions can contribute to pressures for more high-risk energy projects in the coastal zone.

Clearly, the ability of coastal regions to influence the federal marine perspective must come from within and be developed on a broad legislative, judicial, and economic front. The shift to more prudent coastal land uses, alternative water systems, and more practical aquaculture projects are examples of such coastal initiatives. Coastal regions are now learning that similar initiatives could protect them from becoming glorified federal energy colonies.

16

Better Waves

THE VISITOR TO HAWAII MAY BE IMpressed that no offshore oil platforms, coal strip mines, or uranium pits mar the islands' beauty. To the resident, though, these industrial voids can be an economic curse. Reliant almost entirely on imported oil, Hawaii has suffered from some of the nation's highest utility rates and gasoline prices. Needless to say, when oil cuts come, the allocation priority for an island chain in the mid-Pacific is not very high. In this bind, the risk of oil blowouts and stripped hillsides can become acceptable, with or without prodding from a federal energy official. Alas, the Hawaiian sun does not shine on any coal deposits, and the tradewinds do not blow over oil deposits. From a conventional energy point of view, Hawaii is one of this planet's more sterile regions.

Ironically, Hawaii is now on its way to that elusive goal of energy independence by cultivating the sun, the tradewinds, sugarcane waste, and other derided renewable energy sources. Other coastal regions are learning to follow suit.

This new act in the national energy drama stems from a significant policy void. Energy officials chastize us for living in "energy sieves." They implore us to weatherproof and solarize our dwellings. Alluring photos crop up in the daily press of the latest research venture in wind, biomass, or solar projects designed to make communities more energy self-sufficient.

Unfortunately, few distribution systems exist to fund, install, and service these energy alternatives. As in the case of alternative water systems, their decentralized nature can run counter to the current centralized energy system, which is controlled by large companies that manage huge power plants in remote locations. Utility company executives analyzing solar and other renewable sources of energy can sound like military chiefs assessing disarmament. To shift from the comforting technical realm of central plants and orderly distribution grids to the task of installing solar collectors, rooftop to urban rooftop, is asking a lot of this mindset. Southern California Edison's initial response to solar energy was to produce it in the central-plant model: a huge experimental solar "power tower" in the middle of the California desert. The sheer cost of the experiment—$140 million, based on the latest cost override—is beginning to unnerve the U.S. Congress, which is the chief financial angel. The project narrowly escaped Senate budget-cutting action in 1980. The power-tower syndrome can overlook the fact that solar rooftop collectors are a proven technology that can contribute to this nation's energy needs *now*.

Citizens can, of course, procure their own special mix of solar collectors, weatherproofing, wind, and biomass converters on the open market. Federal and state tax credits will reward us for doing this. But that's the rub. You must come up with the cash to pay for the system, which can amount to $3,000 and more. Unlike a multinational oil corporation building an offshore oil rig in the Arctic or a utility building a central plant in the desert or on the coast, individual citizens don't always have a handsome line of credit or an expanding rate base to cover front-end costs.

Glamorous photo spreads in leisure sections of newspapers and magazines may depict custom homes designed for passive solar heat or being retrofitted with active systems such as solar water heaters. The proud owner, standing on a porch overlooking a mountain range or the ocean with a glass of chilled white wine in his hand, urges his fellow citizens to strike a blow for ecology and get a tax break in the process. This is precisely the image that gives solar and other renewable options an elitist aura. With all the risks they impose on coastal regions, nuclear and marine oil development retains an aura of practicality.

Hawaii started to break out of the conventional energy bind even before the 1973 energy cutoff. Sugarcane plantation owners realized the cost of imported oil was cutting profits; Louisiana sugar producers had a ready oil supply in their own backyard. The Hawaiian growers built their own power plants fueled by burning sugarcane waste. Sometimes the growers had excess power. They found a ready buyer. The island utility companies found this domestic power source a bargain compared to imported oil.

When the 1973–1974 energy crunch came, Hawaii realized more than ever its crippling dependence on imported oil. Mainland utilities can obtain up to one-quarter of their energy from sources other than oil, such as nuclear power plants and hydroelectric power, but not Hawaii. Mainland utilities can share generated power; to lay underwater transmission lines in the deep ocean depths between islands in Hawaii is too expensive.

Sugar producers were willing to expand and refine their power plants because the utilities were now willing to enter into long-term contracts to buy excess power. New boilers are being designed to burn other biomass sources such as wood chips and wood from pilot eucalyptus energy tree farms. Today, biomass, mostly sugarcane waste, accounts for approximately 13 percent of all the electricity consumed in the state. The city of Honolulu now plans to use its trash as a biomass source rather than use up limited land for more sanitary landfill sites.

Based on successful pilot wind projects, Hawaiian Electric Company (HECO) has entered into an agreement with a private California firm, Windfarms, to purchase up to 80 megawatts of electricity from thirty-two wind turbine generators that are being built to harvest Hawaii's tradewinds. Under a federal grant, HECO is already drawing wind-generated electricity from a large wind-mill mounted on a 100-foot tubular steel tower.

On the big island of Hawaii, the local utility company has agreed to buy energy generated from a joint federal-state geother-mal test facility. With two active volcanos, the Big Island has the United States' hottest geothermal power source.

Rather than stop at these alternative sources, Hawaii is promoting an entire series of energy projects, including solar. Oahu, Hawaii's most populated island, already has 5,000 solar water heaters, second only to the number in California.

Hawaii plans to achieve 100 percent electrical energy self-sufficiency in 1990 by means of this diversified mix and its head start in biomass. It will still have to import oil for transportation, which accounts for about half of its energy consumption. Liquid fuel self-sufficiency will be harder to attain. But once again the sugar fields are coming to the rescue, at least for a portion of the problem. Molasses, a byproduct of sugarcane processing, is a feedstock well suited for ethanol production. Gasohol, a mixture of 10 percent ethanol and 90 percent gasoline, can power motor-ized vehicles. The Hawaiian Sugar Planters' Association, working with federal and state agencies, is developing an ethanol plant.

To support such diverse energy projects, Hawaii has estab-lished the Hawaii Natural Energy Institute, directed by Dr. Paul Yuen. When the Department of Energy decided to hold a na-tional conference on renewable sources, it selected Honolulu as the conference site. Hawaii realizes that its ambitious goal of energy self-sufficiency will not come from just one or two sources, but from a range of sources. If such initiatives succeed, and the chances for electrical self-sufficiency look especially good, Hawaii can reduce dramatically the $800 million it spends annually on imported oil. This money will be going to local sources instead, such as geothermal wells or wind farms, and will thereby help produce local jobs and revenues. Link these energy initiatives with Hawaii's aquaculture efforts and one begins to sense how new resource horizons can open up for coastal regions burdened by unfavorable trade balances and saddled with the risks of air and water pollution posed by dependence on imported oil.

Other coastal regions are now beginning to realize that they have the natural and political resources to undertake energy initiatives. Local bond issues can often fund residential and commercial solar energy and weatherproofing projects. At the same time that they are working to restore a blighted waterfront, Baltimore and Warwick, Rhode Island, have floated bond issues for energy diversification programs.

What happens when a community forms its own municipal utility to realize the promise of renewable energy? Santa Clara, California, is located in the San Francisco Bay region. With a population of 95,000, it is an older community ringed by tracts housing scientists and executives who work in the high-technology firms that are replacing apricot and prune orchards. At the turn of the century, with surplus money left over from a water bond issue, the city decided to buy some used generators and establish a municipal power company. In the days of cheap oil, Santa Clara, like other cities operating utilities, found it cheaper to buy power wholesale from large power companies or federal hydropower projects. When the energy crunch hit in the 1970s, Santa Clara again wanted to diversify its energy sources. Building a huge central plant was beyond its financial means. Onsite solar systems can be installed at much less cost and without the long lead time required to design a conventional power system and procure federal and state permits. Some jurisdictions mandate solar hot water systems in new residential development. The cost of the system can thus be included in the house price and amortized over thirty years. But this type of mandate does little for residents of existing homes. To benefit this substantial segment of the populace, Santa Clara now purchases, installs, and services residential solar systems. It is, in effect, a municipal solar utility, responsible for capital costs and consumer security.

Santa Clara offers both solar pool heaters and solar water heaters. The resident pays a monthly lease that is 20 to 30 percent less than gas or electric rates. Moreover, the monthly rate, covering the fixed cost of solar equipment, is not subject to the frequent rate hikes that gas and electricity users must endure. A service connection fee of $300 and the lease payment both qualify for state and federal tax credits. You don't have to be in the high-income tax bracket to benefit from Santa Clara's solar program. The city's utility reserve funds solar purchases. The city can buy in bulk to lower the unit price.

Santa Clara can buy from local solar suppliers. The city trains installers and hires local people during summer, the peak installation season. This renewable energy alternative can thus keep jobs, equipment dollars, and tax revenues at home, in sharp contrast to imported oil and massive central plants located in remote regions. Major urban states like New York and California pay millions in out-of-state plant taxes.

Santa Clara solar engineer Robin Saunders estimates that solar systems in the city save up to 400,000 therms of natural gas annually, the equivalent of 5,000 barrels of oil. Advocates of large plants love to invoke such modest figures when attempting to prove that solar systems are little league when compared to conventional plants. ("There's not enough power in a solar collector to suntan Bo Derek," has been one standard line in utility circles.) For over a decade, Pacific Gas & Electric Company (PG&E), the private utility that serves northern and central California, has been pouring millions of dollars into one large plant that has yet to match the output of just one Santa Clara solar collector. Because of unresolved seismic and safety design questions, the Diablo Canyon coastal nuclear plant has yet to obtain an operating license. As in the case of decentralized water systems, decentralized or onsite energy systems can be much more flexible in adjusting to economic and technical change. (The Center for

Law in the Public Interest has requested a study on conversion of the idle Diablo Canyon plant to a nonnuclear facility. Utility companies in Virginia and New Jersey have terminated work on two nuclear plant projects and are considering conversion to coal.)

Impressed by the Santa Clara model, the California Energy Commission is funding a program in which six communities have formed a joint solar utility. As in Hawaii, the California Solar Utility Development Authority works with a whole range of renewable options, including energy tree farms in lumber communities, small-scale hydroelectric power in farm irrigation districts, and apartment weatherproofing in urban Los Angeles. To develop capital, the solar utility can dip into municipal budget reserves, as Santa Clara did, and can apply for federal grants and a line of credit with banks. It can float bonds. Lease and loan payments can go into a revolving fund.

The most promising prospect for a municipal solar utility could eventually be photovoltaic (pv) panels. Unlike solar water heaters, pv panels on a rooftop can generate enough electricity to serve a household's needs, with a surplus to feed into energy grids. (Some pv collectors can double as new roofs.) The present high cost of pv systems could be reduced as a mass market develops. A municipal company could buy the panels wholesale, lease them to homeowners (including some who need new roofs), and receive revenues from pv power exported to energy grids. (In time, utility officials may converge upon the resident with a sunny rooftop to gain his solar rights with the same generous enthusiasm of wildcat drillers seeking mineral rights.)

California is now mandating the state's large private utilities to fund such solar options. A homeowner can qualify for a low-interest loan or cash rebates for a solar water heater. Is there some sort of free lunch involved here? After all, the homeowner is already getting tax credits. By installing a solar heater, the owner is conserving central-plant capacity and helping to postpone the need for new plants. The modest rooftop collector is thus being regarded as a capital investment just as worthy of being carried by the entire utility rate base as a nuclear plant on a coastal fault or a coal-burning plant in the Nevada desert. And you don't need to worry about meeting air quality standards, disposing of radioactive wastes, or importing more oil. The state-mandated program, expected to reach 375,000 residential customers, could save the equivalent of one million barrels of oil annually. Net savings have been estimated at $433 million over a twenty-year period.

Such a shift in energy strategies can generate a variety of jobs—carpentry, plumbing, electrical work, sheetmetal work, insulation—locally rather than hundreds of miles away at a remote coastal or desert site. Don't be surprised if hardhat construction workers eventually shuck their pro-nuke bumper stickers for T-shirts emblazoned with "Sun Power." In areas of high unemployment, onsite solar and weatherproofing programs can be linked with job training. Such joint programs can go far to overcome the elitist or "hippie power" image of renewable energy.

Across the continent, Maine is beginning to shift to renewable energy options, focussing on wood for fuel. Small dams originally built to power textile mills are being reopened in New England to provide low-head hydroelectric power. Community bonds or loans can help fund such systems.

As in Hawaii, large private utilities are now more willing to recognize the potential of renewable sources. PG&E projects that 54 percent of its new generating capacity will come from renewable or alternative sources, including wind and solar. Of its total generating capacity, PG&E says 43.3 percent will come from renewable sources by 1991. At the same time, because of energy conservation and efficiency programs, PG&E has cut its projections of future energy demands by 25 percent. As a result, the utility has been cancelling or postponing large central plants once planned for the coast and the desert. Instead of opposing or accepting high-risk coastal energy development, coastal regions are now developing low-risk, low-pollution alternatives that do not require heavy capital investments.

Other interesting energy perspectives are opening up on the waterfront. Fuel prices have had their impact on commercial shipping and on commercial and recreational fishermen. A freighter can burn $10,000 in fuel each day, and some must cut their speed in half to conserve. One highly touted energy alternative—nuclear propulsion—costs even more. A maritime world running out of cheap oil may learn to run up synthetic sail.

Once jeered by his fellow fishermen as a "rag" sailor, Honolulu-based R.W. Davies saves $5,000 per fishing trip by tapping the same power that brought Captain Cook to Hawaii and Columbus to the New World. He turns on his engine to maneuver his steel schooner on the fishing grounds and to negotiate harbor channels. Puget Sound boat builder Bernie Arthur has turned out, at last count, thirty sailing fishboats. Besides saving on fuel, the proud owners save on wear and tear of their standby power source, the engine. One problem is that the sleek hull design can reduce fish-holding capacity.

Truckers and ferry boat operators in coastal New England have been losing freight contracts to an upstart competitor since 1979. The *Lily* is a 39-foot-long sailing freighter that can carry up to 20 tons of cordwood, lumber, foodstuffs, and even a car or two. It can unload on a customer's beachfront. The owners of the *Lily* are building a larger sailing workboat to give onshore truckers more fits.

Many tropical islands are unable to pay marine freight costs and have been dropped from regular scheduled service. They thus can lose access to needed food and medical supplies. The reemergence of commercial sail could be of special benefit for such islands.

The *Norfolk Rebel* is a new 50-foot-long tugatine. That's the name for a sailing tugboat that can fish too. The bowsprit retracts so the *Rebel* can push as well as pull vessels that are dead in the water. The National Marine Fisheries Service is helping to fund the *Rebel*'s first year of operation to get a better idea of the potential of sail.

The new generation of sailing vessels can benefit from new equipment unavailable to old clipper captains. Sails can be made larger and more durable. Antifouling paints can control the organic drag on hulls that slowed the old clippers. Hydraulic gears can mechanize sail handling. Computers can control optimum wind angle. Japan has built a coastal oil tanker whose engine power is augmented by sail. The Federal Maritime Administration, after cancelling further sudsidies for commercial nuclear ships, is now funding a major feasibility study on commercial sail. Urban waterfronts may be hosting a revival of coastal trade, since onshore truckers have much greater difficulty tacking with the wind. Like solar and wind energy, sail can provide coastal regions with a new lease on economic life in the energy crunch.

The need for constructive energy programs at local and state levels is increased by developments at the federal level. Both Congress and the executive branch appear to be tilting more and more toward the hard-energy path. The solar lobby uncovered a memo from the secretary of energy in 1979 that sought to divert solar energy funds to synfuel projects. Federal funding for nuclear research far exceeds that for weatherproofing and renewable-energy loan programs, even though the latter can offer immediate conservation gains without the need for five- and ten-year research programs. An Energy Partnership Act to help fund community energy projects, urged by Sen. Paul Tsongas (D.-MA) and the American Planning Association, was killed by this bias.

As a result of such a policy tilt, federal officials may be more active in preempting local safety and environmental safeguards than in helping community energy initatives. The Department of Transportation wants to preempt local regulation of nuclear waste shipments. Do local regulations shut down interstate commerce and frustrate federal nuclear policies? Many simply require that local officials be notified of shipping plans and that shipments be placed under escort. As is so often the case, preemption is sought without provision for a comprehensive safety program that would satisfy local concerns in the first place. Rather than come up with a definitive solution to radioactive waste disposal, federal agencies are considering storage at sea. And rather than cut out all energy subsidies and thereby let renewable options compete on an equal basis with conventional forms, the Reagan administration has severly cut modest renewal grants while maintaining or increasing nuclear subsidies and synfuel loan guarantees.

This policy bias may serve to resurrect the federal Energy Mobilization Board (EMB) from legislative death. Debate over this proposal to speed up major energy projects highlighted the willingness of proponents of hard-energy technology to waive or relax health and environmental precautions. While Senators J. Bennett Johnston (D.-LA) and Henry Jackson (D.-WA) pushed the EMB, Sen. Alan Cranston (D-CA) branded it a "gangbuster's approach" to energy policy. Rep. Edward Markey (D.-MA) called the proposed health and safety waivers "an energy Gulf of Tonkin resolution."

If such federal paternalism is not motivation enough for state and local energy initiatives, try this: federal energy policy, on paper at least, has been directed to decreasing oil imports. Now influential voices are urging that we *increase* imports. Defense officials and some utility officials feel we need more imports to build up a strategic reserve of oil for the next disruption of supply. To James Plummer of the Electric Power Research Institute, "we are virtually naked" when it comes to oil cutoffs. These people feel that stockpiling oil reserves should be of higher priority than decreasing oil imports.

If this policy is adopted, motorists and homeowners can anticipate another inflation spiral as they compete with the strategic reserve for world oil supplies. The proposed capacity of the strategic reserve is 1.6 billion barrels. That's a lot of oil tankers. Walter Baer of the Rand Corporation thinks we need more than just a strategic oil reserve. Addressing a 1980 energy conference at the University of Southern California sponsored by the Newport Foundation for the Study of Major Economic Issues, Baer urged that plans for coal and nuclear power be elevated to strategic status. To Baer, nuclear plants such as Diablo Canyon, which can't pass muster for operating licenses, could be considered a possible strategic reserve that can be turned on in the next energy crisis. It would be ironic if the next episode in Mideast power politics would save nuclear power from its technical and economic shortcomings.

The self-defeating nature of "strategic" energy planning reaffirms the federal failure to diversify our energy options. Coastal regions now realize they can fill this national void while regaining a degree of economic and political self-reliance.

17

Recourse for the Coastal Rim

IN CIVILIZED SOCIETIES, WE HAVE come to expect that a party whose acts injure another must recompense the victim. But millions of people who live along the coastal rim remain hostage to spills and to liability systems that serve to subsidize high-risk energy technology at the expense of safer forms. The larger and more devastating spills become, the more antiquated and inadequate our systems of liability.

The goal of comprehensive and equitable spill liability does not suffer from lack of dedicated supporters. For years, key members of Congress, including former Senator Edmund Muskie (D.-ME) and Congressmen Mario Biaggi (D.-NY) and Gerry Studds (D.-MA), have been trying to accomplish this. But these legislators find that a comprehensive system of century-old laws designed to reduce or eliminate liability must first be overcome.

Congress passed the supreme form of liability avoidance in 1851. Under the Limitation of Liability Act, a shipowner's liability can be limited to the value of the vessel *after* a collision or grounding. A total loss actually benefits the owner. He can recover the value of the ship through insurance while claims against him may be extinguished by the loss of the vessel. (Imagine what would happen if this concept were applied to auto or airplane collisions.)

I can understand why shipowners and the marine insurance industry would favor loose liability. But why national legislative bodies? During the nineteenth century, many ships were powered by wind and not by oil, which can coat beaches and shut down coastal tourism. Moreover, nations wanted to encourage maritime enterprises. Legislation to minimize liability was—and remains—a much cheaper form of public subsidy than massive financial aid.

Since the *Torrey Canyon* spill in 1967, when the shipowner tried and failed to limit his liability to the value of one remaining lifeboat, reformers have been working to plug major loopholes. Under the 1851 Act, a spiller could only be held liable if his actions were found to constitute gross or willful negligence. This can be hard to prove in court, particularly if you are a fisherman who can't afford a battery of lawyers. Congress does impose strict liability for spills from vessels or offshore oil production operations. Strict liability means simple liability regardless of fault or negligence. Only an act of war, God, or a third party gets you off the hook. Under the spill provisions of the Alaskan Pipeline Act, Congress even eliminated defenses for acts of God and third parties. (Such double standards for spills are common in existing law. Standards for platform or pipeline spills are generally more rigorous; legislators don't have to overcome the historic heritage of lax vessel liability.)

Despite these tougher standards, a spiller can still benefit from limits on the type of damages that victims can claim. Most congressional reforms seek to ensure recovery of cleanup costs, the major federal expense. While offshore oil operators are liable as well for damage to private parties (such as fishermen and tourist operators) and to natural resources (such as public beaches and fish stocks), Congress has so far failed to extend such explicit damage liability to vessel operators. This leaves such major coastal areas as Cape Cod, Long Island Sound, the Chesapeake Bay region, the Florida Gold Coast, the southern California coast, San Francisco Bay, and Puget Sound with an extraordinary degree of nonprotection from the harsh realities of tanker spills.

Parties incurring losses may be entitled to damages, but may then find a limit placed on the amount. The United States has refused to ratify international spill conventions that limit liability for tanker spills to $56.2 million. The *Amoco Cadiz* spill, in which damage claims in excess of $1 billion have been filed, confirms the U.S. view that such limits are too low. However, the United States can become a fiscal victim of its own low liability limits. Current federal law limits the amount of liability based on the relative size of the vessel. There is also a flat ceiling of $30 million. In 1975, a barge collided with a freighter on the Mississippi River in Louisiana. While the United States spent some $1.1 million to clean up the resulting spill, a court limited recovery to less than $400,000. In 1976, a barge under tow grounded in the scenic Thousand Islands area of the St. Lawrence River. Maximum liability of the barge owner was $847,800, or about one-tenth of the actual cost of the cleanup.

Unimpressed by this hodgepodge of federal policies, coastal states like Florida, Maine, Connecticut, New Jersey, and Washington have enacted their own liability regimes. Nine states require unlimited liability for spill cleanups. This trend has inspired the shipping industry and the marine insurance industry to support a federal liability system that would preempt such state systems.

Congress is presently considering a so-called Superfund bill that could become the most comprehensive system of spill liability in the world. It would establish one set of liability laws for all types of spills from all sources. It would establish one fund at the federal level to compensate victims of spills promptly. The government would then assume the task of recovering damages from spillers. Damage recovery would include damage to natural resources, private property, and loss of income (fishing days or tourist income lost because of spills.) The Superfund would be funded and replenished by a per-barrel tax on crude oil. (Congress passed a Superfund bill to cover chemical wastes in 1980.)

Despite such attractive features, Congress has been debating this bill for five years. Some legislators want to include costs of assessing damage as well as restoring damaged or degraded natural resources; other legislators feel that such additional cost items would place too great a burden on the fund. The Reagan administration's enthusiasm for marine oil development does not extend to the Superfund bill, which it was opposing as of spring 1981.

One major stumbling block regards preemption of state liability schemes. The House would preempt state schemes; the Senate would still permit them. Many coastal states don't want to be preempted until the Superfund proves to be workable. Shippers and the marine insurance industry express concern that oil spill victims will shop around for the most favorable liability regime. Ironically, shipowners shop around for the weakest regulatory regimes, registering their vessels under foreign flags of convenience. At the same time, the shipping industry lobbies against strong international conventions on spill liability, thereby forcing countries like the United States and Canada and coastal states like Maine and Florida to act unilaterally.

One possible compromise on the preemption issue would phase out state liability schemes depending on the proven effectiveness of the federal Superfund. Moreover, spill victims could recover from only one fund. A staff member for Congressman Mario Biaggi, primary sponsor of the House bill, cites one prime weakness in state liability schemes. "The funds they establish simply do not have the financial capacity to recompense victims promptly in case of a major spill," observes Rudy Cassani. If the

Superfund had been law, Texas victims of Mexico's IXTOC blowout would have been entitled to submit claims. Payments under the Superfund would not be restricted on the basis of where the oil originates. If the damage occurs within the extended fishery jurisdiction of the United States (200 miles), the Superfund would pay and the federal government would assume the task of recovering from the spiller, even if it involved another nation.

At times, the federal courts can respond faster than Congress to the need for liability reforms. In 1978, Judge Juan Torruella made the first award in U.S. courts for natural resource damage from an oil spill. The judge awarded the Commonwealth of Puerto Rico $6.3 million to compensate for environmental damage from a tanker spill. Is such a monetary award difficult to arrive at, as critics charge? Based on evidence submitted, the judge was able to assess the costs of replacing organisms killed in the spill. He added the cost to replant and maintain mangrove trees, which help retard coastal erosion and shelter marine life communities. The National Oceanic and Atmospheric Administration (NOAA) is utilizing the *Amoco Cadiz* spill to develop more refined assessment tools for aquaculture, coastal property values, tourism, and human health.

Such expansion of damage recovery could, according to some tanker owners and marine insurance officials, exceed the private sector's capacity to insure marine oil enterprises. One suggested solution is to expand government-subsidized insurance for nuclear power plant accidents to oil spills. This tradition should be junked rather than expanded. Perhaps the greatest long-term benefit of adequate liability is to encourage safer forms of energy. While certainly not accident-free, you don't need Superfunds or government subsidies to cover solar spills, windmill collisions, or energy conservation meltdowns. Inadequate liability can be a hidden subsidy for high-risk energy technology. It penalizes the tanker operator who invests in safety while protecting the careless, cost-cutting operator. (Under its new oilspill act, Alaska links a shipowner's mandatory contributions to a spill fund to his safety record and the ship's design and navigation features.)

Transnational spill incidents, as exemplified by the runaway Mexican oil well blowout, promise to be the toughest of all liability loopholes to close. U.S. officials have been asking Mexico to pay millions in damages while bargaining for Mexican oil and gas at prices Mexico considers an insult to its national honor. Mexico, of course, remembers how U.S. water diversion efforts in the Colorado River basin left her with a salty trickle. As Rep. Edwin Forsythe (R.-NJ) noted in hearings on the IXTOC blowout, Mexico "might think we could stand a little oil, since they are taking a lot of salt."

If the Superfund bill had been passed, Texas fishermen and coastal communities could have recovered their spill damages and loss of business income from the fund. The Superfund would permit damage recovery regardless of the origin of the oil. The IXTOC spill and the liability loophole has placed a severe burden on the Texas shrimp fishermen. After being kicked out of Mexican shrimping grounds in the global readjustment of fishing access, the Texas shrimpers prepared to concentrate on coastal waters off south Texas. This area was pre-empted by the IXTOC spill. The shrimpers then moved north only to see record freshwater flows disrupt shrimp production. Caught in this bind, some shrimpers decided to carry Cuban refugees in violation of U.S. law while others have been petitioning Congress for relief from federal vessel loan payments. (That Mexican shrimpers obtain fuel at much cheaper prices increased the competitive burden.)

The South Padre Island recreation and tourist area suffered an estimated $16 million loss in damages and lost income due to the IXTOC spill. The Texas congressional delegation wants the federal government to pay for such damages since they feel their citizens are victims of public inertia to close the liability loopholes.

The United States and Canada had the foresight in 1974 to set up a joint contingency plan to control oil spills in the Atlantic, Pacific and Great Lakes. Thus both nations can combine their resources in containing border spills rather than exchange recriminations. Mexico and the U.S. were negotiating such a joint plan when the ixtoc blowout occurred. If agreement had been reached, U.S. spill control resources would have been able to help contain the oil at the source immediately rather than wait hundreds of miles away for the oil to wash up on Texas beaches and marshes. When the next well blows out either on the American and Mexican side, this option will be available because agreement on a joint plan has finally been reached.

The next step would be reciprocal agreements on liability for damage. When Congress passed the Alaskan pipeline bill, it gave Canadian citizens the right to recover any damages from spills in U.S. courts. The Superfund bill would allow foreign citizens to recover damages from U.S. spills if their nation provides U.S. citizens with the same recourse.

Building on such transnational accords, border nations could agree to formal consultation on proposed projects with trans-boundary impacts. Guidelines to prevent or mitigate adverse impacts, whether it be from river basin diversions or coastal energy projects, could be invoked before and not after the fact. Eventually, the U.S., Mexico and Canada could develop a joint North American surveillance plan to detect illegal discharges from passing oil tankers. During the ixtoc spill, Coast Guard officials received reports that tanker captains would diverge from Gulf routes to discharge oil wastes into the spill and thus avoid detection. Oil cargos could be required to carry chemical "finger-prints" so illegal discharges could be traced. One-third of the spills that occur come from "unknown sources."

But such advances in liability reform and spill detection could become academic without much better tools to assess environmental and economic damage. As in the case of drilling on the outer continental shelf, this will require reliable baseline studies to detect critical short-term and long-term environmental changes, including survival of fish larva. Given the potential federal tilt towards accelerated oil development, coastal states should develop their own assessment capability, perhaps on a joint basis relying on academic resources. The Superfund bill would not pre-empt states from taxing oil activities to establish assessment and oil spill containment systems.

A strong assessment capability would give coastal states stronger legal recourse against careless or risky federal decisions in the marine realm. Strong evidence of damage can work against the ancient legal adage that the "king can do no wrong." The same public trust doctrine that requires coastal states to manage tidelands carefully can be invoked against federal actions that give scant consideration to the long-term productivity of the coastal ecosystem. There is a serious question of whether the federal government should even be permitted to lease critical marine habitats like Georges Bank without first developing the capability to detect significant change, whether natural or man-induced. Without such a commitment, the federal government is acting like an absentee landlord, content to collect ocs rents and royalties while letting oil companies take the rap for any "accidents."

Ironically, as coastal concerns over the environmental risks and costs of marine production mount, original projections of marine oil reserves ebb. Drilling results in "new frontier" areas in the Gulf of Alaska, eastern Mexico, and the mid-Atlantic Coast have been disappointing so far. Estimates of total U.S. undiscovered recoverable marine and gas resources have been continually revised downward since 1975, according to the 1980 Annual Report by the Council on Environmental Quality. In sharp contrast, gains from energy conservation have exceeded original projections.

The conventional marine perspective—the willingness to risk a coastal region's natural and social marine heritage, whether in the form of oil spills, tanker collisions, fishery depletion or nuclear plants on or near active coastal faults—generates the public awareness that may ensure its downfall: a strong sense of community identity that can override the quest for quick economic flings. Conventional marine perspectives remain tied to an industrial economy based on ever-expanding consumption and high-risk technology. A broader perspective can cultivate a post-industrial economy based on a broader mix of technical and non-technical adjustments, from low-risk energy options to more compatible marine uses. Such a marine perspective can and should appeal to a diverse cross-section of the public interested in a more stable, safer, and less centralized system of economic and political governance.

To deplore short-sighted marine exploitation while maintaining the wasteful resource practices that fuel such an exploitation is a no-win proposition. If these practices are reformed, society can regain the degree of resource self-sufficiency necessary to retain control of its destiny. Unlike the native Americans, the fenmen, and other pastoral coastal societies overwhelmed by insatiable resource quests, the modern coastal society possesses the economic and technical power to influence, if not change, traditional resource strategies.

18

Aquapolis: Some Irreverent Thoughts

AQUAPOLIS ... ATLANTIS IN THE Pacific ... Watery Camelot ... Triton City.

These alluring names serve as captions for a spate of schematics that portray cities on the sea. While these schematics come in a variety of colors and sizes, all possess a certain unity of vision. A circle of columns rises above the ocean surface to support a huge ring that resembles a larger-than-life doughnut. Perched on this mammoth doughnut is a sleek high-rise apartment whose glass walls mirror the surrounding ocean. Circling around this glassy complex, like bees around a hive, is a veritable transportation armada: helicopters, jet airplanes, submarines, hovercraft, hydrofoils. A three-dimensional traffic jam seems imminent. Off in the right-hand corner, below the water surface, are some small toothpicklike shapes that suggest magnetic filings or, more likely, all-purpose fish. In the upper right-hand corner, a v shape suggests a bird. No doubt about it, Aquapolis strives for "ecolibrium."

The depiction of the ocean itself is interesting. No waves or whitecaps sully the pondlike sea surface. This ocean has apparently been injected with novocaine. This same well-mannered ocean often graces oil company ads that claim how well technology can clean up oil spills . . . as long as waves, currents, winds, fog, icebergs, darkness, and other ship traffic keep a low profile.

What these sea-going Shangri-las lack is perhaps as significant as what is present. The doughnut appears to have no room for billboards, commercial strips, autos, or even go-carts. Aquapolis, schematically at least, becomes a screen to filter out all the urban discomforts that afflict its terrestrial counterparts. All in all, the schematics would appear to be formidable competitors to the real estate ads that offer snow-bound easterners residential escapes to Florida wetlands or the Arizona desert.

However, the proponents of Aquapolis are not real estate hawkers. They do not talk of tripling your real estate investment or getting in on the groundfloor of supergrowth in the Sun belt. They avoid crass economic appeals. The public, not the speculator, is to benefit as we subdivide the ocean.

As a prelude to their ultimate goals, the proponents generally catalog the woes of present urban and suburban life. The Floating City Development Program at the University of Hawaii speaks of societies that "watch their agricultural foundations crumble as their urban cancers spread." With the pathology of modern terrestrial life exposed, the prescription is presented: "The oceans offer us an opportunity to build our cities, or even move them, almost anywhere we like." An ecstatic article in *NOAA*, published by the U.S. Department of Commerce, opines that "A City with Sea Legs" could be "the prototype of a solution to planetary overcrowding—the opening of the oceans (70 percent of the earth's surface area) to new settlement." With this opening, pressures to urbanize the natural coast would ostensibly ebb. Opportunities to conserve coastal estuaries and agricultural lands would increase. As an urban relief valve, Aquapolis would help immunize the natural coast from "urban cancer."

As if these goals are not sweeping enough, the University of Hawaii's Floating City Development Program would seek to restore "the vitally important sense of community through a delicate balancing of closeness, openness, cleanliness, quiet and aesthetically pleasant surroundings."

I began to wonder how prospective settlers might react to the lure of these schematics. I asked students in my marine affairs course at the University of California at Irvine to respond, not as planners, engineers, or technical writers, but as people who might have the opportunity to live in Aquapolis. Although there was initial interest in liberation from an automotive society—from traffic jams, head-on collisions, smog and so on—some nagging questions began to surface. Would lack of autos symbolize decreased mobility? Would the loss of a commercial strip mean the loss of commercial competition? Would residents be buying at company stores, or living in corporate communities? Another question arose. What would you do on Saturday night? One time-honored marine pastime—gambling casinos—does not quite fit with the image of arresting urban cancer. While bingo might be OK, the most popular attraction on Aquapolis may be the next ferry to the mainland.

Aquapolis would not necessarily be dull for other prospective settlers. Rather than worry about their children running into the street, parents might have a new worry: slips or falls into the sea, particularly on fog-smitten decks. Children could stay indoors all day with parents . . . or parents could start a campaign to build a wall around the outer rim of the doughnut at the risk of suggesting a floating Alcatraz.

To liven things up, some proponents envision their man-made islands floating north for the summer and south for the winter. Others might float across the ocean to conduct trade. This raises another question. What are these islands going to use for energy when they are standing still?

Were such questions and concerns, however mundane and pedestrian, addressed amid the perorations on solving planetary overcrowding? I looked in vain. Indeed, something besides autos and billboards were missing in the schematics. Amid all the pylons, columns, apartment towers and hovering aircraft, I could find little evidence of any residents. Perhaps the scale was not small enough to depict people. (The toothpick shapes that depict fish did reappear on the deck surface of one Aquapolis but I couldn't be sure, even with the aid of a magnifying glass, whether these shapes were meant to depict people.)

Interesting differences can surface between the various schematics. Some proponents assert that their urban creations, being fixed in size, will preempt the specter of sea-going suburban sprawl and maintain the surrounding ocean in perpetual open space. However, an advisor to the University of Hawaii's program, Kiyonori Kikukati of Japan, envisions a core platform that could grow in increments to cover up to sixty square miles. At least core residents won't be able to complain that the view is always the same.

Rather than being set high above the sea surface to avoid waves, some ocean cities are encircled by large breakwaters or floating walls. The Sea City designed by England's Pilkington Glass Age Development Committee incorporates a wall structure —or, as the designers prefer, an amphitheatre—that would tower sixteen stories above the sea surface; 30,000 residents would live in an enclosed lagoon. Why such scenic blockbusters? To deflect gusty winds, large waves, and—perish the thought—stray supertankers. (One artificial oil island off southern California requires a breakwater that rises 40 feet above the sea surface.) To live inside a walled sea city could have all the rustic charm of living beside a river where your view is interrupted by a molded earth levee that resembles a miniature mountain range. Eschew the wall and you retain your marine vista . . . as well as exposure to stiff sea winds and to an occasional wave that may rinse off the deck of the platform. Waves in the Gulf of Mexico run high enough to deposit sand in living quarters perched on offshore oil platforms. While designers anticipated maximum wave heights of thirty-two feet, waves eight feet higher can and do occur.

Some Aquapolis proponents concede that their creations, like their terrestrial counterparts, could outlive their usefulness. Do you declare a ghost Aquapolis a navigation hazard or a historic monument? Some would be designed to be dismantled and moved elsewhere. Other platforms would be designed to be "weighted and sunk into the sea bottom" to join the shipwrecks, discarded ammunition, and old mines that already snag fish nets. While Aquapolis designers insist that all liquid and solid wastes will be recycled, one wonders if some of the hard-to-treat waste production might not wind up in the same place as a surplus Aquapolis.

Another question began to nag at me. Who would be interested enough to fund these pre-packaged living environments so that one day they would, in the words of one admirer, "float on the ocean surface like water lilies"? Given the broad goals of the proponents, I expected to find such sponsors as the Department of Housing and Urban Development, environmental groups, coastal cities and states, and professional architectural and planning groups. Who then was helping to fund the University of Hawaii's Floating City Development Program? The U.S. Navy, the Cement and Concrete Products Industry of Hawaii, Hawaii Dredging Company, Jorgenson Steel Company and Dillingham Corporation. (The program has also been supported by the Sea Grant program within the Department of Commerce and by the State of Hawaii.)

These are not groups associated with an overwhelming day-to-day interest in arresting urban cancer, preserving coastal estuaries and inducing a sense of community through a delicate balancing of openness and quiet. Their particular interests, while hardly as stirring as the solution of planetary overcrowding, are none the less very real. The U.S. Navy must continually face foreign and domestic pressures to give up or close down existing overseas bases and then reinvest in new facilities that may be phased out as well. *Floating* bases, if practical, could be set up, dismantled and shifted from site to site as international tensions and your friends and enemies change. Free from the need to be attached to the seabed, a floating platform would not need to incorporate costly design features against possible earthquake shaking, submarine landslides, seabed scouring, subsidence and other irritating quirks of an "unstable" seabed. Large submarine columns that would extend 200 feet below the sea surface would provide enough relative buoyancy to stabilize the platform and ward off seasickness.

While the Navy's Mobile Ocean Basing System (MOBS) remains in the idea stage, anxious requests for research data come from airport authorities confronted by noise lawsuits and from power plant companies unable to gain a coastal foothold and access to cheap ocean water for cooling purposes. Coal-burning power plants see an offshore site—fixed or floating—as one solution to stringent onshore urban air standards. Another troubled power source is also interested. Presently, nuclear plant contractors must move from site to site to construct their product. Floating nuclear plants would permit a contractor to establish a work force and facility at one site, standardize operations, and float the finished product to offshore sites around the globe. Costs to acquire and prepare a site would be eliminated. (The current record for the longest ocean tow of a petroleum production platform is 5,200 miles, from Japan to New Zealand.) A corporation has been formed to implement this beguiling concept. While contract prospects have dimmed of late, Offshore Power Systems did receive permission to reclaim a saltwater marsh near Jacksonville, Florida, as its construction site. This trade-off seems at variance with the grand claims that urbanizing the ocean would spare critical coastal habitats.

No wonder some sea city promoters fancy themselves floating across the ocean. The cities might be powered by an entire utility, not just a mere engine. They might be able to float up and down the Atlantic coast, offering their power to the highest urban bidder.

The floating platform as industrial godsend has been epitomized in a schematic in *Petroleum Today*. Besides the standard glassy apartment complex, this Aquapolis accommodated a nuclear power plant, an oil refinery, and an airport control tower serving a supersonic runway. This Aquapolis was nothing more than a grand sanctuary for all the technological wonders whose side-effects concern more and more people in coastal areas. These technological wonders even extended below the surface of the water. Here toothpick fish were being drawn into a pipe by some mysterious, unexplained force. Would this pipe feed into a display aquarium? Similar looking pipes in other schematics lead to floating fish canneries. (A fine mesh screen presumably will filter out sharks, scuba divers or Aquapolis inhabitants who fall into the sea on a foggy night or during a Christmas office party.)

No wonder the schematics don't show people strolling the deck, taking the sea air and lounging around boxed trees. Most would be working. Indeed, there would be compelling reasons for not being on the deck either on or off work. Workers may have to live below the water surface in the underwater columns supporting this industrial celebration. What about the promise to restore "the vitally important sense of community through a delicate balancing of closeness, openness, cleanliness, quiet and aesthetically pleasant surroundings"? The industrial operations topside would generate so much noise above and beyond fog horns and bell buoys that residents, according to Aquapolis proponent Dr. Athelstan Spilhaus, would have to be "insulated from aircraft noise. What better insulator than seawater? Hotel accommodations could be built within the huge floats or pylons beneath the sea surface. Travelers would truly have an 'ocean view'—from below!"

I suspect that an "ocean view from below" would not excite potential residents, particularly a wife with two young children who stays "home" and looks through a porthole while her husband toils topside, armed with ear plugs. But then why should a company go out of its way to make Aquapolis an urban paradise, other than to keep workers' minds off such possible diversions as a strike? Why indeed should a company encourage family housing and thereby incur the need for schools and for taxes to support public services? Isn't that what cities on land are for? Oil companies feel no compulsion to turn offshore platforms into family affairs or gilded prototypes to resolve planetary overcrowding. Nor, judging by the many government disposal regulations these platforms require, are they the models of waste recycling that Aquapolis proponents envision.

The specter of a chain of industrial Aquapolis islands underlines the need to assess impacts, particularly if the motive for industrial relocation is to avoid onshore air and water regulations considered overly restrictive. In a National Science Foundation study, Les Watling of the Marine Studies Center, University of Delaware, found a critical lack of knowledge on how organisms tolerate changes in turbidity, light, and temperature in oceanic —as distinct from estuarine—situations. Oceanic organisms, for instance, exhibit a much narrower tolerance to salinity changes than estuarine organisms. Concluded Watling, "Until many of these aspects of the oceanic environment are investigated, it will not be possible to adequately stipulate what precautions must be taken in order to avoid serious environmental damage during the construction and operation of an artificial island."

Some Aquapolis proponents appear to recognize the need for caution rather than rhetoric. "Quite frankly, we know comparatively little about the oceans that cover most of our planet," observes Dames & Moore, an engineering firm that helped investigate a proposed offshore nuclear facility for Public Service Electric & Gas Company of New Jersey. "Therefore, many of the reservations concerning offshore nuclear siting cannot be dismissed lightly." Wind and waves can make transfer of men, fuel, and equipment a far more unpredictable and risky task for an offshore facility than for an onshore one. A stormy sea coincident with the need to land an emergency repair task force could prove especially disconcerting. Breakwaters to protect floating platforms from waves or errant ship traffic can pose serious siting problems. The seabed, commonly composed of weak and unconsolidated sands, silts, and clays, can settle and shift. Once in place, a breakwater can be undermined by scouring if the potential for erosive currents is not anticipated.

A breakwater might be secure enough to withstand the impact of an errant oil tanker, but this brings us to another design problem. The protected power plant, nuclear or nonnuclear, might turn into the most efficient oil recovery system yet devised. Spilt oil could be sucked into the plant's cooling system, but the plant itself would probably have to shut down even if its onshore clients were contending with a chilly winter.

Industrial islands, floating or stationary, may pose international problems. By relocating hazardous activities seaward, a nation is not eliminating but transferring the risks, in this case to the marine environment, which all nations share as a fishing and recreational resource. Adjacent coastal nations, particularly in semienclosed seas like the Mediterranean and the North, may resent such risk transfer, particularly if the industrial islands proliferate. Proponents of the New Jersey floating nuclear facility concept have invariably talked in the plural, much to the distress of Delaware.

Fortunately, there may be some lead time for more assessment. With one prominent exception, Aquapolis schemes at this point appear to be in a state of suspended animation. One real life version did materialize—for a while anyway—at the 1975 International Ocean Exposition in Okinawa. It was basically a spacious oil production platform with boxed trees and a marine exhibit hall. The architect of this temporary conversion, Kikukati of Japan, is presently seeking funds for a pilot project in Tokyo Bay. Hawaii's Floating City Development Program, according to ocean engineering professor John Craven, is in a "fallback position," with study of prospective occupants limited mainly to power plants, deep-sea mining ventures, and other "candidate industries." While initial federal approval for an offshore oil port in the Gulf of Mexico off Texas has been received, oil companies are reluctant to move ahead because of concerns over government safeguards designed to prevent monopolistic practices in handling oil shipments. New Jersey's offshore nuclear facility proposal has been shelved.

Atlantic Richfield Corporation operates a floating concrete barge 20 miles off Java in waters 135 feet deep. An underwater pipe network brings petroleum to the barge from submarine fields; a facility aboard the barge processes the petroleum to a liquefied state prior to transfer to tankers. Consolidated Edison has placed small power plants on barges moored off New York City. A floating liquefied natural gas facility has been proposed as an alternative to an onshore facility in southern California.

By bringing an interesting twist to the concept, one man has propelled the floating platform concept into the real world. Daniel Ludwig is described by the Associated Press as the "only remaining known billionaire in the U.S." Ludwig, an octogenarian who still likes to walk to his New York City office, gained his fortune by sticking with a tried and true marine enterprise, shipping. In the 1930's, he learned how to build tankers with other people's money. He used contracts with oil firms to ship their future output as collateral to build the ships. By World War II, he was building tankers for the United States, with the understanding that the tankers would revert to him at war's end. One postwar scene enchanted Ludwig—the deserted military shipyards of Japan. At this time the world was not short of oil but of oil tankers. Ludwig gained control of the shipyards. He was soon peddling the world's first supertankers while Greek shipping tycoons scampered for surplus liberty ships. By the time the Greeks were ordering supertankers, Ludwig was investing early and well in another advance: container ships.

Sometime later, Ludwig focused on a coastal lagoon in Baja California, where gray whales that migrate from the Bering Sea mate and calve. Soon the whales were sharing the lagoon with barges serving the world's largest solar salt evaporation project. (It remains to be seen how long the whales can coexist with the increasing lagoon barge traffic. The lagoon may contain another mineral—oil.)

More recently, Ludwig acquired a rain forest in Brazil's Amazon basin. The jungle—some 4 million acres in all—is being replaced by a commercial tree plantation. How can you build an industrial complex so remote from roads, power plants, and other industrial infrastructure? Halfway around the world, in a Japanese shipyard, two floating platforms were constructed—one equipped with a power plant, the other with a pulp mill. The platforms were towed across the oceans and up the Amazon basin to the remote site in 1978. Ludwig's industrial complex can produce 750 tons of pulp for papermaking daily. He has beat the Aquapolis visionaries to the economic punch.

But Ludwig has problems onshore. The trees don't grow fast enough. Bulldozers replaced hand labor so the jungle, with its 125 tree species, could be cleared faster and planted with 2 commercial tree species. But the bulldozers also cleared away the topsoil. Growth of the money trees is lagging. The bulldozers have been retired in favor of hand labor.

Ludwig still does not know if the floated-in factory will make his billion-dollar jungle flyer another winner. The project has inspired one profitable development—a jungle shantytown that provides scarce housing for workers as well as bars, brothels, and brawls.

Such instant industrialization emphasizes again the need to assess the social as well as environmental impacts of floating platforms. Will such capital-intensive, non-labor-intensive projects foster long-term prosperity in developing nations or result in an exhausted landscape and a boom and bust economy?

The shipping industry is more interested in whether Ludwig's use of floating platforms can help lead it out of a global recession. The tanker market Ludwig helped develop over three decades ago is now glutted. U.S. shipyards eagerly point out to prospective industrial clients that floating facilities, unlike land-based facilities, may qualify for federal shipbuilding subsidies. Commercial plantships, when and if they materialize, have been declared eligible for federal vessel loans by act of Congress.

Japanese shipyards, operating at 40 percent capacity, try to drum up business with visions of luxury gambling casinos afloat off the Middle East, where gaming is banned on land. But Atlantic City and Las Vegas don't have to worry. No more Ludwigs have materialized to fund a fleet of floating platforms. One Japanese shipyard, as was discussed in Chapter 16, has turned to a traditional source of power for ships—the wind—to perk up its prospects.

Ironically, the fixed artificial island concept is being updated and modernized to compete with its floating counterparts. The Dutch would like to relocate hazardous industrial operations to Sea Island, a proposed dike and fill operation in a shallow portion of the North Sea. But a Dutch report finds that such a concentration of hazardous activities could have a disastrous "domino" effect if just one refinery or power plant had an accident. In other words, Sea Island might be sitting on a man-made volcano. The report also warns that it might be hard to recruit workers who would be separated from their families. A peninsula could be built for homesick workers, but this would be costly and would obstruct shipping. The Dutch have beached Sea Island for the time being.

Nigel Chattey, a New York City consultant, envisions a similar project in the New York Bight. The project is called ICONN, short for Island Complex Offshore New York, New Jersey, and Connecticut. The New York State Department of Commerce has helped fund the ICONN study, and unions have provided verbal support. Huge dikes would be constructed on an underwater plateau called Cholera Bank, now used as a dumping grounds. With the dikes in place, the enclosed waters would be calm enough to receive floating platforms bearing smelters, refineries, power plants, fertilizer firms, and other industrial refugees. If desired, the "wet polder" could be drained, with the industrial complex left low and dry—that is, below sea level. Views of coastal residents would remain unimpaired.

The dikes would require almost as much fill as was excavated from the Panama Canal. The seabed ooze, covered with accumulated garbage, may not suffice. Undaunted, Chattey would dredge the moribund Erie Canal so it could be reopened, using the spoil for the ICONN dikes. Coal from the West could then be shipped across the Great Lakes, through the revived canal, and down the Hudson to coal-burning power plants on Cholera Bank, downwind of energy-hungry New York.

ICONN has attracted considerable publicity, but Cholera Bank still remains undeveloped. Once more, the costs of the project can make meeting—or circumventing—onshore environmental and safety regulations look cheap. (Reviving the Erie Canal could put the United States in hot water with an oil-rich neighbor, Canada. Joint American-Canadian participation in the St. Lawrence Seaway project is predicated on not diverting any seaway traffic to the Erie.)

Can environmentalists be conveniently blamed for the slow progress in realizing sea-city visions? Hardly. As in the case of nuclear plant technology—on land or at sea—the Aquapolis visions can overlook simple human considerations. They require complex institutions to regulate as well as operate them, are relatively inflexible in adjusting to economic and social changes, and are capital-intensive. While construction trade journals exult about going "Down to the Sea in Concrete," few utilities are committing themselves to floating nuclear plants. Otherwise, as in the case of terrestrial nuclear plants, Congress might be asked either to oversee or to subsidize such risky technical leaps into the marine environment as a way to reap more revenues from the outer continental shelf and circumvent coastal states concerned with safeguarding natural marine values.

Aquapolis may come to play a broader social role than just a cover for another company town. Speculation and research into its potential should certainly not be discouraged. (The flexibility and maneuverability of a floating platform—as distinct from a fixed or stationary platform—could benefit a number of current marine activities.) However, Aquapolis, like other technical visions projected for the marine realm, deserves more serious review if we as a society are truly to benefit from, rather than be victimized by, ocean development.

Must we wait on sea cities to arrest urban cancer or avoid planetary overcrowding? Baltimore's Harborplace is a new $20 million commercial center with over 114 cafes and specialty shops. Glass-enclosed pavilions shelter a festival marketplace. You can reach it by a pedestrian overpass. A blighted waterfront is being recycled as the Inner Harbor Renewal Area. The restored bayfront helps Baltimore reverse city-center decline.

Two aging piers help revitalize Seattle's urban center. The piers now accommodate an aquarium and a waterfront park. Visitors can view marine life in Puget Sound through a subsurface viewing dome. (There are no overnight accommodations in this Aquapolis.) The aquarium even operates a fish hatchery. In its first year, the aquarium drew over 650,000 people to a site once occupied mainly by pigeons. To ensure that the $2.50 admission does not exclude some urban residents, the aquarium has ten free days each year. While it may not be as glamorous as a floating sea city, Seattle's Waterfront Park and Aquarium has proven to be a far more practical means of enhancing people's lives.

Once described as the "dearest place to live in all New England" by Herman Melville, New Bedford, Massachusetts fell on hard times as the whaling industry and then the textile industry declined. The once prosperous waterfront became the hard core of community blight, with a rental vacancy of up to 35 percent in 1975. A plan to raze the area inspired formation of the Waterfront Historic Area League (WHALE). This private, nonprofit group urged owners to restore historic whaling era buildings rather than submit to demolition. Federal community development funds helped restoration efforts. Utility companies removed a maze of overhead lines and wires. Street asphalt was removed to reveal the cobblestones below. Sidewalks were landscaped. Maurice Joseph, a sixty-year-old native of Belgium, opened a restaurant in a former whale oil candleworks built in 1810. Today, the derelict waterfront prospers as a commercial district, attracting both fishermen and tourists. It attracted 200,000 visitors in 1976 and some 750,000 visitors in 1980. "We are a working waterfront, not a museum," says one local merchant.

Savannah, Georgia, has transformed a derelict waterfront into a thirty-acre esplanade that reunites residents with their aquatic heritage. Warehouses are being recycled as restaurants and loft residences. A piazza hosts fairs and festivals. Urban residents don't have to jet to a luxury resort to enjoy a waterfront stroll. The waterfront has its own version of floating platforms: recreational boaters that tie up to the urban dock.

A once-popular beach resort had become a blight on the waterfront of Warwick, Rhode Island's second largest and fastest growing city. Summer cottages deteriorated into hovels. Two hurricane surges speeded up the cycle of decay. One hurricane destroyed 300 homes. After designating the area a Hurricane Danger Zone, Warwick restored it as a beach, complemented by a tot lot, scenic overlook, bikepath, and fishermen's shelter. Today, the area is not only safer but more scenic and popular. Residents can enjoy the same type of waterscapes that inspired Whistler, Homer, and Turner a century ago.

Thus, while Aquapolis promotions continue to receive considerable press fanfare, these working projects are bringing more practical aquatic visions to where the people are. Rather than depend on technology for an aquatic site, they restore the urban coast. This is precisely the type of opportunity so easily overlooked in the technological visions of a conquered ocean.

This practical focus on the urban coast ties in with other critical needs. Derelict wharves and piers that present a fire and navigation hazard can be replaced. By providing aquatic outlets in the urban environment, these waterfront initiatives provide an alternative to expensive commutes to more distant aquatic resorts. The return on clean water is brought home to the urban resident, who must pay the bill for restoring this nation's waterways. By reopening obsolete and decaying waterfront parcels, New York City would have a far more lively civic resource than ICONN to help counter the lure of the sun belt.

These projects can renew a sense of community self-reliance as well. In Brooklyn, a former ferry slip had become an eyesore. During their lunch hour, local sanitation officials graded the site and removed weeds, rotting timbers, derelict cars and oily debris. Boulders from a subway construction project helped redefine the wasted shoreline. A hospital donated cinder footpaths now flanked by olive trees and roses. A local merchant provided oak kegs for seats. Participants in an alcoholic rehabilitation program helped construct a timber "ship" crewed by local children. The eyesore is now a community waterfront park maintained by Unidad Y Progresso, a local group that employs teens during the summer. The park's cost: less then $10,000. When I look at the schematics conjured up by the new generation of Captain Nemos and then at Brooklyn's Grand Street Park, I realize how easily glamorous technological visions can lead us astray.

19

Sea Miners and Sea Minerals: The Elusive Connection

THE SMALL ROCK IN MY HAND RE-
sembles others in my back yard, except that this particular rock
originally lay beneath three miles of seawater in the middle of the
Pacific Ocean. Peculiar traits become apparent on closer inspection. This rock is surprisingly light in weight, so light that it
couldn't be used as a paperweight. It is round and lumpy, not
worn smooth like a beach pebble. It resembles the charred and
overcooked baked potatoes that sometimes result from my efforts
in the kitchen.

The rock is a manganese nodule, and the presence of rocks
like it on the ocean floor has caused a considerable global stir
about the prospect of deep-sea mining. This prospect can incite
visions of a marine mineral rush, serve to embarrass the U.S.

Congress, provide cover for deepwater submarine snatching, and disrupt international conferences. This type of social excitement is normally associated with gold, silver, and other precious metals. The rock in my hand accomplishes this without even sustaining a single commercial mine. What properties do these much-publicized nodules possess to inspire such expansive visions and global ill-feeling?

The prospect of new mineral bonanzas is always an important stimulus to maritime thrusts, probably more so than the prospect of new fish stocks. With their domestic silver mines played out, the ancient Greeks took to the sea to scout out new foreign sources. In the fifteenth century, Italian city-states, short of gold to mint coins, funded overland trips into the interior of Africa to locate new sources. They were beat to the punch by Portugal, whose explorers went by sea along Africa's east coast. (The intrepid explorers did not stop till they reached the spice-rich islands in the Java Sea.)

The possibility of laying claim to new mineral sources can encourage nations to subsidize prospective miners handsomely. This inclination is not lost on enterprising individuals. When seeking funding for his explorations in the Panamanian jungles, Balboa wrote the Spanish court in 1513, "All the caciques and Indians of that province of Comogre tell me that there are so many pieces of gold in the houses of the caciques on the other sea as to make us lose our minds. They say that gold is found in quantity in all the rivers of the other coast and in large nuggets." A century later, James I released Sir Walter Raleigh from enforced residency in the Tower of London. The king's displeasure over Raleigh's knack for alienating the Spanish Court ebbed as the venerable explorer spoke of a "mountain covered with gold and silver ore" that he had stumbled across while exploring the New World in his glory days. Raleigh eagerly agreed to lead another expedition to uncover the metallic mountain. The ore was to be refined in a ship equipped with giant bellows and brick furnaces.

However, such mineral messiahs risk considerable political backlashes if their visions don't pan out. Balboa found no gold while thrashing about in the Panamanian jungles. Even his discovery of "the other sea"—the Pacific—did not spare him from a death sentence laid down by a political rival. When Raleigh returned empty-handed from the New World, James I put him back in the Tower. Raleigh left the Tower for the last time to have his head chopped off.

Today, with all our technical sophistication, we would not lose our minds to gold-covered mountains . . . or would we? We are not running out of metal ore per se, but of high-grade, easily extractable deposits. A "vicious triangle of constraints" results, according to Dr. Douglas Fuerstenau, a mining professor with the University of California at Berkeley. The lower the grade, the more energy has to be expended and the more environmental damage can result, whether we strip mine more hillsides in Appalachia and Colorado or dig deeper copper pits in Arizona. Access to cheap sources of energy can be as critical as access to an ore deposit.

The first large oceanographic expedition, that of Britain's H.M.S. *Challenger* in the late nineteenth century, retrieved the first nodules. Scientists disagreed over whether the potatolike lumps came from submarine volcanos or as "gifts from outer space." The nodules were thought to contain only one commercial mineral, manganese.

The nodules emerged from obscurity after World War II. After conducting a marine mineral research program at the Scripps Institution of Oceanography, Dr. John Mero wrote *The Mineral Resources of the Sea* in 1965. He nominated the nodules as a prime new source of minerals. Mero is somewhat of a standard fixture at conferences that promote the ocean as a vast untapped resource. He is often sandwiched between one speaker who talks of food from the sea and another speaker who talks of drugs from the sea. His presentations are straightforward and pleasantly free of the boosterism and vague assertions of a latter-day Balboa or Raleigh. Nor are there any jingoistic references to America's maritime destiny. Mero accompanies his presentations with visual aids that elicit oooh's and aaah's. Underwater photos reveal nodules lined up on the seabed like marbles on a display counter. Dots on a world ocean map identify nodule sites. The dots are numerous.

Despite an unassuming, calm demeanor—or perhaps because of this—Mero's presentation can come across as a virtual fairy tale come true, a miner's dream. Mero, through laboratory analyses, stressed that the nodules contain not just one but four commercial metals: manganese (used to strengthen steel), copper, nickel, and cobalt. The United States must import almost all of its manganese, nickel, and cobalt. To reach such a mineral windfall, prospective miners would not have to tunnel through hard rock. As Mero wrote, "We have, in the ocean, materials that are available without removing any overburden, without the use of explosives, and without expensive drilling operations for sampling and ore breakage . . . there will be no drifts to drive, shafts to sink, or townsites to construct in developing a deep-sea mine." Are these deposits located in fog-bound, cold waters such as the polar seas? The most promising deposits, according to Mero, occur in the tropical Pacific not too far from Hawaii. For miners accustomed to jungles, deserts, and snow-covered mountains, a much more comfortable era of mining appeared to beckon.

Could there possibly be any better news to disclose about these nodules? Yes, and Mero invariably saves it for the last. Unlike fish or timber, mineral deposits are not renewable. That is why miners, whether from Ancient Greece or today's world, must locate new sources. Metals found in the nodules precipitate out of the sea solution. They collect around a core that may be a shark tooth or a squid beak. Nodules are being formed through this process even now. As Mero claimed in his book, "Once these nodules are being mined, therefore, the mineral industry would be faced with the very interesting situation of working deposits that grow faster than they can be mined." Minerals that grow! What more could miners ask for? One is almost prepared to hear that the obliging nodules, like marine munchkins, will line up in the presence of a seabed mining bucket or vacuum.

There appears to be only one problem. Nodules occur in deep water beyond the continental shelf, deep being on the order of two, three, and four miles. One skeptic likened recovery to "trying to pick up peas with a straw from the top of the Empire State Building—at night."

The mining consortiums that formed to investigate Mero's tantalizing visions indicated that the deep-sea location was not necessarily a technical problem. Field tests showed that nodules could be sucked up by vacuum pipes and, where the seabed might be irregular, with a chain of buckets. Indeed, the location appeared to possess potential political advantages. Deep-sea miners would operate far beyond crowded coastal waters, seemingly beyond the purview of national governments, tax demands, and requirements for union crews or American-built ships. No need to worry about million-dollar mistakes such as coastal oil spills, which haunt the oil industry, trigger national indignation, and inspire environmental lawsuits. As Mero wrote, "These ocean floor sediments have other advantages when being considered as a material to mine, that of being politically-free and royalty-free materials."

To miners, these mundane rocks signified a whole new liberated climate in which to work. No more tense confrontations with concerned environmental delegations, demanding union negotiators, or adamant public regulators. Occasional seasickness or sunburn seemed a small price to pay for such prospective benefits, including a liberty port like Hawaii.

However, the miners' glee is not universally shared. Mero himself suggested one possible caveat to his optimistic visions: "that of fomenting inane squabbles over who owns which areas of the ocean floor and who is to collect the protection money from the mining companies."

In 1966, during the launching of an oceanographic research vessel, President Lyndon Johnson observed that we should not "allow the prospects of rich harvests and mineral wealth to create a new form of colonial competition among the maritime nations. We must be careful to avoid a race to grab and hold the lands under the high seas. We must ensure that the deep seas and the ocean bottoms are, and remain, the legacy of all human beings." This inspiring vision was meant to discourage national seaward claims that might control or limit mining access to the nodules.

A year later, Malta's Ambassador to the UN, Arvid Pardo, turned this solemn presidential announcement around in a manner that shook up the expectant miners. To Pardo, terms like "legacy of all human beings" meant that the international community, instead of safeguarding access for corporate miners, should control exploitation. Most developing nations immediately embraced Pardo's concept that the nodules on the deep seabed were part of the "common heritage of mankind."

Miners once worried about national claims were now confronted by the specter of an international claim to every single nodule in those tantalizing underwater photos. But one American institution was not so dismayed by Pardo's reformulation of the ocean commons. The Defense Department was concerned that developing nations, anxious to reject their colonial past, would limit transit through strategic straits and coastal waters. The U.S.'s UN delegation, encouraged by the Defense Department, decided to favor international control over the deep seabed as an incentive for developing nations to maintain transit rights. In 1970, by a nearly unanimous vote, the UN General Assembly declared that the resources of the sea beyond national jurisdiction are "the common heritage of mankind."

Seabed mining, once a poor political cousin to fishing, navigation, marine oil development, and marine pollution, suddenly became a prime catalyst for the Third United Nations Conference on the Law of the Sea (LOS). Given the initial optimistic projections of nodule wealth, there appeared to be ample room to compromise on an international seabed authority to protect claims of miners while sharing a portion of royalties with the world community.

To American miners, the political assets of the nodules began to ebb. After locating seabed deposits and developing recovery technology, a miner's return on this investment might be determined by an amorphous body of "international do-gooders, bleeding hearts, and political pipsqueaks" inclined to cream off the revenues from such private risk-taking. The specter of public controls now became quite acceptable to the American mining community, but only if they were administered by the United States. (The head of one mineral exploratory venture working the waters between Hawaii and the United States referred to this stretch as "the American Ocean.")

The seabed miners turned landward towards Washington, D.C., and the U.S. Congress. The marvelous story of self-renewing minerals strewn over the deep-ocean floor now unfolded in committee hearing rooms, complete with slides of recovered nodules. The more influential congressmen might receive a nodule suitable as a decorative paperweight or doorstop. Congressmen who asked about technical problems were reassured the main problem was "political." American miners just wanted a "stable" regulatory regime within which to work. The congressmen were impressed. Here was clear evidence of the ocean's much-publicized wealth and the American know-how that could tap it. Russia and Japan might out-compete the United States in harvesting world fish stocks, but not in the race to scoop up marine nodules.

Amid such heightened expectations, seabed mining would now be transformed and altered by pressures unique to the Congress. Congressional committees often compete to claim jurisdiction over critical new issues. Intensive marine development is a legislative bonanza in this regard. The Senate Foreign Relations Committee, which handles international issues, supports the concept of international accords that reduce national tensions while protecting American interests.

The miners wanted a committee more sympathetic to their needs and less concerned with international protocol. Such a committee exists. The Senate Interior Committee continually chastises the Foreign Relations Committee for its alleged propensity to give away national interests—even those three miles below the mid-Pacific—in the search for international peace.

In 1973, a seabed mining bill made its debut in an Interior subcommittee. The late Senator Lee Metcalf declared it was time to decide "so far as ocean mining legislation is concerned, whether we fish, cut bait, or haul for shore." The bill's purported purpose was to establish an "interim" seabed mining agency. The United States would recognize seabed mining claims by U.S. companies until an international agency materialized. Any investment money U.S. companies would lose because of ultimate international restrictions would be reimbursed by the United States Government. The Department of Commerce estimates that this generous guarantee could cost U.S. taxpayers as much as two billion dollars. With such a guarantee enacted into law, the United States would have a strong fiscal incentive never to approve an international agency, or only one with minimal regulatory powers. (One congressman asked a mining official if the United States should share in the profits as well as the risks of deep-sea mining. The official preferred that the United States limit its role to the latter.)

Through long and hard experience with miners on public lands, the United States has learned to limit claims in size and in the time of the lease to discourage speculators and monopolists. Despite this experience, the original seabed bill would permit almost timeless claims covering thousands of square miles. Lease blocks could be as large as 60,000 kilometers, or one and a half times the size of Switzerland. Such concessions to private enterprise rival the concessions that Spanish explorers sought from the Spanish Court. As some observers pointed out, the miners could not have written a more satisfactory bill.

As it turned out, miners did write the bill. After admitting to a *Washington Post* reporter that the bill was introduced at the request of the American Mining Congress, Senator Metcalf conceded that the bill was "preposterous."

Is the Senate Interior Committee a mere tool of the mining industry willing to jeopardize the integrity of the Senate? To the committee, the "preposterous" bill was only intended as a prod to an international settlement that would not be weighted in the interests of the developing nations. Through such maneuvering, marine visions can quickly take on a high-pressure political reality as anxious political competitors serve to fulfill each other's worst fears.

The bill and its later versions have attracted other interesting provisions. One perennial provision is that American seabed mining firms must use American ships with American crews and process all nodules in the United States. Predictably, maritime labor unions and American shipbuilders are the backers for such America-only provisions. As one union official asserts, his members do not want to see "runaway seabed mining operations." Like officials of developing nations, American union officials understand that marine development is by no means an everybody-wins, nobody-loses proposition. Prospective deep-sea miners must consider such protectionist features to gain necessary political support, even when it creates another critical problem. To reduce financial risks, America's would-be lords of the seabed wish to enter into joint ventures or consortiums with foreign mining interests. The America-only terms jeopardize such contracts. Other industrial nations translate and redraft the American seabed bill to protect their own shipbuilders and unions.

The American seabed miners, once excited by a politically free mining environment, now lobby for political protection and even subsidies. Are such favors being sought to make an uneconomic marine enterprise economic, as has so often happened in the past? The mining industry invokes a broader public purpose. While manganese, copper, cobalt, and nickel deposits exist on land, some are located in developing nations considered "unstable" or "hostile"—that is, liable to jack up prices or indulge in metal embargos. The names of these nations are invariably recited in an ominous tone: Gabon, Zaire, Zambia. As one mining lawyer, Northcutt Ely, explained, "If the United States continues to be dependent on foreign sources for manganese, nickel, copper, and cobalt, the economic welfare and national security of the United States will be in jeopardy." An oil embargo today, a mineral embargo tomorrow. Seabed mining would remove this dire threat. Developing nations would have one less means of plucking the Yankee eagle.

To developing nations, such arguments only serve to buttress their fears of a seabed grab. In the LOS sessions, the developing nations, banding together as the Group of 77, have proposed an international seabed authority. This authority would exclude private mineral leases and do the mining itself. Revenues would go into a global fund for developing nations. To American miners and their congressional supporters, this position serves to prove that developing nations want to make seabed mining a keystone for a new international economic order.

An unexpected event contributed to this political snarl. At one point news went out throughout the world that Howard Hughes was building a huge new ship, the *Glomar Explorer,* to mine seabed wealth. Developing nations became convinced that a seabed fortune was up for grabs. American seabed mining consortiums, meanwhile, redoubled their efforts to get the U.S. Congress to pass a bill to preempt international seabed control.

Oddly enough, no Hughes official showed up to support such a bill. To bill opponents, this prominent absence demonstrated that not all American miners needed to be propped up by such self-serving legislation. To proponents, the Hughes plunge underscored the imminence of such mining and the urgent need for legislation to protect such intrepid American miners. In 1974, the *Glomar Explorer* retrieved a curious piece of ore: part of a sunken Soviet submarine. American officials were content to take pride in such technical bravado. To developing nations, the *Glomar Explorer* episode reconfirmed the need for an international seabed authority to preempt imperial shenanigans. Nations that were reaching accord over fishing navigation, and other traditionally thorny ocean issues remained polarized over seabed mining.

The mining debut of another American corporation stirred matters up even more. To Lockheed Corporation, the location of the minerals suggested the need for advanced engineering skills that only an aerospace corporation could wield. Moreover, as a miner, Lockheed might share in the mineral windfall and open up new revenue horizons beyond the Defense Department. That Lockheed needed a federal loan guarantee to ward off bankruptcy in the early 1970's emphasized the need for new corporate income horizons. In a joint venture with oil company firms like Standard Oil of Indiana, Amoco and Royal Dutch Shell, Lockheed formed the Ocean Minerals Company.

While most miners shy away from promoting their exploratory efforts, aerospace firms eagerly trumpet their projects ("technical challenges") to gain public support, both economic and political. Slick magazines began carrying cutaway drawings that showed a ship on a pond-like sea sucking minerals from the seabed. "Harvesting the bounty of the ocean," proclaimed the ads. "Lockheed knows how." U.S. legislators who had taken political flak for "bailing out" Lockheed now realized that the same corporation, along with other miners, was seeking another government guarantee, this time against any losses resulting from formation of an international seabed authority. This type of risk transfer seemed less and less appealing to Congress.

To UN delegates in New York, the ads were one more indication of how industrial nations were about to secure another resource monopoly.

The fate of the world fisheries tended to harden the position of the Group of 77. At the behest of Latin America, most developing nations promoted the concept of a 200-mile-wide exclusive economic zone off each coastal nation. In effect, the coastal waters, where fish stocks are most abundant and easily harvested, would be controlled by coastal nations, depending on the length of their coastlines. The biggest winners turned out to be industrial nations in the northern hemisphere, including the United States, with its two-ocean coastline, and Denmark, which controls the largest island in the world, Greenland. With so much of the living marine resources beyond the reach of the new international economic order, the fate of the deep-sea nodules took on added import. Projections of their potential wealth seemed to rise. If the Group of 77 could not land fish, they would try for the potatolike lumps in the ocean depths.

The United States at first withheld support of a 200-mile zone as leverage to get developing nations to accept a seabed authority with only limited powers. When Congress, under pressure from U.S. domestic fishermen, went ahead and unilaterally adopted a 200-mile zone, the leverage—whatever its value—vanished.

Today, of all the predictions Mero made sixteen years ago, the most pessimistic turns out to be the most realistic: that seabed mining would foment "squabbles over who owns which areas of the ocean floor and who is to collect the protection money from the mining companies." Doesn't this political snarl permit African nations to employ metal embargoes and pluck the Yankee eagle at will? To the contrary, no such metal embargoes have evolved. A cartel, to succeed, requires (1) a virtual resource monopoly and (2) political cohesion among the few countries where the resource is located. In raising the metal embargo specter, deep-sea miners often fail to list all existing metal suppliers. For instance, the second largest known land reserve of manganese lies in Australia. For a manganese cartel to work, Australia must jeopardize its extensive U.S. trade to favor a country like Gabon, which imports virtually nothing from Australia. And America's largest foreign supplier of nickel and copper is Canada.

The alluring image of self-sufficiency through intensive marine development can counter another major national goal: two-way trade relations that enable nations—developed or developing —to buy our finished products. The countries that supply us with minerals found in the nodules generally buy more from the United States than we buy from them. If we use the oceans in a way that drastically reduces imports, we will reduce the ability of other nations to buy our goods—whether fish, nodule metals, computers, or TV sitcoms.

Why weren't such contradictions raised before the seabed mining debate became so polarized? They were. One U.S. researcher cautioned, "The existence of diverse producers, the elasticities of demand for and supply of the four minerals, and the impossibility of export discipline and policy cohesion among producers argue strongly against the possibility of sustained influence over the international market in any of the major minerals found in manganese nodules." Richard Raymond of Johns Hopkins University wrote these words in the *Marine Technology Society Journal* in June 1976. His insight was completely submerged in a flurry of corporate and congressional press releases warning of a prospective metal embargo. Jack Barkenbus of the Scripps Institution of Oceangraphy warned, "While the dependency issue is real, any attempt to portray the U.S. as a helpless victim of unified conspiratorial designs distorts reality . . . We import over half of our cobalt consumption from one nonindustrial country, Zaire. While this may appear ominous it should be recognized that the amount of cobalt we consume annually is quite small—approximately 6,500 tons/year—and that the U.S. has stockpiled cobalt for a number of years. At last count, the U.S. had stockpiled enough cobalt to supply six full years of increasing consumption!" Barkenbus sent these comments to a congressional hearing on seabed mining in 1974. His comments ended up in small print at the end of a 500-page-long published committee hearing. Such print overburden can defy the most steadfast seeker of objective information. Realistic marine assessments have played and always will play second fiddle to what corporate and political leaders want to hear. Balboa and Raleigh understood this 300 years ago.

Ironically, even with a mining regime, national or international, little or no mining would be taking place. Scientists now believe that the nodules form at a much slower rate than Mero originally predicted. But exploitation, much less depletion, does not appear to be around the corner. Some mineral messiahs have long since hauled for shore because of problems that can't be blamed on international do-gooders or conniving Gabon officials.

In 1978, prices of nickel and copper were, according to the *Wall Street Journal,* "sharply depressed by world-wide overproduction from land mines."

While nodule miners were warning Congress of the prospect of strategic mineral cutoffs, copper was dropping in price, from $1.41 in 1974 to 53 cents in 1977. Prices began to rise again in 1980, but not because of actual market demand. "What's driving up the price of copper is sheer speculation and jumping on the bandwagon. It's an unreal market," one New York copper merchant told *Los Angeles Times* reporter Barbara Bry. Some copper customers, unwilling to bid against speculators, are turning to alternative materials, such as plastic piping. Alternative materials are often overlooked when dire predictions of metal embargoes are being invoked.

Meanwhile, the projected costs of mining the seabed are spiraling. Mining equipment must be more durable than research equipment that makes a few seabed grabs and returns to an onshore marine laboratory. The equipment must withstand water pressures of six to nine thousand pounds per square inch, salt-water corrosion, and near-freezing temperatures. Mining consultant Manfred Krutein of Irvine, California, says that it can take twenty to sixty minutes to get one nodule from the seabed to the ship. A slurry method may shorten this time. This vertical distance can severely complicate a ship's ability to maintain a steady position, much less its ability to relocate on a particular site. Imagine if you had to extract gravel with a hovering helicopter, and a two-mile-long pipe as the link. You would have to hover through wind gusts and clouds while changing the length of the pipestring as the terrain below changes from hills to valleys. You would have one advantage over the marine miner; you could at least eyeball the land below.

One potential risk involves the miles of pipe required to reach the seabed, which amounts to a considerable linear weight suspended from the ship. The pipestring itself stretches under this weight, like a spring under tension. The relationship of the suspended pipe to the ship becomes somewhat analagous to that of a drawn arrow to a bow. If part of the pipe falls off, the remainder may spring back and hurtle through the ship's hull. Currents in the water column or a nodule collecter snagged on the seabed can snap the pipe.

The *Glomar Explorer* periodically comes out of mothballs to engage in what it was originally supposed to do. The central well in the ship's hull, through which the pipe is lowered, is so large that, upon being closed, it occasionally traps large, man-eating sharks. I doubt if deep-sea miners ever anticipated such surprise shipboard aquariums.

Another overlooked technical factor is that ore deposits may be expensive to process even though they are of high grade. The separation of various metals from the host rock can be very costly. Rocks rich in silica pose such problems, and nodules are rich in silica. The solution to the separation problem may create another problem: the need for large amounts of energy to fuel processing. According to nodule researchers with Kennecott Copper Corporation, the cost of a nodule processing plant will be nearly twice the cost of the mining operation itself. The vicious triangle of constraints embraces nodule mining with a vengeance.

The major environmental and social problems posed by marine nodule mining, when and if it becomes feasible, involve the need for onshore processing sites. Hilo, Hawaii, which was once agog over the idea of becoming the world's seabed mining capital, is now concerned that a processing facility may pollute the air and compete for scarce energy. The processing facility will produce copious tailings containing toxic elements such as arsenic. The municipal host will have to share shrinking space in its existing coastal dumpsites, make new sites available, or both. If dumped in coastal waters, the wastes may pose risks to marine life and to existing recreational uses. Mining firms say marine disposal can be properly controlled, but their zeal to be exempted from discharge controls in the U.S. Clean Water Act belies such confidence. After the Duluth region in Minnesota eagerly accepted an aluminum-mining operation, its water supply from the Great Lakes was imperiled by pollution from aluminum tailings. The

Duluth experience tends to temper municipal excitement over mineral booms. "Who wants to be the Pittsburgh of the tropical ocean?" says one Hilo resident who is not about to lose his mind over manganese nodules.

Even if a mining firm finds a tolerant community and learns to separate metals from silica-rich nodules, it may face competition from other firms processing immense silica-rich ore deposits that are mined on land. In other words, metal sources on land may continue to out-compete marine sources. Formation of mineral sources on land benefits from one advantage that the marine environment lacks: weathering. Geologist Preston Cloud, who is with Baas Becking Geobiological Laboratory in Australia, cites this difference as one reason that visions of a marine mineral cornucopia can be as overinflated as Raleigh's gold-covered mountain. The solar salt evaporation industry already faces stiff competition from synthetic sources and from underground salt deposits.

The elusive career of seabed mining surfaced at a recent university conference on underwater mining. Like those at other such conferences, speakers bemoaned the lack of such mining. One speaker who was involved in marine mining a decade ago reassured his audience that opportunities still do exist, particularly "opportunities in ocean mining education." The speaker is presently employed as a university professor. The fate of disappointed miners has improved since Raleigh's time.

Today, a new cast of corporate celebrities joins the hard-rock mining concerns that first pursued Mero's nodule visions. This new cast includes such names as Sun Oil, Mobil Oil, Standard Oil of Indiana, and Royal Dutch Shell. Why are multinational oil companies participating in seabed mining consortiums? According to the *Wall Street Journal*, these corporations prefer to invest in tax write-offs for research. Such hedges on deep-sea mining can serve a dual purpose, since oil deposits as well as hard-mineral deposits may occur in the deep seabed. Will the occurrence of submarine oil deposits adjacent to or underneath a layer of nodules supply enough energy to process nodules at sea or on shore? Just the mention of such magic combinations will probably suffice to keep the prospect of nodule mining alive and kicking.

Ironically, as technical drawbacks are becoming more apparent, the political snarl is undergoing new twists. In 1980, Congress passed a deep-sea mining bill to establish an interim mining regime pending adoption of an international regime. The more questionable provisions in the original bill—investment guarantees, large lease blocks, wholesale environmental exemptions, America-only vessels and processing sites—have been dropped or considerably toned down. A set amount of royalties will go into an international fund pending establishment of an international regime. The bill does not permit commercial mining to begin until 1988. This delay is meant to encourage agreement on an international regime.

The draft Law of the Sea treaty, meanwhile, has come up with an international regime concept acceptable to many national delegations. An International Seabed Authority would control deep-sea mining. Private corporations, national ventures, and the Authority itself would be permitted to mine. How can the Authority, without any real capital or equipment, expect to get into the mining business? A private or national contractor must submit two prospective minesites. One minesite and the appropriate mining technology will be transferred to the Enterprise, which mines for the Authority. Each contractor must make the technology available to the Enterprise "on fair and reasonable commercial terms," and, under certain conditions, to some coastal developing nations. The Enterprise must first make good faith efforts to obtain technology on the open market.

Some LOS delegates talk of acquiring the *Glomar Explorer* for the Enterprise. Taking a cue from U.S. mining advocates, the Authority might seek to require that private leaseholders transport, process, and market nodules through Enterprise facilities. All parties to the LOS treaty would be obligated to lend interest-free capital, based on a scale of assessments for the regular UN budget, to fund the Enterprise's first mining project. The projected cost is $1 billion, of which the U.S. share would be about $250 million, depending on how many nations sign the treaty. Some nations may refrain from signing to avoid such financial obligations. Other nations may not sign until they see how the Authority operates.

The Authority would set production ceilings on each lease so land producers would not be unduly affected. The Authority could compensate land producers who "suffer serious adverse effects" from reduced prices caused by seabed mining. Lease royalities would go toward such payments. The major commercial nodule mineral is nickel. Its recovery will generate manganese far beyond market demand. If sold or dumped on the world market, land producers would suffer.

With such broad powers, the Authority could easily tilt in favor of mixed mining efforts or predominantly Enterprise efforts. The Enterprise can seek bank loans. It is exempt from any taxes. There are incentives for nations or corporations to gain mining access through joint ventures with the Enterprise.

Who controls the Authority? The draft treaty tries to spread voting control among three groups—developing nations, Western industrial nations, and the socialist nations of eastern Europe. The hope is that no one group will dominate; the fear is that two groups will form an alliance. To counter this latter option a unique voting formula has been created. A three-tier system would divide up policy decisions by differing voting majorities. Major leasing issues would require a consensus, defined as the absence of a formal objection by any member state. Less momentous matters would be decided by two-thirds or three-fourths votes.

While the 1980 U.S. LOS delegation felt the regime represented a reasonable compromise, the 1981 delegation appointed by the Reagan administration echoes concerns of American interests over the "giveaway" of the deep sea nodule. One appointee: Kennecott Copper lobbyist Leigh Ratiner. This attitude, according to Elliot Richardson, the former head of the U.S. Delegation and a prominent Republican who campaigned for Reagan, could jeopardize the entire LOS process, including provisions for navigation rights that U.S. maritime and naval interests consider so vital.

Given the expectations of seabed wealth and the tensions between industrial and developing nations, the draft LOS mining scheme represents considerable progress, but with a high economic price. The miners' dream of a politically free mining environment is being replaced by the penultimate in social consciousness. Bankers may decide that there are safer risks than funding *Glomar Explorers* controlled by an Authority with a three-tier voting formula.

Will mining revenues help close the economic gap between industrial and developing nations? Francis LaQue, a retired mining engineer and an executive with the International Nickel Company of Canada, is now a research associate at the Scripps Institution of Oceanography. LaQue claims that nodule revenues "cannot be expected to make a substantial contribution to narrowing this gap." This holds true even in the unlikely event that, by year 2025, all the world's needs for nickel were to come from nodules. According to LaQue, lease revenues would run from a low of $2 billion to a high of $9 billion by 2025. The total annual aid needed by developing nations in 2025, based on various projections, will be about $550 billion. Who gets first shot at any revenues? The Authority does—to fund its own costs and to retire any debts, such as loans on the *Glomar Explorer* or a reasonable facsimile.

Once again, human expectations of the ocean far exceed its potential. The 120 developing nations applying for development grants from the Authority may be in for a rude awakening on the largesse available from the vaunted marine treasure chest. Undeterred, three countries are competing to be the headquarters site for the Authority: Fiji, Jamaica, and Malta. One possible compromise may be to rotate the headquarters site.

I am particularly struck by the tenacious hold that a marine mineral rush continues to exercise on the public imagination when I drive to a local dump. Such dumps continue to usurp coastal wetlands and coastal canyons as we produce more solid urban waste. Here metals abound in the form of discarded TV sets, refrigerators, inner-spring mattresses, and aluminum frame chairs. These urban dumps must rank as one of our greatest untapped ore deposits. And they grow faster than nodule deposits. All types of commercial minerals, not just a select few, are present. It generally requires less energy to retrieve and recycle these metals than to process virgin ore from rock. Our metal-rich dumps probably stand a much better chance of saving us from metal embargoes, whenever they might occur. We need no elaborate terrestrial version of a *Glomar Explorer* to mine these deposits. Nobody is going to get seasick. The principal overburden is the stench of decomposing garbage. This decomposition even provides a source of cheap energy: methane gas.

Recycling the metals and the gas can extend the lifespan of these urban dumps and reduce the pressure to recruit more coastal canyons and wetlands. Recently I've noticed a new addition to the dump scene. Sometimes three or four people are busy retrieving the discarded TV sets, inner-spring mattresses, refrigerators, auto parts, and bike frames. This metal harvest is thrown into a battered metal bin. These people are part of a pilot recycling project. Nationwide, such projects out-harvest and out-produce the marine metal industry. And yet no congressman or reporter beats a track to these urban dumps to herald a new mineral cornucopia.

As the scavenging gulls swirl overhead and a parade of trash-laden cars and trucks kick up dust clouds, one senses just how deeply the ocean as resource cornucopia can become ingrained in the popular imagination. Clearly, mining urban dumps—whether in the northern or southern hemisphere—can and will provide far greater environmental and social benefits at far less economic cost than reliance on the vaunted marine mineral rush. In the United States, 13 million tons of metals wind up in municipal solid waste systems each year. Only .6 million tons is recycled, according to Congress's Office of Technology Assessment.

Should we offer liberal patents and exclusive leases for these urban ore deposits to mineral companies? Should we promote an international technological olympics to exploit urban dumps and engage in a race with Russia, Japan, and China to see which nation can best exploit its trash? Perhaps we can finally rid ourselves of the vision of the ocean as resource cornucopia and stop being the victims of our own marine delusions. When the global community finally realizes that no marine mineral bonanza exists to support either a new international economic order or a corporate windfall for the industrial nations, perhaps more attention can be directed to sustaining marine processes vital to the ocean's renewable resources.

20

Blinders
for the Ocean

THE AMERICAN RESEARCH VESSEL
docked at Recife, Brazil. The scientists and crew were looking
forward to shore-side liberty after retrieving seabed rock samples.
To their surprise, Brazilian officials brusquely boarded the vessel.
The crew could not leave the ship and the ship could not leave
the port. In short, they were under detention. The ship did leave
a day later, minus the rock samples, which were confiscated by
the authorities. The ship's crime was the lack of a permit to
dredge for rocks. The lowering of a dredge into the coastal waters
of Brazil without a permit had been a crime as grave, at least on
the statute books, as smuggling. The scientists suspect that most
of their samples lie on the port bottom, waiting to perplex future
researchers and dredgers.

Today more and more marine scientists risk similar predicaments based on the proximity of their research projects to land and to seaward-creeping nationalism. The very core of their scientific capacity—freedom to investigate the coastal zone, the most fertile and useful portion of the seas—is entrained in debates about who is to benefit from marine exploration. As a result, two of the most dedicated professionals in the world—the scientist engaged in the rigorous pursuit of truth, and the government official seeking to protect his nation's patrimony—are at cross purposes over the retrieval of rocks. Our technical ability to research and understand the ocean is expanding, but our ability to deploy this technology can be restricted by political barriers as stultifying as the religious barriers that confronted Galileo.

Because of inadequate equipment and unsophisticated theories of water movement, oceanography as an organized field of study did not really commence until the late nineteenth century. Most of what appears in marine science books has been learned in this century. The pioneer oceanographers of the late nineteenth century and early twentieth century were men of broad vision and limited resources. They could not afford to be specialists. Sir John Murray was a scientist on the first oceanographic expedition, the *Challenger* expedition sponsored by Great Britain in 1872. He would study plankton under the microscope and then shift to analyzing ooze and rocks dredged up from the Atlantic depths. He practically founded a new subscience—marine geology. Pioneer oceanographers like him were as bold and innovative as the marine explorers and artists who preceded them.

No scientific suppliers existed to provide these oceanographers with the latest in technical instrumentation. For transportation, they often had to recruit a man-of-war and its crew, and might find themselves wrangling with a skeptical naval captain over where they could conduct research. For lab space, they would remove cannons. To retrieve seabed samples, they would arm a hand lead used in soundings with sticky lard or tallow. One sounding could take two hours. One dredge sample could take an entire day. On special occasions, the resourceful *Challenger* crew would cool a bottle of champagne in a trawl full of dredged ooze from the chilly seabed.

These pioneers could not depend on speedy vessels to shorten sea time. The sail-powered *Challenger* took over three years to cover 68,000 miles while probing the world oceans. Much of the equipment was left snagged on the seabed. Of the 243 members of the crew, 61 deserted. There were two drownings, one suicide, one accidental poisoning, and ten cases of syphilis.

It took nineteen years to publish the *Challenger*'s fifty-volume report. This was a pretty fair output of work, considering that there were only six scientists on board. Their sampling work eventually resulted in the discovery of 4,714 new species.

Alexander Agassiz covered some 10,000 miles of tropical sea tracks. He too lost countless dredge samples to snags and to the weight of hauls that broke the rope. As a result he replaced rope with more durable steel wire and then improved on the winches used to retrieve the dredge. When Fridtjof Nansen explored the northern seas, there were no aircraft for backup rescue or short-wave radios for communication. There were no engine-powered sleds to traverse ice fields. Nansen devised lightweight gear that now benefits backpackers as well as polar scientists. He put sail on sledges. To enable his research vessel to withstand crushing ice, he devised a hull made out of oak that was 2 feet thick. He relied on the Eskimos for another research vessel—a kayak.

In his greatest contribution to oceanography, Nansen recognized the need for critical analysis of motion and transport in the sea. No batteries of computers existed to speed up the laborious analysis of thousands of temperature and salinity readings. Nansen enlisted the aid of Europe's brightest physicists and mathematicians, who developed the fundamental equations used in oceanography. "No one can call himself an oceanographer who does not have the mathematical background to understand and apply these equations," according to one of today's leading marine scientists, Dr. Joel W. Hedgpeth.

Improved equipment tended to raise the cost of marine research. Oceanographers thus had to develop considerable skill at attracting sponsors. Wealthy yachtsmen with an amateur interest in marine matters were a popular target. Agassiz had the best of both worlds. Independently wealthy as a mining engineer, he could fund his own tropical voyages. Japanese scientists would later fund their research expeditions by catching and selling fish.

Governments would often sponsor marine research as a sign of national prestige. Great Britain provided the *Challenger* expedition with a navy ship and a navy crew. But governments could be undependable and inconsistent. Murray had to use his own money to publish the massive *Challenger* report, and contributors had to settle for a complimentary copy of their work.

To compensate for such political fickleness, oceanographers learned to share human and financial resources without regard to nationality. To identify thousands of *Challenger* geological and biological samples, British scientists recruited German, Norwegian, French, and U.S. scientists, including Agassiz. The British press and some British scientists were upset by use of "foreign naturalists," but one British scientist, Charles Darwin, defended this practice. Later, Murray would dig into his own pocket again to fund a research cruise in the northeast Atlantic. Norway provided the vessel, the *Michael Sars,* and one of the founders of fishery biology, Dr. Johan Hjort. The cruise results provided the basis for Hjort's book, *The Depths of the Ocean,* which helped extend public understanding of the marine environment beyond Captain Nemo's visions.

A global community of marine scientists slowly emerged capable of launching joint expeditions and agreeing on uniform standards for reporting scientific observations. Murray, Nansen, and Hjort realized that knowledge of fish stocks would be critical if fish and fishing were to be sustained. They instigated the formation of the International Council for the Exploration of the Sea (ICES) to study fisheries of the North Sea and North Atlantic. Their foresight was eventually forgotten in the international competition to overfish these stocks.

The need for oceanographers to think in global terms fostered some unique careers. In the wake of World War I, over one million homeless people were scattered across war-torn Europe. The world turned to Nansen, the respected and innovative Arctic explorer, to resettle these people. Many were stateless, estranged from their homeland by revolution and terrorism. Nansen devised a passport that enabled these forsaken people to cross national borders on their way to a new life. It was known as the Nansen certificate or passport. Subsequently, a severe famine struck Russia. Some thirty million people were starving. Nansen, his head balding but his carriage as erect as when he traversed Greenland by sled, was called upon by the International Red Cross to organize food relief to the world's largest nation. Twenty-three years after receiving international accolades for exploring the Arctic, Nansen received a new award, the Nobel Peace Prize.

These pioneer oceanographers came to cherish the long lonely times at sea. To Harald Sverdrup, who coauthored a classic oceanographic text, *The Oceans,* the chief value of a voyage to polar seas was the long nights and isolation, which gave him time to think. For Nansen, a return to urban civilization made him yearn even more for the pitching deck of a vessel and the expanse of sea and sky. "I tell you deliverance will not come from the rushing, noisy centers of civilization. It will come from the lonely places," said Nansen.

No one was concerned at that time about possible conflicts of interest or about the point at which basic research became applied research. During the *Challenger* project, Murray learned of deposits of phosphate, a rich fertilizer source, on a lonely island in the Indian Ocean. At his urging, Great Britain annexed Christmas Island and let a concession for exploiting the phosphate. Murray himself was the concessionaire. The taxes Britain received from the phosphate works exceeded the value of its support for the *Challenger* expedition. Murray pointed this out in seeking public support to publish the *Challenger* results, but he did not get very far, and finally dug into his own pocket. The short, stocky Scotsman was still going strong in his early seventies when an automobile accident took his life.

These marine scientists did enjoy one distinct advantage as compared to their counterparts on land. Scientists must obtain permission to trespass on private lands. Suspicious farmers are not prone to distinguish between earnest scientists and possible poachers. Scientists who take soil samples and archeologists who conduct digs often enter into extended negotiations with property owners. And if your research interest extends across national borders, you must obtain governmental as well as private permits. The pioneer oceanographers did not have to worry about this. There were no trespassers on the oceans. They had in effect an open passport to study the marine environment.

The vast surface area and depth of the oceans would seem likely to frustrate the most indefatigable researcher. However, the ocean tends to concentrate its most critical features in an area smaller than the combined size of our land masses. The coastal zone off the major continents is where major ocean currents occur and where up to 90 percent of the biological activity occurs. Here atmosphere and ocean interact and shape our climate. Here most of the world's undersea earthquakes occur. Here many of the answers concerning the history of the earth are to be found. Here too the human impact on the ocean is most intense.

The proximity of land to prime marine research areas provides research expeditions with handy access to onshore facilities and to water, food, and emergency medical care. And scientists are no more immune from the lure of liberty ports than sailors.

In our time North American marine scientists try to keep contact with their Latin American counterparts, though there are precious few to make contact with. Latin America, Africa, and much of Asia had turned inward to develop an agricultural economy. The land had become the main theater for war, as well; the need for a navy and for maritime technology was thus diminished. Since industrial nations dominated shipping, there was little incentive to develop a merchant marine. South America's first marine institute was not founded until 1923 in Argentina. Chile followed suit twenty years later.

While science and society tended to remain estranged in the Southern Hemisphere, they tended to become increasingly allied in the north. The United States has realized that to stint on marine research in an age of submarine warfare, amphibious landings, and ocean testing of atomic bombs is a false economy. In World War II, for example, the U.S. Marines made an amphibious assault on the small Pacific island of Tarawa. They lost a thousand men when landing craft ran aground on reefs and exposed the marines to Japanese gunfire. The landing went off on ebb tide, which intensified the deadly effect of the reefs. The most recent map of the reef area was over a century old. One hour of a marine scientist's time could have helped avert the butchery. Japanese marine scientists published more up-to-date information in many U.S. scientific publications prior to World War II. Marine naturalist Ed Ricketts tried to interest naval officials in this rich lode of precise intelligence, but was ignored. Since then, the navies of the major industrial nations have become generous sponsors of marine research.

I remember visiting a calving ground for the gray whales in Baja California in 1966. An oceanographic vessel with extensive electronic gear was attempting to eavesdrop on the whales. The acoustical scientist in charge later wrote a paper entitled "The Silent Whale," in which he speculated that whales, like submarines, can run silently to avoid attracting attention. This remote exercise was funded by the U.S. Navy, which was interested in identifying the difference between whale and submarine sounds in the depths of the ocean.

Today marine research is a high-technology enterprise that only a few nations can afford. Approximately 75 to 90 percent of the world's ocean research capability—the critical mass of scientists, ships, and instruments—resides with six nations: the United States, the USSR, the United Kingdom, West Germany, Canada, and Japan. Some European states possess a limited ocean capability, primarily regional: Norway, Sweden, Denmark, East Germany, France, Spain, Portugal, Italy, and Poland. Six nations thus have the power to carry out most major marine research projects.

But they are no longer free to roam at will in the coastal zone. Technical advances have become hostage to political changes. Murray's style of applied research following his discovery of the phosphate deposits is a thing of the past.

As developing nations extended their borders seaward to control exploitation, many marine scientists assumed that they would be exempt from controls. They thought of themselves as seeking knowledge about the ocean, not exploiting it. After all, the knowledge they generate gives coastal nations the capability of harvesting marine resources in the first place. To U.S. legal scholar William Burke, freedom of scientific access "is the primacy upon which progress can be made in conquering and preserving the ocean environment for the shared benefit of all people." As a sign of good faith, marine scientists reiterated their willingness to notify coastal nations of research cruises ahead of time. This concept is referred to as "prior notification."

But coastal developing nations tend to see no difference between marine research and the ultimate exploitation of their resources. As one Brazilian diplomat observed in a United Nations debate, "In the last analysis, every particle of scientific knowledge could be translated into terms of economic gain or national security. In a technological society, scientific knowledge means power." Indeed, marine scientists in the United States continually reaffirm how pure research eventually pays off. Even the appearance of research technology belies any clear-cut distinctions. Some equipment used in geophysical research, such as the seismic survey and drilling equipment, resembles oil exploration gear. When the *Pueblo* was seized off Korea, the U.S. Navy described it as an "environmental research ship." As if such similarities between basic and applied research are not enough to make coastal officials suspicious, marine scientists must take repeated measurements to monitor marine processes. To coastal officials, such monitoring appears to put their coastal waters under constant surveillance.

Marine scientists often assure coastal officials that there will be "open publication" of any and all results coming out of coastal surveys. Ironically, this assurance can backfire. Historically, discovery of a mineral deposit in a developing nation can unleash political power struggles, sometimes financed by foreign interests seeking lucrative exploitation leases. The last thing a coastal nation wants is "open publication" of a possible new submarine oil deposit, an underutilized fish stock, or an outfall that pollutes regional waters.

Many coastal nations thus assert a very broad control over marine scientific access. This concept is referred to as "prior consent."

Let's say you are in charge of organizing an oceanographic expedition. The principal research area will be off Brazil, but you plan to conduct research all along the South American coast. To start, the State Department's Research Vessel Clearance Office sends you a standard form. You must name all the researchers and technicians and enclose their curricula vitae. Next you must outline your proposed route, your field stations, and when you will be at these stations. (What happens if you cannot maintain this schedule because of sea storms or mechanical failures? You'll ask for clarification later.)

Next you must declare that ship space will be reserved for observers and researchers from the host nation. You call the State Department. How much space is enough? You are told that the more space available, the more likely it is that permission will be granted. (You begin to revise upward your budget estimates for food.)

You must provide a copy of all information the expedition obtains. This can mean providing plankton samples and seabed grabs, as well as computer readouts of temperature and salinity.

You must secure permission from each nation whose coastal waters you will be passing through, regardless of how short a period of time is involved. And nations often have differing requirements. Colombia, for example, requested that 30 percent of the cost of one expedition in its coastal waters be paid to specified Colombian institutions. The expedition sponsor, Scripps Institution of Oceanography, decided to go elsewhere.

Your ultimate goal—publication of your research—may well be determined by a foreign official. Some nations insist on prior approval of publication. Most if not all scientists will bypass coastal waters rather than submit to such a condition.

The response to your application comes in due time. It is yes, but with a condition. If you delay or change the schedule, you must apply for prior consent again.

To what degree is marine research actually being inhibited by the need for prior consent? Are requests routinely granted once made? In 1977, ten coastal nations denied requests from one U.S. marine institute, Woods Hole. The University National Oceanographic Laboratory System, which coordinates cruises by the U.S. Academic Fleet, reported that about half the cruises scheduled in 1976 were denied access to coastal waters. Eighteen nations were involved in denying clearance. In a survey of U.S. access requests from 1972 to 1978, Dr. Warren Wooster, a prominent marine scientist at the University of Washington who has served on the U.S. delegation to the LOS conference, found that one-third of the requests "have encountered serious difficulties" involving denial or inordinate delays.

Most European nations are more cooperative in providing coastal access. However, one nation with considerable coastal frontage, the Soviet Union, rigidly controls scientific access.

The global mobility that helped oceanography overcome its late maturity as a science is thus in jeopardy. A scientist laying out a stationline must balance scientific opportunities with potential legal barriers.

It is important in this respect to note how wide-ranging marine processes can be. You can't forecast hurricanes from the penthouse of a Florida hotel; the hurricanes that punish our shores begin to form on the other side of the Atlantic. Migratory patterns and spawning behavior of certain marine animals, such as billfish, tuna, and whales, can be transoceanic. With the blow-out of the Mexican oil well IXTOC I, oil spills have become trans-national in impact. To restrict access, particularly in an area as important as the coastal zone, is to severely handicap marine research and assessment.

It is fortunate that the collision between freedom of scientific research and national coastal claims did not occur earlier. If it had, the *Challenger* expedition might never have happened. Our knowledge of coastal upwelling, of the geology of continental shelves, and of migratory patterns of fish could have been severely retarded.

Doesn't some sort of transnational agency exist to certify bona fide research projects and hear appeals when a coastal nation rejects a research request? It could also develop a set of uniform research standards and could help shape research in terms of the needs of developing nations. Such an agency does exist. The Intergovernmental Oceanographic Commission (IOC) was created as a UN agency in 1960. The IOC has helped sponsor over 200 scientific expeditions. It has also sponsored conferences on the use of remote-control instruments to expand research horizons. In 1969, Commission-member states reaffirmed the IOC function "to promote the freedom of scientific investigation of the ocean for the benefit of mankind." In a harbinger of things to come, South American officials voted against this. One dissenting delegate regarded IOC "as a rich man's club, dominated by the world's nuclear, industrial and oceanographic giants." Another delegate pointed out that, in its first thirteen years, no Asian or African was included on the Commission staff, except for some Japanese officials. South American nations felt this void reflected international power politics rather than any measure of support for marine science.

Today, IOC delegates from industrial nations, who stress science's "impartial search for truth" occasionally find themselves branded as corporate lackeys and military handmaidens by delegates from developing nations. The IOC staff must walk a tightrope between the contending doctrines of prior consent and

---

prior notification. IOC was the leading coordinator for the International Decade of Exploration in the 1970s. One of its responsibilities was to ensure coastal access for research vessels. Would the IOC opt for prior notification or prior consent? The IOC managed to carve out a position designed less to ensure access than to avoid the issue. The IOC would pass on a research state's request for access to a coastal state, urging "favorable consideration." In other words, the research scientist could save some time by applying directly to the coastal state.

The IOC remains a prominent victim of the clash over scientific access. As a National Academy of Sciences report notes, "The role that the developing countries envisage for the IOC is an increasingly restrictive and regulatory role which would carefully direct scientific research towards the development of resources, rather than encourage the free development of non-resource oriented research."

The draft Law of the Sea (LOS) convention says coastal states may "in their discretion withhold their consent" to marine research projects "of direct significance for the exploration and exploitation of natural resources, whether living or nonliving." However, the coastal state—not the scientist—determines whether or not a project is "of direct significance." Since developing nations argue that most if not all research leads to exploitation, it would be hard to devise a project so abstract and ethereal as to avoid coming under this rubric. Moreover, coastal states that are eager to shape research to their own immediate needs will often be more receptive to projects that can be linked to their own marine development goals. That after all is how some developing nations view the issue of coastal research access: a means of bargaining for transfer of technology.

Some developing nations recognize the need to take their own scientific initiatives. Argentina, Brazil, and Chile are expanding their scientific capabilities. Depending on how it allocates its marine oil revenues, Mexico could eventually develop a competence rivaling that of major industrial nations, particularly with its proximity to major U.S. marine institutes. Smaller nations can also develop meaningful capabilities. U.S. biologists single out Peru as having contributed significantly to upwelling research during the International Decade of Exploration. In the wake of its bitter experience with the anchoveta, Peru has recognized that a generous marine patrimony can be lost through its own acts and not because of foreign exploitation.

Regional sharing of resources and manpower may become more common, too. Petrobas, Brazil's national petroleum company, recently invited noted U.S. marine geologist K.O. Emery to participate in joint shelf research off Brazil. In return for his technical expertise in mapping the shelf for exploration purposes, Emery was allowed to study the longest continuous coastline of any country on the Atlantic. This is a big step for Brazil. One Brazilian oceanographer has observed that "a wave of stupid nationalism considers collaboration in science almost like the crime of 'collaborationism' in war."

The draft LOS Convention also proposes the establishment of regional marine scientific and technical centers "to stimulate and advance the conduct of marine scientific research." Here scientists from both developing and developed nations could formulate joint research programs. Once member states assent to a joint program, permission to enter each other's coastal waters would be assumed, eliminating the burdensome application process. Under this kind of arrangement, American research centers could help train and assist scientists in developing nations. The promise of new marine research technology, from underwater cameras to remote sensing buoys, would no longer be shackled by arbitrary marine boundaries. The American Sea Grant College Program already has a modest international component in which U.S. institutions work with institutions in developing nations. The University of Hawaii, in cooperation with the University of the South Pacific, helps meet marine public service needs in eleven Pacific island nations, such as Fiji and the Solomon Islands.

Under the draft treaty, a coastal state is to provide other states "with a reasonable opportunity" to obtain information "to prevent or control damage to the health and safety of persons and the environment." A regional center could ensure that such an opportunity is made available in assessing damaging pollution episodes that cross national marine borders.

Ironically, the clashes between developed and developing nations over the LOS treaty often disclose bitter regional differences. Argentina and Chile can't agree on a joint marine border whose placement will determine control over rich fish stocks. For over a century, Peru has been involved in bitter, sometimes bloody, border disputes with Chile to the south and Ecuador to the north. The possibility that a border dispute could leave a joint facility in one nation's control tends to curb enthusiasm for joint projects.

What would those free-roaming pioneer oceanographers think of today's state of affairs? Their excitement over technical advances would probably give way to incredulity over political restraints. But one pioneer sensed what was coming. Nansen's distaste of "noisy centers of civilization" was not a mere personal preference. In his refugee and famine work, he was impressed at how readily aid could come from people directly, and how it could be withheld arbitrarily by nation-states. The United States cooperated in the relief of the Russian famine; European nations did not. Some even blocked grain shipments. Grain surpluses were available. Dockers who could have handled these shipments were unemployed at the time. But their governments withheld aid to the Russian peasants because of Russia's political nature. While the very spirit of Communism ran directly counter to his own individualism, Nansen could not understand how societies that considered themselves civilized could use drought as a political weapon to punish other human beings. Nations, he wrote, "are little more than a collection of predatory beasts." He felt it was incumbent upon smaller nations like Norway to foster global institutions and global norms to curb nationalistic power plays.

Stateless persons needed a Nansen passport fifty years ago. A similar approach is required today to ensure that scientists can cross national marine borders without undue political restrictions.

More positive forms of distributing the benefits of scientific knowledge must be developed, such as regional marine programs that cross national borders. As American scientist Victor Weisskopf noted in *Science*, "Science cannot develop unless it is pursued for the sake of pure knowledge and insight. But it will not survive unless it is used intensely and wisely for the betterment of humanity and not as an instrument of domination by one group over another."

21

The Dump
of Last Resort

No HIGH-LEVEL RADIOACTIVE wastes are to be dumped in the ocean. This bold-sounding agreement, also called the London Ocean Dumping Convention, was ratified by the requisite number of nations and came into force in 1975. The ban was inspired by the infiltration of the marine ecosystem by radioactive residues from atom bomb tests in the 1950s and 1960s. By 1975, most nations—except for France— were willing to forgo atom bomb testing in the oceans.

Nations that signed the convention were also confident that alternative means of handling radioactive wastes from nuclear reactors, such as storage in inert glass or in salt mines, would evolve. The United States was so confident that, in 1970, it banned dumping or discharge of all nuclear wastes, both high and low level. Trace amounts of radioactivity, however, continued to be released in cooling discharges from nuclear power plants.

But the European community would not have signed a convention with such an all-embracing ban. The United Kingdom, the Netherlands, Belgium, and Switzerland do not have as much land as Canada or the United States to spare for long-term storage of mounting nuclear wastes. They insisted on continued outfall discharge and dumping of low-level radioactive wastes, at least until the expected technical alternatives materialized. Such a radioactive waiver calls for special safeguards.

The European nuclear community has agreed on a threshold standard for high-level radioactive wastes. However, the nations involved have yet to agree on the amount of low-level radioactive discharges that the surrounding seas can safely handle, minimum containment standards for barrels used for dumping wastes, and an adequate monitoring system to detect leaking barrels and illegal discharges. In 1977, European nations dumped 5,605 metric tons of packaged radioactive wastes into the Atlantic, most of it 500 miles west of Ireland in what is sometimes referred to as the ocean commons.

This rather casual attitude towards radioactive dumping is not exactly a shining example for developing nations intent on pursuing their nuclear futures. Why, if dumping of low-level wastes is considered so safe, do the European nations go to the expense of dumping the wastes well beyond their coastal waters in ocean depths that are much harder to monitor for leakage? The European community certainly has the technical and financial resources to monitor and control radioactive dumping. This would be cheaper and more reliable than having each nation duplicate such efforts, assuming of course that the United Kingdom, the Netherlands, Belgium, Switzerland, and their sister nations each have their own system for monitoring drums on the seabed and radioactive residues discharged via outfalls. But each nation prefers to consider control of such dumping an internal affair, just like road building and the local garbage pickup, even though an accident, miscalculation, or outright dumping violation could have impacts well beyond one nation's borders.

The price for such a policy could be high. The dangers from indiscriminate or inadequately controlled radioactive dumping have not changed since the ambitious convention was ratified. But the pressures to risk such dangers have increased oppressively. A light-water nuclear reactor can produce 30 tons of spent radioactive fuel and 46,000 cubic feet of low-level radioactive wastes each year. Capacity for onsite storage rarely extends beyond two or three decades. By the year 2000, several hundred thousand tons of highly radioactive spent nuclear fuel will have accumulated on this planet.

The energy crunch and accompanying pressures to exploit all available energy sources have now materialized, but the means of storing nuclear wastes permanently and safely have not. One much-touted alternative, fuel reprocessing, can generate wastes ten times the original volume of the spent fuel. These new wastes can require long-term isolation, long-term being on the order of magnitude of the whole of man's recorded history. (One primary end product, plutonium, can be used to make nuclear weapons.) As the Council on Environmental Quality observes in *The Global 2000 Report*, "No nation has yet conducted a demonstration program for the satisfactory disposal of radioactive wastes and the amount of wastes is increasing rapidly."

Once more, the ocean could become an escape hatch for human oversights. Japan, which ratified the London Ocean Dumping Convention, is small geographically but big on nuclear energy. Japan is running out of storage space for nuclear wastes, and recently planned to dump what it termed low-level radioactive wastes contained in 10,000 drums in the Pacific east of Iwo Jima. Emissaries were dispatched to Pacific island nations to assure government officials that the dumping operation would pose no threat to the environment.

The officials were not impressed. The people of the Pacific islands are intimately acquainted with the accidents that can result from the use of nuclear energy. They remember the tuna catches that had to be confiscated because of high radioactive counts after bomb tests in the mid-Pacific. They remember that some of their people were forced to move from one island so atom bomb tests could proceed and that radioactive residues made the island uninhabitable for years. They are aware of accidents like Three Mile Island and the protests in Japan and the United States over proposed nuclear plants. They know how the oceanic currents can transport people and goods over long distances—after all, many of their forefathers rode these currents to colonize tiny islands separated by hundreds of miles of open ocean. They also know how these currents can transport the errors of mankind, including leaks and spills.

The Japanese proposal triggered a new-found sense of community among the widely scattered island nations. The Micronesians had seen some of their islands recruited for the U.S. atom bomb tests; the Polynesians were still unable to prevent French atom bomb tests in their midst, despite global protests; and the Melanesians were determined to retain a nonnuclear heritage. All protested the Japanese proposal. John Kosi of Papua New Guinea told the Japanese that if the nuclear wastes were so harmless and the concrete containment so sure, then they should be confident enough to store the wastes back home. As it turns out, drums of nuclear waste are already being dumped in the Sea of Japan by South Korea. South Korea has been doing this for ten years, but waited till 1980 to disclose this practice publicly.

Australia joined the Pacific island nations in protesting Japan's dumping proposal. After temporarily postponing the dumping proposal, Japan announced it would participate in a joint feasibility study of the storage of radioactive wastes in the Pacific Ocean basin. The other participant was the United States. Why would the United States, which has halted such practices in its own coastal waters, want to participate in such a study? While no longer so enthusiastic about nuclear energy, the United States still remains entrained in the nuclear predicament, and wants to discourage Asian nations from joining the nuclear bomb club. Japan, South Korea, the Philippines, and Taiwan could possibly develop their own atom bombs by reprocessing spent nuclear fuel. Nuclear garbage dumps somewhere in the Pacific could be an alternative to such a prospect.

The United States has even considered a $2 billion proposal to entomb radioactive wastes in concrete silos on Palmyra, a series of islets a thousand miles south of Hawaii; it already uses a small Pacific island, Runit, to store "hot" soil from Eniwetok and other atom bomb test sites. Closer to home, states like Illinois, Washington, South Carolina, and Nevada are restive about serving as national nuclear waste depositories. States with vacant salt mines don't want to become the next nuclear way stations. The United States is running out of land storage possibilities as communities become more concerned about the reliability of storage systems. The Nuclear Regulatory Commission wants to recommence study of ocean disposal. The Federal Interagency Task Force on Nuclear Waste Management seconded this idea and added another: burial under the ocean floor. And the U.S. Navy wants to dump obsolete nuclear subs in the ocean. Once again, the ocean emerges as a possible dump of last resort. The Navy is currently trying to locate a nuclear submarine reactor it scuttled 120 miles off our Atlantic coast in 1959.

The burial twist first emerged in the context of dumping nuclear drums in deep-sea trenches. These trenches can form where the massive continental plates collide. One plate can slip beneath the other and sink toward the earth's molten core. It was suggested that the drums might be swallowed up in this process and melted into liquid rock beneath the earth's crust. Ergo, permanent storage. Professor James Porter of the University of Georgia has pointed out some shortcomings in this alluring idea of a trapdoor to the interior of the earth. Only the subsurface plate sinks, not the overlying sediments (where the drums would reside), which are exposed to frequent seismic activity associated with deep-sea trenches. The burial idea has thus shifted its focus to inactive regions of the deep seabed covered with clay oozes. The drums would sink into the ooze and the ooze would serve as a critical buffer to contain any leakage that might result.

However, certain aspects of the ocean are much less hospitable to the safe-for-all-time vision. In 1974, the Environmental Protection Agency (EPA) contracted for underwater photographs of drums containing radioactive waste dumped 40 miles off San Francisco between 1946 and 1966. The drums were made of metal and had concrete caps. The photographs revealed drums that had ruptured because of corrosion and high pressures. The ruptured drums, thoughtfully labeled HAZARDOUS TO HANDLE, were being colonized by sponges and anemones.

The discovery of the not-so-tight drums led to another question: what impact, if any, was leakage from the ruptured barrels having on marine life? The dump site happened to be in the Farallon Islands area, a marine habitat rich in fish, seabirds, and marine mammals.

When you shut down an old municipal sewage outfall, you don't have to worry about monitoring it many years hence for potential toxic leaks. But, as the ruptured drums off the California coast indicated, this is not the case with an old nuclear dump site. On land, you can at least inspect such drums with the naked eye, and you don't have to worry about marine corrosion and hydrostatic pressures. Monitoring a nuclear dump site in the ocean is a far more demanding challenge. It is expensive, and the equipment, such as submersibles and remote underwater TV cameras, is not in abundant supply. EPA and the National Oceanic and Atmospheric Administration (NOAA) find themselves in budgetary competition to obtain such expensive technology. The biological pathways that radioactive residues can take once loose in the marine environment are almost as numerous as marine life itself. Tracing them can require extensive sampling.

In 1980, EPA reported to a congressional subcommittee that one-fourth of the 47,500 drums were leaking, but that no dangers from the leakage had been detected "so far." Unimpressed by the speed and technical depth of the EPA investigation, Subcommittee Chairman Rep. Toby Moffett (D.-CN) urged that the Farallon

---

site be monitored more frequently, perhaps every six months, through a joint agreement between EPA and NOAA, which has the ocean-going gear to do the monitoring task. Getting these two federal agencies to work together, however, can be as difficult as getting the sovereign nations of Europe to work together in nuclear matters.

Across the continent, in Reading, Vermont, a former navy pilot named George Earle IV read about the Farallon dumping with special interest. He decided to break thirty-three years of silence to describe three secret missions in which he was ordered to dump drums of radioactive waste into the Atlantic. Officials know that 33,998 barrels of nuclear wastes were dumped off the mid-Atlantic coast, but the details of Earle's secret missions came as somewhat of a surprise. While serving as a navy pilot, he had been ordered to drop the drums from a B-17. This was the first time that EPA was aware of such aerial dumping. The old records on dumping often don't even indicate the specific contents of the drums.

Thus, while some federal agencies would like to open up the possibility of more ocean dumping of nuclear wastes, EPA copes with the exacting task of attempting to monitor thousands of aging drums strewn offshore. And how do you pinpoint the location of drums dropped from an airplane? Perhaps the nuclear legacy left to us should give us pause when we think of the type of legacy we want to leave to future generations.

What happens if monitoring indicates the need to recover and repackage some of the leaking barrels? This brings up another overlooked advantage—if that's the right word—of land storage. You don't need an underwater salvage unit to repair or empty a defective drum on land. Pushing a drum overboard is pretty easy compared to trying to recover the drum some thirty or forty years later. If the drums happen to lie mired in the deep seabed ooze, bringing the *Glomar Explorer* out of mothballs may not even suffice.

The fact that the "radioactive ring around America," as one congressman described the nuclear dumpsites, has yet to be implicated in a damaging incident should not necessarily be cause for comfort. Toxic agents loose in the environment do not always reveal their deadly nature with the dispatch of cyanide slipped to a marked victim. It can take time for toxic wastes to build up to lethal levels and for us to recognize this poisonous spiral. It took over thirty years from the time DDT was introduced in the United States for awareness of its toxic side effects to develop and for restrictions on its use to be implemented. Some seventeen years passed between the time mercury-laden catalysts were first discharged in Minamata Bay in Japan and the first appearance of nerve disorders in fishermen and their families, and three more years passed before the cause of Minamata Disease—mercury-laden shellfish—was identified. It took another fourteen years before a chemical factory was held responsible for the disease and ordered by a court to compensate victims, some of whom were already dead. While we like to think we are now much more aware of the potential for such toxic buildup, we still do not know the volume of radioactive wastes the seas can safely dilute, the amount already present there, and the accumulated leakage from corroded or imploded drums. It is no wonder that Pacific island nations have become concerned over proposals to export nuclear wastes into their part of the watery planet.

To some nations, the long-term buildup of toxic wastes, inadequate monitoring, and the difficult task of relocating old marine dump sites can be regarded as more of an opportunity than a threat. Nations with dim economic prospects, such as some of the Caribbean islands, may be willing to hire themselves out as waste repositories to industrial nations with vexing toxic surpluses. Land space on an island might crimp such plans. Or would it? The waste importer might choose to transship toxic cargos to a special fleet of ocean dumping vessels. If the toxic trade got off the ground, importers might compete with discounts on large volumes, a no-questions-asked policy on drum contents, and the kind of client anonymity Swiss banks brag about.

Recently, city officials in Washington, D.C., were ready to export their mounting sludge problem to Haiti via ocean tanker.

The deal broke down when Haiti discovered that the sludge would be delivered raw rather than composted. At last word, the same officials were trying to sell Antigua, a modest island east of Haiti, on the virtues of a sludge run.

The U.S. State Department finds such a "solution" to America's mounting waste production very disturbing. What might be the reaction if a disease outbreak in a third world nation was linked to toxic wastes exported by the United States? How would coastal nations react if their waters were being polluted by toxic wastes dumped by a hired handler of U.S. waste production? The State Department has intervened to quash hazardous waste shipments by American firms to Sierra Leone and the Bahamas. While the United States exerts some controls over exports of toxic substances, it is only now beginning to address the need for a hazardous waste export policy. The State Department would at least like to be notified of such shipments so it can alert the host nation to potential dangers and the need for precautions.

Interestingly enough, there has been an awareness of the need for such controls for some time. The London Ocean Dumping Convention banning dumping of high-level radioactive wastes also banned dumping of highly toxic materials such as mercury. But compliance with such bans is at the discretion of each nation. Some nations have not even bothered to sign the convention. The more governments clamp down on land disposal of toxic wastes without controlling the production of such wastes, the more the pressures will mount for ocean disposal, regardless of contrary-sounding international conventions or the concerns of island nations.

This ominous trend surfaced during the controversy over the leaking nuclear drums in the Farallon Islands area. California officials roundly berated federal agencies for failing to monitor the drums adequately. But these same officials have been so derelict in toxic waste planning that only one hazardous waste disposal site exists to serve the Los Angeles–San Diego region. Do the many chemical and oil firms in the region carefully pack up their hazardous wastes and haul them many miles to this one remaining facility? "I wouldn't be surprised if the more unscrupulous people are throwing it down the sewers," Kieran Bergin of the Los Angeles County Sanitation Districts told the *Los Angeles Times.* Such suspicions were heightened when a sister facility to the one remaining toxic disposal center closed. Officials expected to see an upsurge in truck traffic diverted from the closed facility. But the daily truck counts remained about the same. A midnight run to the nearest manhole can seem a very attractive alternative to long-distance hauls of hazardous wastes.

Amid reports of the leaking nuclear drums and the illegal sewer dumping, Beverlee Myers, director of the California Department of Health Services, observed, "We simply cannot continue to produce the kinds of toxic wastes this society is generating and expect to continue as a civilization." An ocean exposed to illegal toxic discharges and surreptitious dumping raises a particularly disturbing prospect. Scripps Institution of Oceanography marine scientist Edward Goldberg is concerned that such casual introduction of pollutants could lead to long-term buildup of toxic material. "Widespread mortalities and morbidities" in ocean organisms could result, writes Goldberg. Once this occurs, he warns, there would be "no turning back. The great volume of the open ocean makes the removal of a toxic substance, identified by a catastrophic event, an endeavor beyond mankind's capabilities with the technologies of today or of the foreseeable future."

Semienclosed seas such as the Mediterranean and the Baltic are particularly vulnerable to such toxic backlashes. But one coastal nation's vulnerability stands out above all the rest. Once toxic wastes infiltrate the marine food chain, the consequences are most likely to be felt in the country with the greatest amount of coastal waters covered by extended jurisdiction. And that happens to be the world's leading producer of toxic waste compounds, the United States.

This vulnerability should prompt some reforms in our ambivalent attitude towards production and control of toxic wastes. For starters, the United States should expand its ability to detect and assess toxic compounds loose in the marine environment. The goal of such assessment should be to determine the ocean's finite dilute capacity, pollutants that threaten to exceed this capacity, and the main source or sources of such pollutants. The United States should not assume that any nation or group of nations will be undertaking this technical task in the near future, given shrinking public budgets and rising inflation. The pressures for illegal ocean dumping are present now and will intensify.

Must such an expanded marine assessment system mean tremendous amounts of money and sophisticated technology? In other words, would such a system contribute more to the well-being of hi-tech firms than to the goal of effective ocean monitoring? Dr. Goldberg has identified one monitoring device that is already in place throughout the globe, can perform in polluted or brackish waters, can sample on a continuous basis, and never needs to be replaced or repaired. It is the mussel, a filter-feeder that can pick up minute amounts of pesticides, trace metals, and radioactive residues. This "sentinel organism" is so sensitive that one can actually pinpoint a pollutant source by comparing the relative concentrations of the pollutant found in mussels along a coastal stretch. (A mussel watch used by EPA has revealed high unexplained levels of the radioactive element curium at Cape Charles, Virginia.)

The United States must also develop a program that links the continued high production and use of toxic substances, both chemicals and nuclear matter, with the capacity for safe storage and disposal. It makes no sense for local jurisdictions to restrict or reduce this capacity while still tolerating the production and use of hazardous material. This behavior guarantees careless disposal of toxic wastes on land and in our coastal waters. If the states or local jurisdictions do not implement adequate disposal programs, the federal government may have to mandate such planning before illegal dumping of toxic wastes becomes a national epidemic. Continued development of nuclear energy should be linked to a specific, cost-effective program for long-term storage of nuclear wastes. Shuffling such wastes from one "temporary" site to another cannot substitute for such a program. Neither can hazy assumptions about deep-sea disposal or schemes to export wastes to the Caribbean.

It should be anticipated that producers of toxic substances may "run away" to nations with weak or lax toxic controls. Nations that want to export toxic substances to the United States should be required to disclose their toxic controls. They should be willing to sign reciprocal agreements that provide for mutual access to each country's toxic discharge and assessment data. The United States should not do business with nations that limit or exclude access to their coastal waters by pollution-monitoring teams.

As a result of such reforms, the United States would be in a much better position to influence management of toxic wastes at the international level. The United States and the European community could work more closely to establish uniform standards for control and assessment of toxic wastes. The United States can provide technical assistance to developing nations that want to set up toxic control programs. It can cooperate with the regional seas program sponsored by the United Nations Environmental Programme (UNEP) to expand pollution assessment in the Caribbean. UNEP has also formed a Global Environmental Monitoring System (GEMS) and an International Register of Potentially Toxic Chemicals. While the program titles are impressive, funding support from member states is not. GEMS's major marine focus has been on oil pollution. The Register has published twenty-eight data profiles on chemicals impacting the Mediterranean.

The leading role of the United States in developing alternative energy sources can help demonstrate to other nations that safer and more effective energy choices exist that don't require stockpiling of toxic radioactive wastes. Some developing nations have been skeptical of solar and renewable alternatives. They feel such alternatives may be promoted in the third world so that industrial nations can monopolize oil and nuclear energy sources.

The energy initiatives in states like Hawaii and California may help counter this skepticism.

Sooner or later, a working group of internationally respected scientists must be formed to monitor toxic levels in the ocean, to indicate when particular pollutants are reaching a hazardous level and to identify the sources of such pollutants. A UN advisory committee, the Joint Group of Experts on the Scientific Aspects of Marine Pollution (GESAMP), is responsible for issuing periodic (every three or four years) reports on the health of the ocean. While the International Atomic Energy Association wants GESAMP to develop a model of the dispersion of wastes dumped in the deep sea, limited staff and funds are severely crimping these critical assessments.

Eventually, the global community must gain the capacity to identify and move against a careless dumper, possibly through trade sanctions. While coastal nations retain complete control over land-based sources of marine pollution under the draft LOS treaty, dispute-settlement procedures in the treaty may provide some recourse for nations damaged or threatened by transboundary pollution. If we continue to regard national sovereignty as a license to pollute, we will sacrifice the most basic form of national security, a healthy biosphere.

22

Vigil for a Watery Planet

W̲E HAVE YET TO LEARN HOW TO protect the vital processes that sustain the ocean and our own marine ambitions. The community of nations must respond to the challenge; the pervasive character of the ocean will permit no less.

Clearly we have overestimated the ocean's ability to provide us with needed resources. These estimates were inspired less by careful assessment than by our faith in technology and our hope that the ocean, big as it is, can perpetuate the same relentless exploitation that has depleted too many resources on land.

Our belief in the ocean as a fish bonanza has caused many nations to build fishing fleets well beyond the capacity of the stocks to sustain such frenetic effort. Today, these same nations must plow money into patrol vessels to resist foreign intruders and control the relentless competition for diminishing fish resources. Efforts to assess stock limits effectively and to reduce costly excess capacity are lagging. As a result, it is almost inevitable that more stocks, particularly transboundary stocks caught in a political no-man's-land, will be depleted. Caught up in a marginal economic situation and squeezed by catch quotas, commercial fishermen are sometimes tempted to bend the rules or turn to other marine enterprises that require modest but swift vessels. This is the sort of human predicament that grandiose marine expectations can foster.

Our faith in the ocean as a cheap, all-purpose dump deters us from the inevitable task of controlling our mounting waste production, particularly of toxic compounds. As a result fishermen must confront the continuing prospect of having hard-won fish catches confiscated for high toxic counts. When fishermen spot a school on their sonar screen or see birds diving on a boil, they have no way of judging whether the fish meet health standards.

Our eagerness to urbanize the active beach zone means that more major coastal disasters are inevitable. On our Atlantic and Gulf coasts, there are any number of billion-dollar urban disasters waiting to happen. The density of coastal resident and resort populations is making early-warning and evacuation systems obsolete; now we must face the prospect of death losses in the hundreds and even thousands. When we regard a landform as dynamic as a beach as mere real estate, we are inviting catastrophe.

Our willingness to turn the coastal zone into an oil patch and an industrial quay means that key marine habitats and estuaries will remain hostage to massive oil spills. We can lambaste multinational oil companies and substandard tankers sailing under the Liberian flag all we want for risking spills, but it is our collective failure to diversify our energy options that fosters this predicament. The promotion of the glamorous marine technology—deep-sea mining, floating cities, desalinization of seawater, and ocean ranching—can divert attention away from more realistic resource alternatives, such as mining our urban dumps, cultivating inland fish ponds, and reclaiming our sewage.

Will intensive marine development be monitored closely so adverse impacts can be controlled? As congressional hearings into oil spills and nuclear waste dumping indicate, our ability to monitor and assess changes in the marine environment adequately is limited. In key habitat areas, such as Georges Bank, we do not even have reliable baselines or an adequate understanding of critical processes to detect early warning signs of environmental stress. As on the land, our desire to exploit can race ahead of our ability to control the impacts of such exploitation. We must expect less from the ocean if we do not expect more from our ability to understand and protect its critical processes.

The style of governance that has evolved on this planet clearly abets such predicaments. Each and every nation retains the right, if not always the capability, to deplete fish stocks and alter marine ecosystems regardless of how wide-ranging the effects are. One nation can discharge wastes that degrade the coastal waters of an entire region. When states do unite in such situations, it is often in order to protect each other's right to pollute.

The UN Law of the Sea conferences have provided an opportunity to develop regional standards to control the careless exercise of sovereign rights and provide meaningful recourse for states damaged by a neighbor's reckless acts. Yet once again, the promise of a marine bonanza has diverted attention away from such key issues. Nations generally prefer to compete for a piece of the resource action, as in the case of deep-sea mining. As a result, nations compete for resources that don't exist in the abundance expected, while the resources that do exist are being lost to careless exploitation, pollution, and habitat destruction. In an age when the major pollutant was human sewage and when fishermen hand-cast nets, such political inertia was understandable. Today, as mechanized fishing fleets prowl the sea and toxic waste production exceeds safe disposal capacity on land, this inertia casts doubt on our ability—or political will—to control our destiny in a rational, humane manner. We still consider national security in terms of territorial rights, national borders, missiles, and standing armies. Yet the most basic form of national security—a healthy biosphere—is left mainly to political chance. Nations have become expert in spying on each other's affairs. But we still lack a regional or global assessment system to detect key climatic and marine changes that could affect the health and security of all nations. We can not even agree on whether the earth is cooling or heating, or whether we should expect sea levels to rise or drop.

Some people predict the demise of this or that sea in ten or twenty years. Such predictions assume an assessment capability that simply does not exist. Moreover, they tend to regard environmental change as a simple matter of life or death. But we do not so much destroy or "kill" ecosystems as create ecological mutants that reflect the unstable, erratic nature of the social order to which they are hostage. The more nations compete to divert water from major river basins, the more downstream estuaries and seas will experience drastic changes in biota and abrupt declines in fish catches. We can wind up with aquatic systems like the Great Lakes that must be propped up by multi-million-dollar cleanup and stocking programs. We may end up transforming our planetary home into a haunted house that repeatedly shocks us with unpredictable, mystifying changes springing from our failure to understand and assess the consequences of our own acts.

It is the communities along the coastal rim that are exposed most frequently to such shocks and surprises. This is where the much-promoted marine bonanza can deteriorate into stock collapses, oil spills, tanker collisions, rusting canneries, and derelict waterfronts. Here the full weight of historical resource exploitation can come to roost with a vengeance. Citizens of these regions must face up to the import of their own contradictory attitudes: protesting offshore oil drilling while contributing to the demand, branding coastal oil refineries as hazardous while permitting condo complexes to urbanize hurricane-prone beaches, opening up tastefully designed seafood restaurants that overlook bays plagued by polluted urban runoff and constricted river inflow.

It is in the coastal regions that the need to rise above conventional resource horizons can be felt the most. And it is in these regions that one can see exciting new resource horizons open up. Who would have predicted ten years ago that the laid-back Aloha State, Hawaii, would be working so diligently to get off the hydrocarbon high and to develop safer and more economically sound energy sources? Who would have predicted that commercial sail would supplant nuclear propulsion as the latest trend in advanced ship design? Or that Jersey City, New Jersey, whose motto is "Everything for Industry," would turn down three refinery proposals in order to restore its blighted waterfront and its polluted air? Who would have predicted that the Thames Estuary, written off as fishless except for eels in the 1950s, would be clean enough to host haddock, shrimp, flounder and eighty other fish species in the 1970s? Or that sewage salvage would outstrip the promise of desalinization and iceberg towing?

Who would have predicted that the Mediterranean nations, split by century-old differences in politics, language, and religion, would agree to a joint convention to control the pollution of the sea that they once fought their battles on, and to pledge money as well as good intentions? Who would have predicted that China's historic emphasis on inland fish production would be regarded as a worthy alternative to capture fisheries and mariculture?

To this writer, such events mark a truly historic turning point for humanity. They symbolize people's ability to shift from traditional, exploitive resource practices to practices based on new, more ecologically sound perspectives. This shift is as daring and bold as Columbus's venture across the Atlantic or the descent of a scientist to the deep seabed.

This shift to new perspectives has often been regarded as the province of the affluent and the coastal elite. And yet Jersey City and the Mediterranean nations hardly qualify in this respect. Their quest for a cleaner waterfront is a revolt against the notion that such a prospect is a luxury of the well-to-do.

For the Mediterranean nations, a healthier sea is a prerequisite for retaining a critical economic component. Coastal tourism provides far more income to these nations than marine oil development or commercial fishing. If the sea is not cleaned up, the tourists will be taking their dollars to the Caribbean, and the Mediterranean nations will be faced with an even worse balance of trade. In their quest to control marine pollution, these nations are learning to share limited human and technical resources in monitoring pollutants and in forming regional spill control centers. The cause of pollution control is even forcing historical rivals like Greece and Turkey to work together. One spinoff from improved sewage treatment is the opportunity for water reclamation, which, in turn, opens up opportunities in aquaculture, coastal agriculture, and reforestation. And joint antipollution efforts have fostered joint projects to restore marine plant communities and endangered species such as the monk seal.

Plato criticized his countrymen many centuries ago for clearing away forests and letting the topsoil wash away into the sea. The condition of their sea has finally forced the Mediterranean nations to confront the true cost of such attitudes. If the process of renewal can be sustained, these nations stand to gain a greener land as well as a more productive sea. When these prospects are linked with onsite energy alternatives and inland aquaculture projects, one can see how a coastal region bypassed by history can gain a new economic lease on life.

The Mediterrean initiative, which has been vigorously supported by the UN Environmental Programme, suggests that regional rather than global frameworks may be more suitable forums to achieve transnational governance. The Baltic nations are working at a regional level to protect the Baltic; the Scandinavian nations have even agreed to permit citizens access to each nation's court system to seek recourse for environmental damages. Canada and the United States have been working jointly on pollution control projects in the Great Lakes. The degree to which Mexico and the United States benefit from their common marine resources will depend more and more on the success or failure of similar bilateral accords.

If regional accords are the coming trend, it is high time for the nations of the Pacific Basin to get together. There has been too much emphasis on unilateral and bilateral efforts to figure out how to use the Pacific as a dump and not enough attention to what's best for the ocean itself. If the entire basin seems too large and politically diverse to function as a regional forum, then two subregions—north and south—could be utilized. These forums could establish independent scientific advisory panels to review critical issues such as the nuclear dumping proposal by Japan. While the United States and Panama have shown foresight in establishing a joint environmental commission that would review any sea-level canal projects, the need remains for a review process separate from the two major project beneficiaries (three if Japan participates), given potential impacts that could span both the Caribbean and Pacific regions. The assessment systems necessary to monitor the biosphere with the same critical precision that nations exert in spying on each other may eventually evolve from such regional perspectives.

Some people may have a feeling that the ocean has somehow let us down in not living up to our grandiose expectations. But the opportunities that stem from a more modest assessment can be exciting. Is it so bad after all to settle for historic uses such as marine recreation, shipping, and food fisheries? Given proper management, such uses can persist long after the last marine oil well is capped and the last nodule is scooped off the deep seabed. The delegates to the Law of the Sea conferences deserve commendation for reaffirming rights of transit in coastal waters and international straits. Maritime transportation, because of its ability to carry large quantities of goods at reasonable prices, will become even more important as land and air transportation systems cope with spiraling fuel costs. And the latter two systems cannot run up sail.

The coastal initiatives in alternative energy, water, and fish production projects can open up new economic and political horizons. We may no longer have to feel we are part of some modern Greek tragedy in which oil spills, nuclear risks, and depleted fish stocks are necessary evils.

Will our children become adults in a world still competing relentlessly for whatever marine "riches" still exist? It is much too early to tell. Certainly there is a growing and reassuring awareness of the self-defeating nature of such exploitation. How long can citizens, particularly those along the sensitive coastal rim, retain confidence in governments that expose their living space and their health to a growing array of environmental insults, whether it be tanker oil on a summer beach or dumped chemicals that find their way into fishermen's catches? How can nations be truly sovereign when the health of their citizens can be endangered by transboundary water pollution?

These predicaments on our watery planet will intensify if we fail to account for our acts in a rational way. We need not exist in a haphazard state of environmental warfare. Like good sailors, we can leave a clean wake.

APPENDIX I
SELECTED INFORMATION
ON WORLD FISHERIES
AND AQUACULTURE

Value of 1978 Landings of Finfish and Shellfish from Georges Bank

SPECIES	1978 LANDINGS (TONS)			1978 VALUE (IN THOUSAND DOLLARS)[2]		
	U.S.	OTHERS	TOTAL	U.S.	OTHERS	TOTAL
Cod	23,749	8,903	32,652	12,991	4,870	17,861
Haddock	12,101	10,180	22,281	8,555	7,197	15,752
Yellowtail flounder	7,658	58	7,716	10,223	77	10,300
Pollock	5,529	4,413	9,942	2,057	1,642	3,699
Redfish	2,632	82	2,714	995	31	1,026
Silver hake	6,394	3,607	10,001	1,893	1,068	2,961
Red hake	151	813	964	37	197	234
Herring	2	—	2	+[3]	—	+[3]
Mackerel	2	242	244	1	141	142
Other finfish	16,563	1,803	18,366	6,824	743	7,567
Squid *(Illex)*	120	675	795	26	147	173
Squid *(Loligo)*	7	40	47	7	42	49
Sea scallops[1]	5,569	12,145	17,714	31,131	67,891	99,022
Lobster	1,691	286	1,977	6,908	1,168	8,076
Other shellfish[4]	1,019	—	1,019	763	—	763
TOTAL	83,187	43,247	126,434	82,411	85,214	167,625

1. Meat weight.
2. U.S. value applied to United States and others.
3. Less than $1,000.
4. Primarily red crab.
SOURCE: National Marine Fisheries Service, Northeast Fisheries Center. Reprinted from *Final Supplement to Environmental Statement* (North Atlantic States Offshore Oil Lease Sale No. 42), Bureau of Land Management, 1980.

U.S. and World Commercial Fishery Catches, 1950–78

| YEAR | U.S. COMMERCIAL CATCH AND EXVESSEL VALUE | | | WORLD COMMERCIAL CATCH, LIVE WEIGHT (IN MILLION METRIC TONS) | | | | | |
| | LIVE WEIGHT (IN MILLION METRIC TONS) | | | | | MARINE | | | |
	PUBLISHED BY U.S. (EXCLUDES WEIGHT OF MOLLUSK SHELLS)	PUBLISHED BY FAO (INCLUDES WEIGHT OF MOLLUSK SHELLS)	EXVESSEL VALUE (IN BILLION DOLLARS)	FRESH-WATER	PERUVIAN ANCHOVY	OTHER[1]	TOTAL	GRAND TOTAL
1950	2.2	2.6	0.3	2.4	—	18.7	18.7	21
1951	2.0	2.4	.4	2.6	—	20.9	20.9	23.5
1952	2.0	2.4	.4	2.8	—	22.3	22.3	25.1
1953	2.0	2.7	.4	3.0	—	22.9	22.9	25.9
1954	2.2	2.8	.4	3.2	—	24.4	24.4	27.6
1955	2.2	2.8	.3	3.4	—	25.5	25.5	28.9
1956	2.4	3.0	.4	3.5	0.1	27.2	27.3	30.8
1957	2.2	2.8	.4	3.9	.3	27.5	27.8	31.7
1958	2.2	2.7	.4	4.5	.8	28.0	28.8	33.3
1959	2.3	2.9	.4	5.1	2.0	29.8	31.8	36.9
1960	2.2	2.8	.4	5.6	3.5	31.1	34.6	40.2
1961	2.4	2.9	.4	5.7	5.3	32.6	37.9	43.6
1962	2.4	3.0	.4	5.8	7.1	31.9	39.0	44.8
1963	2.2	2.8	.4	5.9	7.2	33.5	40.7	46.6
1964	2.1	2.6	.4	6.2	9.8	35.9	45.7	51.9
1965	2.2	2.7	.4	7.0	7.7	38.5	46.2	53.2
1966	1.9	2.5	.5	7.3	9.6	40.4	50.0	57.3
1967	1.8	2.4	.4	7.2	10.5	42.7	53.2	60.4

Year								
1968	1.9	2.5	.5	7.4	11.3	45.2	56.5	63.9
1969	1.9	2.5	.5	7.6	9.7	45.4	55.1	62.7
1970	2.2	2.9	.6	8.4	13.1	46.6	59.7	68.1
1971	2.3	3.0	.7	9.0	11.2	48.3	59.5	68.5
1972	2.2	2.8	.7	5.7	4.8	53.7	58.5	64.2
1973	2.2	2.9	.9	6.0	1.7	57.4	59.1	65.1
1974	2.3	2.9	.9	6.0	4.0	58.9	62.9	68.9
1975	2.2	2.9	1.0	6.4	3.3	58.9	62.2	68.6
1976	2.4	3.2	1.4	6.2	4.3	61.6	65.9	72.1
1977	2.4	3.1	1.5	6.3	.8	64.1	64.9	71.2
1978	2.7	3.5	1.9	6.1	1.2	65.1	66.3	72.4

1. Includes diadromous (salmon and other anadromous fishes and catadromous fishes such as eels). There are 2,204.6 pounds in a metric ton.

NOTE: There is a discontinuity of data in the world commercial catch of freshwater and marine fish prior to 1972 compared to data from 1972 to 1978 due to an FAO revision of the mainland Chinese catch as published in *Yearbook of Fishery Statistics 1978*, Vol. 46. The mainland Chinese freshwater fish catch was revised downward and the marine fish catch was revised upward.

SOURCE: *Fishery Statistics of the United States*; *Fisheries of the United States*; *Yearbook of Fishery Statistics*, Various issues, Food and Agriculture Organization of the United Nations (FAO). Reprinted from *Fisheries of the United States*, National Marine Fisheries Service.

World Commercial Catch of Fish, Crustaceans, Mollusks, and Other Aquatic Plants and Animals (Except Whales and Seals), by Countries, 1974–78

COUNTRY	LIVE WEIGHT (IN THOUSAND METRIC TONS)				
	1974[1]	1975[1]	1976[1]	1977[1]	1978
Japan	10,805	10,524	10,662	10,763	10,752
USSR	9,257	9,975	10,134	9,352	8,930
China, mainland	4,400[2]	4,500[2]	4,600[2]	4,700	4,660
United States	2,929[3]	2,920[3]	3,160[3]	3,085[3]	3,512[3]
Peru	4,145	3,447	4,343	2,541	3,365
Norway	2,668	2,542	3,416	3,460	2,647
India	2,255	2,266	2,174	2,312	2,368
Republic of Korea	2,024	2,134	2,405	2,419	2,351
Thailand	1,516	1,553	1,660	2,190	2,264
Denmark	1,835	1,767	1,912	1,807	1,745
Chile	1,158	929	1,409	1,349	1,698
Indonesia	1,336	1,390	1,483	1,572	1,655
North Korea	1,400[2]	1,500[2]	1,600[2]	1,600[2]	1,600[2]
Iceland	945	996	992	1,378	1,579
Philippines	1,371	1,443	1,393	1,511	1,558
Canada	1,042	1,033	1,133	1,270	1,407
Spain	1,510	1,518	1,475	1,394	1,380
Vietnam	1,014[2]	1,014[2]	1,014[2]	1,014[2]	1,014[2]
Brazil	740	772	659	748	858
France	808	806	806	760	796
Mexico	442	499	572	670	752
Malaysia	526	474	517	619	685
Bangladesh	822	823	826	835	640
Republic of South Africa	648	642	640	603	628
Poland	679	801	750	655	571
England and Wales	534	497	520	525	548
Burma	434	485	502	519	540
Argentina	296	229	281	392	537
Nigeria	473	466	497	504	519
Scotland	538	468	503	468	479
Ecuador	174	263	315	476	476[2]
Namibia (S.W. Africa)	840[2]	761[2]	574[2]	404[2]	418[2]
Federal Rep. of Germany	526	442	454	432	412
Italy	426	406	420	380	402
Senegal	357	363	362	289	346
Netherlands	326	351	285	313	324
Faeroe Islands	246	286	342	310	318
All others	7,450	7,323	7,323	7,594	7,646
TOTAL	68,895	68,608	72,113	71,213	72,380

1. Revised.
2. Data estimated by FAO.

(notes continued on next page)

THE OCEANS: OUR LAST RESOURCE

Projected Production, Employment and Revenues from Aquaculture in Hawaii, 1978 to 2000

YEAR	PRODUCTION YIELD (IN THOUSAND POUNDS)	ACRES	EMPLOYMENT DIRECT JOBS	INDIRECT JOBS	TOTAL JOBS	WHOLESALE REVENUES (IN THOUSAND DOLLARS)
1978	427	149.0	34	49	83	$ 931
1980	2,600	606.5	82	157	239	6,382
1985	16,785	2,429.0	313	641	954	32,644
1990	47,075	5,768.0	644	1,490	2,134	71,410
1995	93,975	12,109.0	1,273	2,879	4,152	147,988
2000	198,125	28,100.0	2,805	6,217	9,022	334,567

SOURCE: *Aquaculture Development for Hawaii*, Hawaii Department of Planning and Economic Development, 1978.

3. Includes the weight of clams, oysters, scallops, and other mollusk shells. This weight is not included in U.S. landings statistics shown elsewhere.

NOTE: Statistics for mariculture, aquaculture, and other kinds of fish farming, seaweed harvesting, etc., are included in country totals. Statistics on quantities caught by recreational fishermen are excluded.

SOURCE: *Yearbook of Fishery Statistics, 1978*, Vol. 46, Food and Agriculture Organization of the United Nations (FAO). Reprinted from *Fisheries of the United States, 1979*, National Marine Fisheries Service.

U.S. Marine Fishery Resources that Are Depleted, in Imminent Danger of Depletion, or Under Intensive Use

SPECIES/SPECIES GROUP	CONDITION

Northwest Atlantic and Middle Atlantic Bight (Canadian Border to Virginia–North Carolina Border)

FINFISH

American dab (american plaice)	Intensive use
Black sea basses	Intensive use
Bluefish	Intensive use
Cod	Intensive use/Imminent danger
Flukes	Imminent danger
Grey sole (witch flounder)	Imminent danger
Haddock	Depleted
Mackerel	Imminent danger
Menhaden	Depleted
Ocean perch (redfish)	Intensive use
Scups or porgies	Intensive use
Red hake	Imminent danger
Sea herring (Atlantic herring)	Depleted
Silver hake	Intensive use
Winter flounder	Imminent danger
Yellowtail flounder	Depleted

SHELLFISH

American lobster	Intensive use
Blue crab	Intensive use
Hard clams	Intensive use
Oysters	Intensive use—depleted
Softshell clam	Intensive use
Pandalid shrimps	Depleted
Sea scallop	Depleted
Surf clam	Intensive use

Southeast U.S. Coast (Virginia–North Carolina Border to Florida Keys East of Long. 81°W)

FINFISH

Atlantic mackerel	Imminent danger
Menhaden	Depleted

SHELLFISH

Shrimps	Intensive use
Spiny lobster	Intensive use
Stone crab	Intensive use

Gulf of Mexico (Florida West of Long. 81°W to Mexican Border)

FINFISH

Groupers	Intensive use
Menhaden	Intensive use
Snappers	Intensive use

SPECIES/SPECIES GROUP	CONDITION

SHELLFISH

Oysters	Intensive use—depleted
Shrimps	Imminent danger
Spiny lobster	Intensive use
Stone crab	Intensive use

Southwest U.S. Coast (Cape Mendocino, California, South to Mexican Border)

FINFISH

Pacific barracuda	Imminent danger—depleted
California yellowtail	Intensive use
Hake (Pacific hake)	Imminent danger—depleted
Pacific Bonito	Imminent danger
Pacific mackerel	Depleted
Pacific sardine	Depleted
Rockfishes (including Pacific Ocean perch)	Intensive use
Sea herring (Pacific herring)	Intensive use
White sea bass	Intensive use

SHELLFISH

Abalones	Intensive use—depleted
Dungeness crabs	Intensive use
Pismo clam	Intensive use—depleted
Shrimps	Intensive use—depleted
Spiny lobster	Imminent danger

Northeast Pacific (Cape Mendocino, California, North to Canadian Border)

FINFISH

Cod (Pacific cod)	Intensive use
Flounders (Pacific flounders and soles)	Intensive use
Hake (Pacific hake)	Imminent danger—depleted
Halibut (Pacific halibut)	Depleted
Rockfishes (including Pacific Ocean perch)	Imminent danger—depleted
Sablefish (black cod)	Intensive use

SHELLFISH

Dungeness crabs	Intensive use
Razor clams	Intensive use
Shrimps (Pandalid shrimps)	Intensive use

Alaska

FINFISH

Alaska pollock	Depleted
Flounders (Bering Sea only)	Depleted
Halibut	Depleted
Pacific cod	Imminent danger
Rockfishes (including Pacific Ocean perch)	Imminent danger—depleted
Sablefish (black cod)	Imminent danger

SHELLFISH

Dungeness crab	Intensive use
King crab	Intensive use

SPECIES/SPECIES GROUP	CONDITION
Shrimps	Intensive use
Tanner crabs (Gulf of Alaska)	Intensive use

Insular Fisheries of the Caribbean
Species lists to be developed.

Insular Fisheries of the Pacific
Species lists to be developed. (Most coastal Hawaiian stocks are depleted.)

Highly Migratory Species
FINFISH

Albacore	Intensive use
Bluefin tuna (both Atlantic and Pacific)	Imminent danger—depleted
Yellowfin tuna (Atlantic)	Intensive use
Yellowfin tuna (Pacific)	Imminent danger

Anadromous Species

Alewife (a river herring)	Depleted
American shad (a river herring)	Intensive use—depleted
Atlantic salmon	Depleted
Blueback herring (a river herring)	Depleted
Hickory shad (a river herring)	Intensive use—depleted
Pacific salmons	Intensive use—depleted
Sea run trouts	Intensive use—depleted
Striped bass	Intensive use—depleted

SOURCE: Prepared by the National Marine Fisheries Service, National Oceanic and Atmospheric Administration, Department of Commerce, August 1975. Reprinted from *A Legislative History of the Fishery Conservation and Management Act of 1976*, U.S. Congress.

National Aquaculture Organizations and Associations

American Fish Farmers Federation
P.O. Box 158
Lonoke, Arkansas 72086
President: Jim Malone, (501) 676-2800
Vice President: Wayne Elmore,
    (501) 676-6642

American Fisheries Society
5410 Grosvenor Lane
Bethesda, Maryland 20014
Phone: (301) 897-8616
Executive Director: Carl R. Sullivan
President: Richard A. Ryder
President Elect: John J. Magnuson
Publications: *Transactions* (bimonthly)
    $10, *Fisheries* (bimonthly with
    membership dues)

American Salmon Growers Association
6427 So. Island Drive
Sumner, Washington 98390
Phone: (206) 863-5537
President: Greg Ferguson

Catfish Farmers of America
P.O. Box 34
Jackson, Mississippi 39205
Phone: (601) 353-7916
President: Turner Arant
Vice President: Kelly Farmer
Secretary: Stan Hudson
Treasurer: W.S. Edwards
Executive Secretary: Mark Freeman

**Fish Culture Section of the American
    Fisheries Society**
P.O. Box 4004
Monroe, Louisiana 71203
Phone: (318) 343-4044
President: Janice S. Hughes
President-Elect: Robert Piper
Vice President: Ian Pritchard
Secretary: Nick Parker
Treasurer: Harry Westers
Publication: *FCS Newsletter* (quarterly)

**Inland Commercial Fisheries
    Association**
Box 2565
Oshkosh, Wisconsin 54903

Phone: (414) 424-3057
Executive Director: Vern Hacker
President: Virgil Young
Vice President: Nephi Grasteit
Secretary/Treasurer: Michael Hoeft
Publication: *This and That* (quarterly)

**New England Collaborative for
    Aquaculture**
240 Alden Road
Fairhaven, Massachusetts
02719
President: Frank Baker
Vice President: Tom Keller
Vice President: Dick Colagiovanni
Secretary/Treasurer: Mark Howland
Meetings: Spring and Fall throughout
    N.E.
Publication: *The New England
    Aquafarmer*

Ontario Trout Farmers' Association
R.R. #2, Holland Centre
Ontario, Canada NOH 1RO
Phone: (519) 794-2684
President: Wayne Thompson
Administrator: Nigel J. Robbins
Publication: *Ontario Trout* magazine

Pacific Oyster Growers Association
270 South Hanford Street
Seattle, Washington 98134
Phone: (206) 625-1481
President: W. Arnold Waring
Vice President: David McMillin

Shellfish Institute of North America
400 North Capitol Street,
Suite 323
Washington, D.C. 20001
Phone: (202) 783-2803
Executive Director: R. Josh Lanier
President: Ralph V. Pausina
Executive Vice President: Weston F.
    Conley, Jr.
Vice Presidents: Bob O. Bower, Ted
    Blount, William Shields
Financial Secretary: John E.P. Borden
Publication: *Soundings*

Southern Southeast Regional
   Aquaculture Association, Inc.
P.O. Box 6916
Ketchikan, Alaska 99901
Phone: (907) 225-9605
Executive Director: Ronald W.
   Wendte
President: Roger Ingman
Vice President: Jack Jacobsen
Publication: *Spawning News* (quarterly)

United States Trout Farmers
   Association
P.O. Box 171
Lake Ozark, Missouri 65049
Phone: (314) 365-2478
Executive Director: Tim Pilkington
President: Ed Murrison
Eastern Vice President: Ben Watson
Western Vice President: Keith Brown
Secretary: Russ McCleary

Treasurer: Hugo Kettula
Publication: *Salmonid* (bimonthly)

U.S. Aquaculture Council and U.S.
   Aquaculture Federation
P.O. Box 276
Lacey Springs, Virginia
Phone: (703) 433-2395
Chairman: Fern Wood Mitchell

World Mariculture Society
174 Pleasant Hall, Div. of Cont.
   Education
Louisiana State University
Baton Rouge, Louisiana 70803
President: Carl J. Sindermann
President-Elect: Guthrie Perry
Vice President: George S. Lockwood
Secretary: Margie Lee Gallagher
Treasurer: Samuel P. Meyers
Publications: Newsletter (quarterly)

SOURCE: *Aquaculture Magazine, 1981 Buyer's Guide,* Little Rock, Arkansas.

State Aquaculture and Fish Farming Associations

Alabama

Alabama Catfish Farmers, a division of the Alabama Farm Bureau Federation
P.O. Box 11000, Montgomery, AL 36198
Phone: (205) 288-3900, ext. 312
Division Director: Jimmy Carlisle AFBF
State Chairman: Bill Easterling

Arkansas

Catfish Farmers of Arkansas
1818 Fairway, Stuttgart, AR 72160
Phone: (501) 673-1788
President: Charles Day
Vice President: John Eaves

California

California Aquaculture Association
P.O. Box 5293, Carmel, CA 93921
Phone: (408) 372-6010
President: George S. Lockwood
Vice President: Hugh Staton

California Fish Farmers Association
P.O. Box 448, Niland, CA 92257
Phone: (916) 645-1183 or
(714) 348-0547
President: Keith Brown
Vice President: Tony Vaught
Secretary: George Ray
Treasurer: Bob Hulbrock

Florida

Florida Tropical Fish Farms Association
P.O. Box 1519, Winter Haven, FL 33880
Phone: (813) 293-5710
President: Ross Socolof
Vice President: Dave Walker
Secretary: Arlen Wetherington
Treasurer: Richard Atcheson
Past President: Johnny Williams

Kansas

Kansas Commercial Fish Growers
Association
Box 237, Pretty Prairie, KA 67570
Phone: (316) 459-6589
President: George Adrian

Vice President: Brent Culver
Secretary/Treasurer: Lynn Vern Krehbiel

Louisiana

Louisiana Crawfish Farmers Association
University Station, Knapp Hall
Baton Rouge, LA 70803
Phone: (504) 388-4141
President, Eastern Div.—John E. Thibaut
President, Western Div.—Ricky J. Broussard

Maine

Maine Aquaculture Association
P.O. Box 535, Damariscotta, ME 04543
President: Jon Smith
Vice President: Tom Archambault
Secretary/Treasurer: Dick Clime
Newsletter: Bimonthly column in *Commercial Fisheries News*

Mississippi

Catfish Farmers of Mississippi
P.O. Box 1609, Jackson, MS 39202
Phone: (601) 354-6569
President: Lester Myers
President-Elect: Mark Lupher
Secretary: Tommy Peaster
Treasurer: Rodney Henderson

Missouri

Missouri Fish Farmers Association
P.O. Box 171, Lake Ozark, MO 65049
Phone: (314) 365-2478
Executive Director: Tim Pilkington
President: Dwight Emerson
Vice President: Wayne Luecke

Rhode Island

Rhode Island Aquaculture Association
P.O. Box H, Kingston, RI 02881
Phone: (401) 539-2858
President: William Silkes

Secretary: Bruce Rogers
Treasurer: Deborah Westin

Texas

Fish Farmers of Texas
P.O. Box 2948, College Station, TX
77841
President: Jack Giffin
1st Vice President: Wallace Klussmann
2nd Vice President: Billy Edwards

Wisconsin

Wisconsin Trout Growers
Box 115, Lewis, WI 54851
Phone: (715) 653-2271
President: Larry Brunner
Vice President: Mike Foster
Secretary: Hugo Kettula
Newsletter: *Creel* (quarterly)

Processor and Marketing Associations

American Catfish Marketing Association
P.O. Box 1609, Jackson, MS 39205
Phone: (601) 948-5938
Acting Executive Secretary: James H.
Smith
President: Joe Glover
Vice President: Paul Barrett
Secretary/Treasurer: Richard True
Membership: Processors of domestic
Farm Raised catfish

Mississippi Catfish Farmers Marketing
Association
Belzoni, Mississippi
Phone: (601) 247-3392
Executive Director: Robert L. "Mac"
McClellan
Annual Meeting: February

SOURCE: *Aquaculture Magazine, 1981 Buyer's Guide,* Little Rock, Arkansas.

APPENDIX II
HAZARDS OF OFFSHORE
OIL DEVELOPMENT

Potential Hazards to Marine Mammals and Seabirds From Offshore Oil Resource Development and Production

ACTIVITY OR FACILITY	CHRONIC HAZARDS	EPISODIC/CATASTROPHIC EVENTS
Exploration		
Seismic profiling	Noise, "startle" effects	Subsurface noise—
Drilling		Concussion
Boat traffic	Prop hits	Siltation
		Opacity increases
		Downstream pluming
Operation	Disturbance near	Disturbance in
Onshore facilities	reproductive areas of	construction
Staging areas	sensitive mammal	
Pumping stations	and bird populations	
Tank farms	(depends on site)	
Separation plants	Introduction of terrestrial	
Refineries	predators	
Offshore facilities		
Production platforms		Blow-out
Well-head	Leakage/seepage	
Support		
Crew and supply boats	Sub-surface noise and	
Aircraft	propeller hits	
	Noise in air	
Transport		
Pipelines	Leakage	Rupture
Pumping buoys	Leakage	
Barges and tankers	Bilge Oil	Collision or grounding

ACTIVITY OR FACILITY	CHRONIC HAZARDS	EPISODIC/CATASTROPHIC EVENTS
Cleanup		
Oil on water		
Skimmers		
Burn-off		
Chemicals		Pollution—air
Grounded oil		Pollution—water
Booms		Disturbance of sensitive
Straw		bird and mammal
Chemicals		populations on islands by human intrusion and aircraft activity

SOURCE: *Santa Barbara Channel Marine Sanctuary,* County of Santa Barbara, 1978.

Numbers of Operational Oil Spills from Tankers in United States Harbors

OPERATION	CAUSE								UNKNOWN	TOTAL INCIDENTS
	HUMAN ERROR				MECHANICAL FAILURE					
	TANK OVERFLOW	BILGE/BAL PUMPING	IMPROPER OPERATION	OTHER ERROR	VALVE–PUMP	PIPE–HOSE	TANK OR HULL LEAK	OTHER EQUIPMENT		
Loading/discharging operations	212	6	39	63	73	51	23	53	145	665
Miscellaneous operations	50	82	50	39	27	11	9	22	53	343
Unknown operations	12	9	16	8	6	5	0	12	51	119
SUBTOTALS	274	97	105	110	106	67	32	87	249	
TOTALS	586				292					1127

SOURCE: U.S. Coast Guard's pollution incident reporting system (January 1974 to August 1975).

REFERENCES

Chapters 2 and 3

FORAGE FISH

Brewer, Gary, and Donna Cooksey. 1979. Biology of the Northern Anchovy in Relation to Its Biomass Utilization. *Biosources Digest* 6(2).

California Cooperative Oceanic Fisheries Investigation. 1977. *Annual Reports,* Vols. XIX and XX. Calcofi Coordinator, George Hemingway, La Jolla, Calif.

Chapoton, Robert. 1973. Biological Considerations and the Gulf of Mexico Menhaden Fishery. *Proceedings—Gulf and Caribbean Fisheries Institute 26th Annual Session,* Oct., 1973, pp. 15–23.

Clepper, Henry, ed. 1979. *Predator-Prey Systems in Fisheries Management.* Sport Fishing Institute, Washington, D.C.

Culley, Michael. 1971. *The Pilchard: Biology and Exploitation.* Pergamon, New York.

Glantz, Michael. 1979. Science, Politics and Economics of the Peruvian Anchovy Fishery. *Marine Policy,* July, 1979.

Hartline, Beverly. 1980. Coastal Upwelling: Physical Factors Feed Fish. *Science* 208(4), April.

Haughen, Charles. 1973. The Status of the Pacific Sardine Resource and Its Management. Marine Resources Technical Report #13. California Department of Fish and Game, Long Beach, Calif.

Henry, Kenneth. 1971. Atlantic Menhaden Resource and Fishery—Analysis of Decline. Technical Report, National Marine Fisheries Service SSRF-642, Washington, D.C.

Kameon, Herbert. 1978. Natural Variability of Anchovy Populations. Testimony submitted to Pacific Fishery Management Council, January 14, 1978, by the President of the National Coalition for Marine Conservation—Pacific Region.

Lasker, Reuben. 1975. Field Criteria for Survival of Anchovy Larvae. *Fishery Bulletin, U.S.* 73(3).

———. 1978. The Relation between Oceanographic Conditions and Larval Food in the California current. *Rapp. R.-V. Reun. Cons. Int. Explor. Mer.* 173.

McHugh, John. 1969. Comparison of Pacific Sardine and Atlantic Menhaden Fisheries. *FiskDir. Skr. Ser. HavUnders.* 15:356–367.

McHugh, John, and Elbert Ahlstrom. 1951. Is the Pacific Sardine Disappearing? *Scientific Monthly* 62(6).

Mais, Kenneth. 1974. *Pelagic Fish Surveys in the California Current.* Fish Bulletin 162. California Department of Fish and Game, Long Beach, Calif.

National Coalition for Marine Conservation. 1976. Letter, December 7, to National Marine Fisheries Service on Atlantic Herring Fishery Management Plan. Signed by Christopher Weld, Secretary. Boston.

New England Fishery Management Council. 1978. Final Environmental Impact Statement/Fishery Management Plan for the Atlantic Herring Fishery of the Northwest Atlantic. Peabody, Mass.

Pacific Fishery Management Council. 1978. Northern Anchovy Fishery Management Plan and Final Environmental Impact Statement. *Federal Register* 43(141): 31651–31879.

Pacific Fishery Management Council, Scientific and Statistical Committee. 1980. Minutes of meeting, July 7–8, 1980, pp. 2, 7–9, on anchovy. La Jolla, Calif.

Paulik, G.J. 1966. Anchovies, Birds and Fishermen in the Peru Current. In W. W. Murdock, ed., *Environment, Resources, Pollution and Society,* pp. 156–185. Sinauer Associates, Stamford, Conn.

Reintjes, John. 1969. *Synopsis of Biological Data on the Atlantic Menhaden.* U.S. Fish and Wildlife Service Circular 320.

Ricketts, Edward, and Jack Calvin; revised by Joel Hedgpeth. 1968. *Between Pacific Tides,* 4th Ed., Chapter 15 (Beyond the Tides: The Uncertain Sea). Stanford University Press, Stanford, Calif.

Schaff, William. 1975. Status of the Gulf and Atlantic Menhaden Fisheries and Implications for Resource Management. *Marine Fisheries Review* 37(9).

Sport Fishing Institute. 1976. California Anchovy Reduction Fishery. In *Sport Fishery Institute Bulletin,* November–December. Washington, D.C.

FISHERY MANAGEMENT

Baker, Robert. 1978. Fish: A Wasted Resource. *New York's Food and Life Sciences Quarterly* 11(4).

Christy, Francis T., Jr. 1973. *Alternative Arrangements for Marine Fisheries: An Overview.* Resources for the Future, Inc., Washington, D.C.

Environmental Defense Fund. 1979. Petition for Amendment of Guidelines for Development of Fishery Management Plans. Prepared by Langdon Warner and Michael Bean. Washington, D.C.

Gulland, J. 1974. *The Management of Marine Fisheries.* University of Washington Press, Seattle.

———. 1978. *Review of the State of World Fishery Resources.* Food and Agriculture Organization, Fish Circular #710. Rome, Italy.

Gulland, J., ed. 1977. *Fish Population Dynamics.* Wiley, New York.

Hedgpeth, Joel W., ed. 1957. *Treatise on Marine Ecology.* Geographical Society of America, Memoir 67, New York.

Hennemuth, Richard. 1978. Man as Predator. Delivered to International Statistical Ecology Program in Jerusalem, September, 1978. (Hennemuth directs the Northeast Fisheries Center, National Marine Fisheries Service, Woods Hole, Mass.)

———. 1979. Marine Fisheries: Food for the Future? *Oceanus* 22(1).

Joseph, James, Witold Klawe and Pat Murphy. 1979. Tuna and Billfish—Fish without a Country. Inter-American Tropical Tuna Commission, La Jolla, Ca.

McGoodwin, James Russell. 1980. The Human Costs of Development. *Environment* 22(1).

May, Robert, John Beddington, Colin Clark, Sidney Holt, and Richard Laws. 1979. Management of Multispecies Fisheries. *Science* 205.

Mitchell, Barbara, and Richard Sandbrook. 1980. *The Management of the Southern Ocean.* International Institute for Environment and Development, London.

Naylor, John. 1977. *Food Resources of the Sea.* Fisheries Division, Food and Agriculture Organization, Rome, Italy.

Office of Technology Assessment. 1977. Establishing a 200-mile Fisheries Zone. Robert Niblock, Program Manager. U.S. Congress, Washington, D.C.

Rawitscher, Mary, and Vern Mayer. 1977. Nutritional Outputs and Energy Inputs in Seafoods. *Science*, October 21, 1977.

Ricker, William. 1969. Food from the Sea. In *Resources and Man.* W.H. Freeman, San Francisco.

Robinson, M.H. 1980. World Fisheries to 2000. *Marine Policy*, January.

Rothschild, Brian J., ed. 1972. *World Fisheries Policy: Multidisciplinary Views.* University of Washington Press, Seattle.

U.S. Department of Commerce. 1976. *A Marine Fisheries Program for the Nation.* Washington, D.C.

———. 1979. *Fisheries of the United States, 1979.* National Marine Fisheries Service, Washington, D.C.

U.S. General Accounting Office. 1979. Progress and Problems of Fisheries Management under the Fishery Conservation and Management Act, CED-79-237. Washington, D.C.

———. 1979. Fishery Conservation and Management Act's Impact on Selected Fisheries, CED-79-577. Washington, D.C.

U.S. House of Representatives, Committee on Merchant Marine and Fisheries. Ninety-sixth Congress. 1979. Fishery Conservation and Management Act. Hearings. Serial #96-17.

———. 1980. American Fisheries Promotion Act. Report 96-1138.

U.S. Senate, Committee on Commerce. Ninety-fourth Congress. 1976. Legislative History of the Fishery and Conservation Management Act of 1976. Washington, D.C.

MARINE RECREATIONAL FISHING

Centaur Management Consultants. 1977. Economic Activity Associated with Marine Recreational Fishing. Report for National Marine Fisheries Service, Washington, D.C.

Clepper, Henry, ed. 1976. *Marine Recreational Fisheries.* Sport Fishing Institute, Washington, D.C.

SEABIRD—FISH INTERACTION

Ainley, David, and James Lewis. 1974. History of Farallon Island Marine Bird Populations. *Condor*, Winter, 1974.

Crawford, Robert, and Peter Shelton. 1978. Fish and Seabird Interrelationships. *Biological Conservation*, September, 1978. (Authors with Sea Fisheries Branch of the Union of South Africa)

Frost, P.G.H., W.R. Siegried, and J. Cooper. 1976. Conservation of the Jackass Penguin. *Biological Conservation,* February, 1976. (Authors with University of Cape Town, South Africa)

Hunt, George. 1978. History, Distribution and Ecology of Marine Birds of the California Channel Islands. Paper delivered to symposium on Channel Islands at Santa Barbara, February 27 to March 1, 1978.

Keith, James. 1978. Synergistic Effects of DDE and Food Stress on Reproduction in Brown Pelicans and Ringdoves. Doctoral Dissertation, Ohio State University. (Keith is with the U.S. Fish and Wildlife Service, Denver office.)

Murphy, Robert Cushman. 1925. *Bird Islands of Peru.* G. P. Putnam's, New York.

Chapters 4, 5 and 6

Alsten, Chris. 1979. Is This the Decade for Aquaculture? Parts 1 and 2. *Compost Science/Land Utilization,* January–February, March–April, 1979.

Bardach, John, John Ryther, and William McLarney. 1972. *Aquaculture.* Wiley, New York. (Chapters 1–4 cover carp.)

Bortz, Brenda, Jack Ruttle, and Marc Podems. 1977. *Raising Fresh Fish in Your Home Waters.* Rodale, Emmaus, Penn.

Fassler, C. Richard. 1979. *Aquaculture in Hawaii: Past and Present.* Uni. of Hawaii Sea Grant Pub. AB-80-05.

Hawaii Dept. of Land and Natural Resources. 1979. Hawaii Fisheries Development Plan. Stanley Swerdloff, Project Manager. State of Hawaii, Honolulu.

Hawaii State Center for Science Policy and Technology Assessment. 1978. Aquaculture Development for Hawaii. Aquaculture Planning Program, Hawaii Dept. of Planning and Economic Development, Honolulu.

Hedgpeth, Joel W. 1980. The Problem of Introduced Species in Management and Mitigation. *Helgolander Meeresunters.* 33, 662–673.

Holden, Constance. 1978. Government Seeking Ways to Encourage Aquaculture. *Science,* April 7, 1978.

Huet, Marcel. 1970. *Textbook of Fish Culture.* Fishing News Books, Surrey, England.

Hunter, Jay. 1980. Future Trends—Freshwater Aquaculture in the U.S. *Farm Pond Harvest,* Summer, 1980.

Lampman, Ben Hur. 1946. *The Coming of the Pond Fishes.* Binfords & Mort, Portland, Oregon.

Lindsey, Cedric. 1980. Salmon farming in Washington moves closer to industry status. *Aquaculture,* March-April, 1980.

Ling, Shao-Wen. 1977. *Aquaculture in Southeast Asia.* Univ. of Washington Press, Seattle.

Lovell, Richard. 1980. Fish Culture in the United States. *Farm Pond Harvest,* Summer, 1980.

National Academy of Sciences. 1976. *Making Aquatic Weeds Useful.* Washington, D.C.

Nishiyama, Tsuneo. 1977. Japanese and Soviet Attitudes Towards Aquaculture. Univ. of Alaska Sea Grant Report 77-2.

Pelzman, Ronald. 1971. The Grass Carp. California Dept. of Fish and Game, Inland Administrative Report No. 71-14.

Pryor, Tap. 1974. *A Marine Plantation for North Kohala.* Systemculture, Honolulu.

Ryther, John. 1979. Aquaculture in China. *Oceanus,* Spring, 1979.

Tamaki, Takehiko. 1974. *Niskikigoi—Fancy Koi.* Tamaki Yogyoen, Tokyo.

Transactions of the American Fisheries Society. 1978. Special section on the grass carp, 107(1).

U.S. Fish and Wildlife Service. Undated. Environmental impact of grass carp. Research proposal prepared by Tom Jackson of the Service's Denver office.

Yeo, Richard. 1977. Hydrilla in California. *California Agriculture,* October, 1977.

Chapters 7 and 8

Bane, G. 1968. *Fishes of Upper Newport Bay.* University of California Press, Berkeley.

California Coastal Zone Conservation Commission. 1974. *Life in the Sea.* Marine element adopted by South Coast Regional Commission. Section 2, pp. 1–19 (Coastal Wetlands) and Section 3, p. 41 (Silt Control). Long Beach, Calif.

California Sea Grant College Program. 1979. California's Coastal Wetlands. Sea Grant Report Series #2, La Jolla, Calif.

Conomos, T.J., ed. 1979. *San Francisco Bay: The Urbanized Estuary.* Pacific Division: American Association for the Advancement of Science, San Francisco.

Council on Environmental Quality, Coordinator. 1978. *Our Nation's Wetlands.* Government Printing Office, Washington, D.C.

Dixon, Peter, and Gordon Marsh. 1973. *Ecological Survey of Aquatic and Terrestrial Resources for the City of Newport Beach.* Newport Beach, Calif.

Frey, Herbert, Ronald Hein, and Jack Spruill. 1970. *The Natural Resources of Upper Newport Bay.* California Department of Fish and Game, Long Beach, Calif.

Gosselink, James, Eugene Odum, and R. M. Pope. 1974. *The Value of a Tidal Marsh.* LSU-56-74-03. Center for Wetland Resources, Louisiana State University, Baton Rouge, La.

Hedgpeth, Joel W. 1962. *Seashore Life of the San Francisco Bay Region and the Coast of Northern California.* University of California Press, Berkeley, California.

———. 1973. Preliminary Notes and Recommendations for the Rehabilitation of Upper Newport Bay, California. Report prepared for Friends of Newport Bay, Newport Beach, Calif.

———. 1979. San Francisco Bay—The Unsuspected Estuary. In T. J. Conomos, ed., *San Francisco Bay: The Urbanized Estuary* (see listing under this title).

McHugh, John. 1966. *Management of Estuarine Fisheries.* American Fisheries Society Special Publication No. 3, pp. 133–154.

———. 1976. Estuarine Fisheries: Are They Doomed? In *Estuarine Processes,* Vol. 1. Academic Press, New York.

Marx, Wesley. 1967. *The Frail Ocean,* Chapter 8. Coward, McCann, New York.

———. 1968. Suicide in the Shallows. *National Wildlife* 6(4).

———. 1969. Nurseries of the Sea. *UNESCO Courier,* March, 1969.

Odum, Eugene. 1971. *Fundamentals of Ecology,* 3rd ed., Chapter 13. Saunders, Philadelphia.

Ricketts, Edward, and Jack Calvin, revised by Joel Hedgpeth. 1969. *Between Pacific Tides,* Part 3: Bay and Estuary, 4th ed. Stanford University, Stanford, Calif.

San Francisco Bay Conservation and Development Commission. 1968. Ownership. In *San Francisco Bay Plan Supplement.* San Francisco.

Stevenson, R.E., and K.O. Emery. 1958. *Marshlands at Newport Bay, California.* Allan Hancock Foundation Occasional Paper No. 20. University of Southern California, Los Angeles.

Sunset Magazine. 1969. Upper Newport Bay . . . Watching the Wildlife. February, 1969.

U.S. Department of Agriculture. Undated. Controlling Erosion on Construction Sites. Soil Conservation Service—Agriculture Information Bulletin 347. Washington, D.C.

U.S. Department of the Interior. 1970. *National Estuary Study.* Seven volumes. Washington, D.C. (Vol. 5 includes brief section on Upper Newport Bay, p. 48.)

TIDELAND LEGAL CASES AND LAW REVIEW ARTICLES

Briscoe, John. 1979. Legal Problems of Tidal Marshes. In T. J. Conomos, ed., *San Francisco Bay: The Urbanized Estuary.*

California Constitution, Article X, Sections 3 and 4.

City of Long Beach v. Mansell. 3 Cal. 3d 462 (1970).

County of Orange v. Heim. 30 Cal. App. 3d 694 (1973).

Illinois Central R.R. v. Illinois. 146 U.S. 287 (1892).

Marks v. Whitney. 6 Cal. 3d 251 (1971).

Note, 1970. The Public Trust in Tidal Areas: A Sometimes Submerged Traditional Doctrine. *Yale Law Journal.* 79:762.

Parker, C.E. 1977. History, Politics and the Law of the California Tidelands Trust. *Western State University Law Review* 4(2).

Taylor, N. Gregory. 1972. Patented Tidelands: A Naked Fee? Marks v. Whitney and the Public Trust Easement. *California State Bar Journal* 47(5).

Chapter 9

Abbott, Isabella, and Eleanor H. Williamson. 1974. *Limu.* Pacific Tropical Botanical Garden, Lawai, Kawai, Hawaii.

Bryce, Armond. 1977. Research and Development Program to Assess the Technical and Economic Feasibility of Methane Production from Giant Brown Kelp. Presented at Ninth Synthetic Pipeline Gas Symposium, Chicago.

Chapman, Valentine. 1970. *Seaweeds and Their Uses,* 2nd ed. Methuen, London.

Doty, Maxwell. 1973. *Euchema* Farming for Carrageenan. Sea Grant Advisory Report, University of Hawaii.

Doty, Maxwell, and Vicente Alvarez. 1975. Status, Problems, Advances and Economics of *Euchema* Farms. *Marine Technology Society Journal* 9(4):30–35.

Friends of Irvine Coast and Laguna Greenbelt. 1978. Open Space and Recreation Plan for Proposed Wilderness Park and Resource Conservation Area.

Haaker, Peter, and Kenneth Wilson. 1974. Restoring the Kelp Beds. *Outdoor California,* September–October, 1974.

———. 1975. *Giant Kelp.* Marine Resources Leaflet No. 9, California Department of Fish and Game, Long Beach, Calif.

Hawaii Department of Planning and Economic Development. 1978. Aquaculture Development for Hawaii, pp. 53–60—Aquatic Plants. Aquaculture Planning Program, Honolulu.

Hunt, Jeffrey. 1974. Cooperative *Gracilaria* Project, Marine Option Program. Windward Community College, Oahu, Hawaii.

Hunt, Jeffrey, and William Magruder. 1979. *Seaweeds of Hawaii.* Oriental Publishing Company, Honolulu.

Jones and Stokes. 1976. Environmental Impact Report and Project Report for Irvine Coastal Community Plan. Submitted to County of Orange and to California Coastal Commission.

Leone, Joseph. 1980. Marine Biomass Energy Project. *Marine Technology Society Journal* 14(2).

Madlener, Judith. 1977. *The Sea Vegetable Cookbook.* Potter, New York.

Mearns, Alan, Doyle Hanan, and Leslie Harris. 1977. Recovery of Kelp Forest off Palos Verdes. Annual Report, 1977, Southern California Coastal Water Research Project, Los Angeles.

Neushul, Michael. 1978. Domestication of the Giant Kelp, *Macrocystis* as a Marine Plant Biomass Producer. In *The Marine Plant Biomass of the Pacific Northwest Coast.* Oregon State University Press, Corvallis.

North, W.J. Annual Progress Reports, Kelp Habitat Improvement Project. 1969 on. California Institute of Technology, Pasadena, Calif.

Pearse, John, and Valerie Gerard. 1977. Kelp Forests. In John Clark, *Coastal Ecosystem Management.* Wiley, New York.

Ryther, John. 1979. Fuels from Marine Biomass. *Oceanus* 22(4).

Scofield, W.L. 1959. History of Kelp Harvesting in California. *California Fish and Game* 45(3), Sacramento.

Wilcox, Howard. 1977. The U.S. Navy's Ocean Food and Energy Farm Project. Naval Oceans Systems Center, San Diego.

Chapter 10

D'Arms, John. 1970. *Romans on the Bay of Naples.* Harvard University Press, Cambridge, Mass.

Hern, Anthony. 1967. *The Seaside Holiday.* Cresset Press, London.

Juvenal. 1965. *Satires.* Translated by Jerome Mazzara. University of Michigan Press, Ann Arbor.

McKay, Alexander. 1970. *Vergil's Italy.* New York Graphic Society, Ltd., Greenwich, Conn.

Petronius. 1959. *The Satyricon of Petronius.* Translated and with an introduction by William Arrowsmith. University of Michigan Press, Ann Arbor.

Pimlott, J.A.R. 1947. *The Englishman's Holiday.* Reprint, 1976. Harvester Press, London.

Turner, Louis, and John Ash. 1975. *The Golden Hordes.* Constable, London.

Chapters 11 and 12

Balsillie, J.H., and D.W. Berg. 1972. State of Groin Design and Effectiveness. *Proceedings 13th Conference on Coastal Engineering.* Vancouver, B.C., July, 1972.

Bascom, Willard. 1964. *Waves and Beaches.* Anchor Books, New York.

Clark, John R.K. 1977. *The Beaches of Oahu.* University of Hawaii Press, Honolulu.

Crane, Jerald. 1972. History of the Marine Structures on Waikiki Beach and Their Effects upon the Beach. Report, Department of Ocean Engineering, University of Hawaii, Oahu, Hawaii.

Dolan, Robert, Paul Godfrey, and William Odum. 1973. Man's Impact on the Barrier Islands of North Carolina. *American Scientist* 61, March–April, 1973.

Godfrey, Paul. 1976. Barrier Beaches of the East Coast. *Oceanus* 19(5).

Harding, Elizabeth. 1980. Nantucket's Shifting Shoreline. *Sea Grant Today* 10(5).

Inman, D.L., and B.M. Brush. 1973. The Coastal Challenge. *Science* 181:20–32.

MacLeish, William, ed. 1980. Special Issue on the Coast. *Oceanus* 23(4).

Parker, Neill. 1979. Weir Jetties—Their Continuing Evolution. *Shore and Beach,* October, 1974.

Seymour, R.J., and D.B. Duane. 1978. The Nearshore Sediment Transport Study. *Proceedings 16th Conference on Coastal Engineering.* Hamburg, Germany, September, 1978.

U.S. Army Corps of Engineers. 1971. National Shoreline Study, North Atlantic Region. North Atlantic Division, New York.

———. 1980. San Diego County, Vicinity of Oceanside, California. Survey Report for Beach Erosion Control. Los Angeles District, September, 1980.

U.S. House of Representatives. Ninety-sixth Congress. 1980. To establish a Barrier Islands Protection System, Hearings. Committee on Interior and Insular Affairs. Serial #91–32.

Walton, Todd, and James Purpura. 1977. Beach Nourishment along the Southeast Atlantic and Gulf Coasts. *Shore and Beach,* July, 1977.

Chapters 13 and 14

Arcata, California. Undated. *Wastewater Treatment, Water Reclamation and Ocean Ranching.* F.R. Klopp, City Director of Public Works.

California Coastal Zone Commission. 1974. Marine Element adopted by South Coast Regional Commission. *Life in the Sea,* Section 3, pp. 37–40, Water Reclamation. Long Beach, Calif.

California Regional Water Quality Control Board. 1980. San Jose/Santa Clara Water Pollution Control Plant, August 1980 Spill. Staff Report, Wil Brehns, Engineer. Oakland, Calif.

———. 1980. Stinson Beach—Status Report on Septic System Corrections. Lester Feldman, Engineer. Oakland, Calif.

———. 1980. San Jose/Santa Clara Water Pollution Control Plant—Fall 1979 Upset. Harold Singer, Engineer. Oakland, Calif.

California Resources Agency. 1978. *Delta Water Facilities.* DWR Bulletin 76, Sacramento, Calif.

California State Water Resources Control Board. 1979. Action Plan: Alternate Wastewater Management Systems. Sacramento, Calif.

———. 1979. Industrial Water Recycling. Office of Water Recycling, Sacramento, Calif.

Center for Law in the Public Interest. 1979. Motion for Summary Judgment prepared by Carlyle Hall and Jan Levine for Plaintiffs, O'Toole v. Irvine Ranch Water District. Superior Court of California, County of Orange, CIV. No. 29-12-52. Los Angeles.

Costle, Douglas. 1978. EPA's Construction Grants Program: Perspective on Costs. *Pollution Engineering*, September, 1978.

Chiang, S. C. A Crazy Idea on Urban Water Management. *Water Resources Bulletin* 7(1).

Davoren, William. 1980. Tragedy of the Bay Commons. Bay Institute Office, U.S. Fish and Wildlife Service, Tiburon, Calif.

Hey, Donald, et al. 1979. Planning for Water Quality: 1776 to 1976. *Journal of the Water Resources Planning and Management Division*, March, 1979.

Irvine Ranch Water District. 1979. Waste Water Management and Action Program —Final Environmental Impact Report. Irvine, Calif.

Kasperson, Roger and Jeanne. 1977. *Water Re-use and the Cities.* University Press of New England, Hanover, N.H.

Marx, Wesley. 1971. *Man and His Environment: Waste.* Pp. 116–124, Harper and Row, New York.

———. 1971. The Fall and Rise of Sewage Salvage. *Bulletin of Atomic Scientists*, May, 1971.

———. 1971. Reclaiming Water. *Sierra Club Bulletin*, April, 1971.

———. 1973. Sewage: The Surprising Resource. *The Nation*, May 7, 1973.

Milne, Murray. 1976. Residential Water Conservation. California Water Resources Center, University of California, Davis, Calif.

Phelps, Charles et al. 1978. Efficient Water Use in California: Executive Summary and Water Rights, Water Districts and Water Transfers. Prepared for California State Assembly Rules Committee. Rand Corporation, Santa Monica, Calif.

Rozengurt, Michael and Irwin Haydock. 1980. Methods of Computation and Ecological Regulation of the Salinity Regime in Estuaries and Shallow Seas in Connection with Water Regulation for Human Requirements. In press. Authors with County Sanitation Districts of Los Angeles.

Schinzinger, Roland, and Henry Fagin. 1979. Emergencies in Water Delivery. California Water Resources Center. Contribution No. 177. Davis, Calif. (The authors are at the University of California, Irvine.)

Shaefer, J.R. Storm Water for Fun and Profit. *Water Spectrum* 2(3).

Uiga, Ants, and Ronald Crites. 1978. *Environmental Changes from Long-term Land Application of Municipal Effluents.* Environmental Protection Agency, Washington, D.C.

———. 1980. Relative Health Risks of Activated Sludge Treatment and Slow-rate Land Treatment. *Journal Water Pollution Control Federation* 52(12).

U.S. Department of Interior. 1976. San Felipe Division: Final Environmental Statement, 2 Vols., FES 76–15. Water and Power Resources Service, Mid-Pacific Region, Sacramento, Calif.

U.S. Environmental Protection Agency. 1973. *Survey of Facilities Using Land Application of Wastewater.* EPA-430/9-73-006. Washington, D.C.

———. 1979. *An Approach for Comparing Health Risks of Wastewater Treatment Alternatives.* EPA 430/9-79-009. Washington, D.C.

———. 1979. A History of Land Application as a Treatment Alternative (William Jewell and Belford Seabrook). MCD-40, Washington, D.C.

———. 1979. Wastewater: Is Muskegon County's Solution Your Solution? John Walker, Office of Research and Development, Washington, D.C.

———. 1979. Water Reuse: A New Emphasis for the Environmental Protection Agency. James Smith, Office of Water and Water Management, Washington, D.C.

———. 1979. *Cost of Land Treatment Systems.* EPA-430/9-75-003. Washington, D.C.

———. 1979. Water Supply—Wastewater Treatment Coordination Study. Contract #68-01-5033. Office of Drinking Water, Washington, D.C.

U.S. General Accounting Office. 1979. Large Construction Projects to Correct Combined Sewer Overflows Are Too Costly. CED-80-40. Washington, D.C.

Van der Ryn, Sim. 1978. *The Toilet Papers.* Capra Press, Santa Barbara, Calif.

Woodworth, William. 1979. *Cistern System for Homeowners.* Monterey Peninsula Water Management District, Monterey, Calif.

Chapter 15

Ball, Milner. 1978. *Law of the Sea: Federal-State Relations.* Monograph No. 1, Dean Rusk Center, University of Georgia School of Law, Athens, Ga.

Comprehensive Planning Organization of the San Diego Region. 1978. Outer Continental Shelf: Early Action Program for Lease Sale No. 48. San Diego, CA.

Conservation Law Foundation. 1979. Nomination of the Area Commonly Known as Georges Bank as a Marine Sanctuary. Boston.

County of Santa Barbara, California. 1978. Santa Barbara Channel Marine Sanctuary. Prepared by Resources. Santa Barbara, Calif.

Hershman, Marc. 1975. Achieving Federal-State Coordination in Coastal Resources Management. *William and Mary Law Review,* Summer, 1975.

Marx, Wesley. 1971. *Oilspill.* Sierra Club, San Francisco.

———. 1973. The Coastal Zone and Oil Spills: Cultural Splits. In *Assessing the Social Impacts of Oil Spills,* Institute of Man and Science, Rensselaerville, N.Y.

———. 1975. Modern Man and the Coastal Zone. In H. J. Walker, ed., *Geosciences and Man: Coastal Resources.* School of Geoscience, Louisiana State University, Baton Rouge, La.

Mohr, John. 1979. Testimony submitted to Environmental Protection Agency, San Francisco, November 6, 1979, opposing discharge permit for Exxon drilling vessel on Cortes-Tanner Bank off California. Author resides in Los Angeles.

National Oceanic and Atmospheric Administration. 1978. Position Statement—Siting of Oil Refinery by the Hampton Roads Energy Company at Portsmouth, Virginia. Washington, D.C.

National Oceanic and Atmospheric Administration. 1979. Georges Bank Marine Sanctuary Issue Paper. Office of Coastal Zone Management, Washington, D.C.

Note. 1978. State Power Yields to Supertankers: Ray v. Atlantic Richfield Company. *Columbia Journal of Environmental Law,* Spring, 1978.

Tribe, Laurence. 1978. *American Constitutional Law,* pp. 376–91. Foundation Press, Mineola, N.Y.

U.S. Department of Commerce. 1978. *U.S. Ocean Policy in the 1970's: Status and Issues.* Washington, D.C.

————. 1978. Proposed Designation of the Flower Garden Bank as a Marine Sanctuary. National Oceanic and Atmospheric Administration, Office of Ocean Management White Paper No. 1. Washington, D.C.

————. 1980. Flower Garden Banks Marine Sanctuary. National Oceanic and Atmospheric Administration—Office of Coastal Zone Management. Federal Register, 45 (125) p. 43205

————. 1980. Final Environmental Impact Statement, Proposed Looe Key National Marine Sanctuary. National Oceanic and Atmospheric Administration—Office of Coastal Zone Management, Washington, D.C.

————. 1980. Final Environmental Impact Statement on the Proposed Point Reyes-Farallon Island Marine Sanctuary. Two Volumes. National Oceanic and Atmospheric Administration—Office of Coastal Zone Management, Washington, D.C.

U.S. Department of Interior. 1979. Letter opposing Portsmouth, Virginia, refinery site signed by Undersecretary James A. Joseph, January 2, 1979. Washington, D.C.

————. 1979. Final Supplement to Environmental Statement—Oil and Gas Lease Sale—Offshore the North Atlantic States—OCS Sale No. 42. Prepared by Bureau of Land Management, New York office.

U.S. Environmental Protection Agency. 1979. Letter to Army Corps of Engineers on proposed Portsmouth, Virginia, refinery. Signed by Deputy Administrator Barbara Blum, January 4, 1979. Washington, D.C.

U.S. House of Representatives, Committee on Merchant Marine and Fisheries. 1980. Ocean Dumping, Hearings. Serial No. 96-40. See pp. 290–404 for testimony on future of the marine sanctuary program.

————. 1980. Hearings, Drilling Mud Research Oversight. Serial No. 96-28.

Zile, Zigurds. 1974. A Legislative-Political History of the Coastal Zone Management Act of 1972. *Coastal Zone Management Journal* 1(3).

Chapter 16

Acton, Jan Paul. 1980. *Electricity Prices and the Poor: What Are the Effects and What Can We Do?* Rand Corporation, Santa Monica, Calif.

Baer, Walter. 1980. Responses to oil supply vulnerability. Presented at Solutions to the Energy Problem Conference, sponsored by Univ. of Southern California and Newport Foundation for Study of Major Economic Issues, Univ. of Southern California, July 11, 1980.

California Energy Commission. Undated. *Alternatives in Energy Options: The Municipal Solar Utility.* Sacramento, Calif.

California Public Policy Center. 1978. *Jobs from the Sun.* Los Angeles.

Center for Law in the Public Interest. 1980. Center's Battle over Licensing of Diablo Canyon Nuclear Power Plant Continues. *Public Interest Briefs*, Spring, 1980. Los Angeles.

Commoner, Barry. 1979. *The Politics of Energy.* Knopf, New York.

Courrier, Kathleen. 1980. DOE Technocrats Downgrade Conservation, Solar Power. Baltimore *Sun*, June 16, 1980. (Author with Solar Lobby, Washington, D.C.)

Energy/LA. 1980. Community-wide Energy Audit. Office of the Mayor, Los Angeles.

Energy Task Force, New York City. 1977. No Heat, *No* Rent. Funded by grant from Community Services Administration, Washington, D.C.

Hawaii Natural Energy Institute. 1980. Annual Reports, 1979 and 1980. Univ. of Hawaii at Manoa.

Lovins, A.R. 1977. *Soft Energy Paths: Towards a Durable Peace.* Ballinger, Cambridge, Mass.

Marx, Wesley. 1980. They're building solar cells, but not for U.S. *Minneapolis Tribune,* op-ed section, March 19, 1980.

National Consumer Cooperative Bank. 1980. "Futures" for Energy Cooperatives (draft). Washington, D.C.

Negroni, Julio. Undated. *Biomass Use for Island Utilities.* Center for Energy and Environment Research, Univ. of Puerto Rico.

Pulliam, Eric and Roger Hedgecock. 1980. Local Leadership for Solar Energy. *Solar Law Reporter,* May/June, 1980.

Saunders, Robin. 1978. Santa Clara Pioneers with Solar Utility. *Public Power,* July–August, 1978.

Totten, Michael, ed. 1980. Local Alternative Energy Futures Resource Handbook. Prepared for Alternatives Conference, Austin, Texas, Dec. 11–13, 1980. Funded by Dept. of Energy—state and local assistance programs, Washington, D.C.

U.S. Congress, Joint Economic Committee. 1979. Employment Impact of the Solar Transition. Washington, D.C.

U.S. Dept. of Housing and Urban Development. Undated. Protecting Solar Access for Residential Development. Guidebook prepared by American Planning Assn., Washington, D.C.

U.S. Senate, Energy and Natural Resources Committee. 1980. Sail Power Bill—s. 2992. Hearings. Washington, D.C.

Yergin, D., and R. Stobaugh eds. 1979. *Energy Future.* Random House, New York.

Zinner, John. 1980. *Los Angeles Solar Energy Book.* Office of the Mayor, Los Angeles.

Chapter 17

Mattson, James. 1979. Compensating States and the Federal Government for Damages to Natural Resources Resulting from Oil Spills. *Coastal Zone Management Journal* 5 (4).

National Oceanic and Atmospheric Administration. 1978. The *Amoco Cadiz* Oil Spill—A Preliminary Scientific Report. Washington, D.C.

U.S. General Accounting Office. 1977. Total Costs Resulting from Two Major Oil Spills. CED-77-71. Washington, D.C.

U.S. House of Representatives, Committee on Merchant Marine and Fisheries. 1977. Oil Pollution Liability. Hearings. Serial No. 95-2.

———. 1979. Oil Pollution Liability. Hearings. Serial No. 96-16.

———. 1979. Blowout of the Mexican Oil Well IXTOC I. Hearings. Serial No. 96-19.

———. 1979. The IXTOC I Oil Pollution Compensation Act of 1979, Hearings. Serial No. 96-41.

U.S. Senate, Committee on Commerce. 1977. Oil Spill Liability and Compensation. Hearings. Serial No. 95-27.

Chapter 18

Craven, John. 1975. Present and future uses of floating platforms. *Oceanus*, Fall, 1975.
————, chief investigator. 1972. Hawaii's floating city development program. First annual report. Univ. of Hawaii.
Dorfman, Dan. 1978. Ludwig's $1 billion gamble. *Esquire*, Aug. 1, 1978.
Fischer, Joseph, and Fred Fox. 1973. Siting constraints for an offshore nuclear power plant. Dames & Moore Engineering Bulletin 42. Los Angeles.
Hoffman, John. 1970. Man-made islands can solve many of our problems. *Ocean Industry*, Feb., 1970.
Kindt, John. 1980. Offshore siting of nuclear power plants. *Ocean Development and International Law Journal* 8(1).
Person, Abraham. 1977. Barge mounted offshore LNG liquefaction plants. Global Marine Development Inc., Newport Beach, Calif. Presented at Oceans '77 Conference, Los Angeles, October, 1977.
Spilhaus, Athelstan. 1972. A city in the sea. *Petroleum Today*, 1972/three.
Talkington, Howard. 1973. Transfer of Navy platform technology to solution of societal problems. *Marine Technology Society Journal* 7(1).
Thomas, Charles. 1972. A city with sea legs. *NOAA* 2(3).
U.S. Dept. of Commerce. 1980. *Improving your waterfront: a practical guide*. National Oceanographic and Atmospheric Administration: Office of Coastal Zone Management, Washington, D.C.
U.S. Dept. of Interior. 1980. *Urban waterfront revitalization: The role of recreation and heritage*. Two volumes. Heritage Conservation and Recreation Service, Washington, D.C.
U.S. House of Representatives. Ninety-sixth Congress. 1979. Future of New York, New Jersey and Great Lakes Ports. Hearings. Committee on Merchant Marine and Fisheries. Serial No. 96-21.
Watling, Les. 1975. Artificial islands: information needs and impact criteria. *Marine Pollution Bulletin* 6(9).

Chapter 19

Agarwal, J.C., et al. 1979. Comparative Economics of Recovery of Metals from Ocean Nodules. *Marine Mining*, Vol. 2, #1–2.
Buzan, Berry. 1976. *Seabed Politics*. Praeger, New York.
Cloud, Preston. 1969. Mineral Resources from the Sea. In *Resources and Man*. W. H. Freeman, San Francisco.
Eckert, Ross. 1979. *The Enclosure of Ocean Resources*. Hoover Institution Press, Stanford, California. Author is at University of Southern California.
Fuerstenau, Douglas. 1978. Some Approaches to the Extraction of Metals from Deep-Sea Manganese Nodules. Presented to the 9th Underwater Mining Institute, San Diego, Calif.

Hawaii Department of Planning and Economic Development. 1978. The Feasibility and Potential Impact of Manganese Nodule Processing in Hawaii. Honolulu, Hawaii.

Krutein, Manfred. 1978. Ocean Mining—Problems and Today's Results. Presented at the 9th Underwater Mining Institute, San Diego, Calif.

LaQue, F.L. 1980. Possible Contribution of Deep Sea Mining to a New World Economic Order. *Marine Technology Society Journal*, 14(1).

Mero, John. 1965. *The Mineral Resources of the Sea*. Elsevier, Amsterdam.

Raymond, Richard. 1976. Seabed Minerals and the U.S. Economy: A Second Look. *Marine Technology Society Journal* 10(5).

United Nations Third Conference on the Law of the Sea. 1980. Draft Convention on the Law of the Sea (Informal Text), Part XI. U.N. DOC. A/Conf. 62/WP. 10/Rev. 3, 27 August 1980.

U.S. House of Representatives, Committee on Merchant Marine and Fisheries.

————. Ninety-third Congress. 1973. Deep Seabed Hard Minerals. Hearings. Serial #93-27.

————. Ninety-fifth Congress. 1977. Deep Seabed Mining. Hearings. Serial #95-4.

————. Ninety-sixth Congress. 1979. Deep Seabed Hard Mineral Resources Act. Report 96-411, Parts 1 and 3.

————. Ninety-sixth Congress. 1979. Law of the Sea. Hearings. Serial #96-9.

Chapter 20

Beebe, William. 1938. *Zaca Venture*. Harcourt, Brace and Company, New York.

Burke, William. 1970. *Marine Science Research and International Law*. Law of the Sea Institute, University of Rhode Island, Occasional Paper No. 8.

Deacon, Margaret. 1971. *Scientists of the Sea, 1650–1900: A Study of Marine Science*. Academic Press, New York.

Erb, William. 1980. Summary of 1979 Clearance Requests. United States Department of State—Bureau of Oceans and International Environmental and Scientific Affairs, Washington, D.C.

Galey, Margaret. 1973. *The Intergovernmental Oceanographic Commission*. Occasional Paper Series, Law of the Sea Institute, University of Rhode Island.

Hedgpeth, Joel W. 1974. One Hundred Years of Pacific Oceanography. In *The Biology of the Oceanic Pacific*. Oregon State University Press, Corvallis.

Herdman, William. 1923. *Founders of Oceanography*. Edward Arnold, London.

Murray, John, ed. 1885. *Report of the Scientific Results of the Voyage of H.M.S. Challenger*.

Murray, John. 1913. *The Ocean*. Williams and Norgate, Ltd., London.

Palacio, Francisco. 1977. Towards a Marine Policy in Latin America. Woods Hole Oceanographic Institute, Woods Hole, Mass.

————. 1980. The Development of Marine Science in Latin America. *Oceanus* 23(2):39–49.

Reynolds, Ernest. 1949. *Nansen*. Penguin Books, Middlesex, England.

Roche, Marcel. 1976. Early History of Science in Spanish America. *Science*, 194:-806–810.

Schlee, Susan. 1973. *The Edge of an Unfamiliar World*. Dutton, New York.

Steinbeck, John, and Edward Ricketts. 1941. *Sea of Cortez: A Leisurely Journal of Travel and Research.* Viking, New York.

United Nations Third Conference on the Law of the Sea. 1980. Draft Convention on the Law of the Sea (Informal Text), Part XIII. U.N. DOC. A/103F.62/WP. 10/Rev. 3, 27 August 1980.

Wooster, Warren, ed. 1973. *Freedom of Oceanic Research.* Crane, Russak and Company, New York.

————. 1976. The Decline of Marine Scientific Reearch. *Marine Technology Society Journal,* 11(2).

————. 1981. Research in Troubled Waters. *Ocean Development and International Law* (in press). Author is with Institute for Marine Sciences at University of Washington.

U.S. House of Representatives. 1980. Hearings, Sea Grant Reauthorization and Oversight. Serial No. 96-28.

Chapter 21

Council on Environmental Quality. 1979. Ocean Disposal of Radioactive Wastes. In 10th Annual Report, pp. 448, 623–625. Washington, D.C.

Council on Environmental Quality and Department of State. 1980. Global 2000 Report to The President. Gerald Barney, Study Director. Two Vols. Vol. 1— Impacts of Nuclear Energy, p. 37. Vol. 2—Artificial Radioactive Materials, pp. 309–310, and Open Oceans, pp. 315–318. Washington, D.C.

————. 1981. Global Pollution. In *Global Future: Time to Act.* Washington, D.C.

Goldberg, Edward. 1976. *The Health of the Oceans.* UNESCO, Paris.

Interstate Electronics Corp. 1974. A Survey of the Farallon Islands Radioactive Waste Disposal Site. Report prepared for U.S. Environmental Protection Agency, Contract 68-01-0796. With 20 colored illustrations, a collector's item.

Lamb, Robert. 1980. Ocean Trenches and Radioactive Wastes. *Environmental Conservation,* Spring 1980. Author with Earthscan, London.

Note, 1980. Pacific Islanders Protest Japan's Nuclear Dumping Plan. *World Environment Report,* August 25, 1980.

O'Reilly, Richard. 1980. Hearing Takes Up Peril of Nuclear Waste off Coast. In *Los Angeles Times,* Oct. 13, 1980.

Tolba, Mostafa. 1980. The Environmental Effects of Military Activity. In The State of the World Environment 1980 Report. United Nations Environmental Programme, Nairobi.

Waldichuk, Michael. 1977. *Global Marine Pollution.* UNESCO, Paris.

Chapter 22

Braudel, Fernand. 1966. *The Mediterranean.* Harper & Row, New York.

Caeser, C. Julius. 1955. *Caesar's War Commentaries.* Edited and translated by John Warrington. Dutton, New York.

Coleridge, Samuel. 1828. Cologne. In *Poems of Samuel T. Coleridge* edited by Ernest Hartley Coleridge. p. 477, 1960 edition. Oxford, London.

Dalpra, C. 1981. Mediterranean Cleanup. *J. Water Pollution Control Fed.* 53 (2). 1980.

Ember, Lois. 1980. Caribbean environmental plan taking shape. *Chemical & Engineering News,* April 14, 1980.

Jenkins, S. H. 1980. Coastal Pollution of the Mediterranean. *Marine Pollution Bulletin,* January, 1980.

Morison, Samuel Eliot. 1974. *The European Discovery of America.* See pp. 30–31 for Columbus's miscalculation of the distance to Asia. Oxford, New York

Muller, Frank. 1979. Divide-up to Clean-up. *Environmental Policy and Law,* Volume 5, 1979.

Note, 1980. The Save-the-Mediterranean plan's in danger—no funds. *World Environment Report,* March 10, 1980

Ronald, K. and R. Dugay. 1979. The Mediterranean Monk Seal. Published for the United Nations Environmental Programme by Pergamon Press, Oxford.

Singer, Grace. 1979. Citizens defend the urban coast. *Bulletin of the Atomic Scientists,* June, 1979.

Slonim, Gilven. 1972. The "Humanities of the Sea." *Vital Speeches.*

United Nations Environment Programme. 1978. Mediterranean Action Plan. United Nations, New York.

INDEX

AGASSIZ, Alexander, 26, 261, 262
American Sea Grant College Program, 271
Amoco Cadiz, 213, 215
Anchoveta, Peruvian, 12, 14, 15, 16
Anchovy, 10, 12, 19–21
Aquaculture, 31–40, 51–60, 63–68, 176, 294
Argo Merchant, 190
Army Corps of Engineers, 148, 149–52, 155
Atom bomb tests, 275

BARRIER islands, 140, 153–54, 155–56
Bays. *See* Estuaries
Beach building, 149–52
Beach erosion, 145–58
Beaches, 135–44; management of, 145–58; urbanization of, 290. *See also* Coastal recreation

CALIFORNIA Fish and Game Department, 20, 82, 90, 111
California Solar Utility Development Authority, 205
Carp, 41–49, 51–57 *passim*
Challenger expedition, 239, 260–61, 263
China, and fish farming, 57, 58–59, 68
Clean Water Act, 172, 251
Clean Water Program, 164
Climatic changes, and marine ecosystem, 5, 15. *See also* Water temperature
Coastal development: and beach erosion, 147; and disaster control, 93: government subsidy of, 155; and marine ecosystem, 111–12
Coastal recreation, 115–34
Coastal Zone Management Act, 189

Cobalt, sea mining of, 240
Copper, sea mining of, 240

DEPTHS of the Ocean, The, 262

ECOSYSTEM. *See* Marine ecosystem
Energy alternatives, 200–210, 293; biomass, 201; in coastal regions, 293; cost of, 200–201; decentralized, 200; geothermal wells, 202, 203; sail, 207–8; solar water heaters, 202; sugarcane, 202; wind farms, 202, 203; wood, 206
Environmental Protection Agency (EPA): and California deepwater oil leases, 193; and Farallon Islands nuclear dump, 280–81; and funding of effluent transfers, 171; and nuclear waste monitoring, 281; and oil drilling, 192; and oil spills, 191; and regulation of aquaculture, 33; and sewage land-disposal, 174; and sewer grants, 160, 164, 165, 172
Estuaries: benthic life in, 85; defined, 70; ecosystem of, 27, 71, 83; effect of silt on, 80, 92; formation of, 80; preservation of, 69–82; public attitude toward, 75–79, 81, 86, 87, 90; ownership of, 72, 73, 83, 84, 87–88, 91; reclamation of, 76–77; and Upper Newport Bay, 69–94; watershed controls and, 92–93

FEDERAL subsidies: of fishing industry, 14, 28; of floating industrial platforms, 231–32; of nuclear energy, 208, 209–10; of oceanographic research, 265; of oil tankers, 189; of sewage treatment, 160, 164, 165, 171, 172; of whale research, 265

and transboundary management of
tuna, 24
Minamata, 282
Mineral deposits, and urban dumps,
255–57
Mineral Resources of the Sea, The, 239
Mining. *See* Sea mining
Mobile Ocean Basing System (MOBS),
226
Murray, Sir John, 260, 262, 263–64

NANSEN, Fridtjof, 261, 263, 272
National Marine Fisheries Service
(NMFS), 18–20
National Oceanic and Atmospheric
Administration (NOAA), 191, 215, 280
Nickel, sea mining of, 240
Nuclear energy, federal subsidy of, 208,
209–10
Nuclear power plants, floating, 226,
228–29, 230, 233
Nuclear Regulatory Commission, 279
Nuclear safety regulations, 196
Nuclear wastes: alternative energy
sources and, 286; amount of, 277;
and Nuclear Regulatory Commission,
279; ocean dumping of, 208, 275–87;
shipment of, 208; storage problem of,
276, 277, 279, 285–86

OCEAN: future of, 2–7; as resource
cornucopia, 2, 3, 5, 256, 257, 289; as
resource grab, 4–5
Ocean currents: effect of, on fish
populations, 15; and nuclear wastes,
278; and sand transport, 137, 138
Ocean dumping, effects of, 284–85,
290. *See also* Nuclear wastes, ocean
dumping of
Ocean management, international,
294–95
Oceanographers: Alexander Agassiz,
261–62; Johan Hjort, 262; and
international cooperation, 262; Sir
John Murray, 260, 262, 263–64;
Fridtjof Nansen, 261, 263, 272;
Harald Sverdrup, 263
Oceanographic research: and American
Sea Grant College Program, 271;

cost of, 262, 265; and exploitation of
marine resources, 266; free access
for, 264, 272–73; government subsidy
of, 262, 265; and Intergovernmental
Oceanographic Commission, 269–70;
and international cooperation, 271;
and Law of the Sea conventions,
270, 271–72; nations participating in,
265–66; political barriers to, 259–60,
266–72
Oceans, The, 263
Oil drilling, 191, 194
Oil leases, 193, 194
Oil platforms, floating, 229–30
Oil resources, marine, 218
Oil spill liability: Alaskan oil spill act,
215; federal regulation of, 213–14;
and Limitation of Liability Act, 212;
limits on, 212, 213; state regulation
of, 213; transnational, 216, 217; and
Superfund, 213–15
Oil spills: *Amoco Cadiz,* 213, 215;
Argo Merchant, 190; IXTOC, 216;
major cause of, 193; monitoring
environmental effects of, 190–91,
215, 217–18; public responsibility for,
290–91; recompensation for, 211–19;
Torrey Canyon, 212. *See also* Oil
spill liability
Oil tankers, federal subsidy of, 189
Outer continental shelf, 188
Oyster farming, 66–67

PACIFIC Fishery Management Council,
20
Pelican, brown, 19, 109
Peripheral Canal, 170

RADIOACTIVE wastes. *See* Nuclear
wastes
Research. *See* Oceanographic research

SALMON ranching, 34–40
Sand, 141–42, 152–53
Sand bars, 138
Sand transport, 137–38, 147, 148–49,
157–58
San Francisco Bay, sewage spill in,
165–66, 167, 168–69, 171